System-on-Chip Design

with Arm® Cortex®-M Processors

System-on-Chip Design

with Arm® Cortex®-M Processors

Reference Book
JOSEPH YIU

arm Education Media

To our families

Contents

Contents

3. AMBA, AHB, and APB

6. Low-power support

7. Design of bus infrastructure components

8. Design of simple peripherals

9. Putting the system together

10. Beyond the processor system

11. Software Development

Foreword

Why Read this Book?

Right now, you are probably surrounded by Arm processors without even knowing they are there. More than 145 billion chips containing an Arm processor have been produced up to now – this is 19 for every human on the planet.

The most surprising thing is that Arm does not produce chips. It just designs the technology and enables its partners to manufacture differentiated devices that integrate them.

Many more of those chips, also called SoCs (system-on-chip), are expected to be produced in the coming years. We even start talking about trillions of devices for the Internet of Things (IoT). Of the total number of SoCs currently out in the market, the great majority use the smallest processors in the Arm product range: the Cortex-M series. Small, very energy efficient and powerful enough for many applications, they are at the heart of many of today's electronic devices.

This book is here to explain how SoCs based on the Arm Cortex-M processor portfolio cores are designed, detail the different elements that compose such a system, explain the different design issues, describe the integration into systems, and discuss how these SoCs are programmed.

A Brief History of Arm

The crazy years marking the history of personal computing began in the 1980s. Acorn, a British company, became very successful with the BBC Micro-computer, which was used in many schools throughout the country. For its future generation computers, the company wanted an updated processor and started a quest for such a component. Unfortunately, none of the available microprocessors were suitable for its needs. Most of them were either too complex or not available and required a large number of external components. The Acorn team then learned about the Reduced Instruction Set Computer (RISC) concept and found it could lead to powerful, yet low-cost, solutions.

At the time, RISC processors were confined to high-end computers, where cost was less of an issue, since no existing RISC processors were exactly suitable. That led the team to embark on the journey to develop their own piece of silicon.

This secret project was named "Acorn RISC Machine" (ARM, in short). The first processor, ARM1, was launched in 1985. It was produced by VLSI Technology in a 3μm technology (almost 500 times larger than the most advanced designs now) and could run at 6 MHz. One of the side-benefits of this simple processor architecture was its lower power consumption (compared to contemporaneous CPUs), which allowed the component to use a lower-cost plastic package without melting it.

At the heart of the processor design was the Arm instruction set, which progressively evolved to optimize the performance and efficiency of new generations of processors. This is a key element of what is called the 'architecture.'

The Arm processors powered several models of Acorn computers, but a major change happened when VLSI Technology, which was manufacturing the components in its factories, signed an agreement with Acorn to re-sell the chips to other companies. This was the first 'Arm license.'

In 1990, after discussions with Apple Computer, who needed a new processor for the Newton project, Acorn decided to spin-off its processor division and form a joint venture with Apple and VLSI Technology. The team then changed the meaning of Arm to 'Advanced RISC Machines', which became Arm Ltd later on.

This evolution came at the same time as a great change in the new company's business model. On the one hand, Arm had unique assets: great expertise in processor design and an original architecture. However, producing chips required caring about fabrication, yield, quality, logistics, sales channels, complex application-specific marketing, or any other tasks that a silicon manufacturer should do to be successful. This was not optimal.

On the other hand, silicon manufacturers had a hard time staying competitive, because they had to excel at these activities while simultaneously investing in design and innovation around processors, at an increasingly fast pace. This was not great either.

The revolutionary idea for the newly-formed company was to become a specialist in R&D and focus on the processor design only. Instead of selling components, Arm would license 'Intellectual Property' (IP in short) to semiconductor manufacturers, who would then use this IP to design their chips, in combination with other elements that would be more application-specific.

Arm Ecosystem

The IP model selected from the start by Arm required a very tight relationship with the other companies using the IP. As the company did not manufacture products, its success was entirely dependent on the success of chip manufacturers embedding the Arm IP into their chips. Conversely, to make sure that they always get the best performance and efficiency for their products, silicon manufacturers had to make sure that the success of their products also benefited Arm, so that part of the increasing revenues would be invested in improved and competitive IP. Together, Arm and partners solidified the symbiosis using a royalty-based model: Arm revenues were largely dependent on the success of the chips containing its IP. This resulted in a strong partnership between the company and its customers, and a great sign of this very special relationship is that customers were called 'partners' (This is still the case more than 25 years after the foundation of the company).

Another great benefit from these partnerships was that each semiconductor 'partner' could focus on a different set of applications, on different market segments, and integrate its own expertise and 'secret sauce' into the design of their products. This business model allowed the creation of a rich variety of products that no single company (even the largest ones) would have been able to put into their product catalog. It also made it increasingly difficult for processor manufacturers using other architectures to compete with Arm because they had to compete with a whole 'ecosystem.' Many of them progressively decided to stop wasting money on processor architecture development and realized that it was much less expensive just to license state-of-the-art IP from Arm.

Another consequence of having several companies using the same processor IP cores was that tools, software, and expertise could be reused from one chip to another. Indeed, a processor requires many tools like code compilers or debuggers: having a larger market for these tools encouraged several companies to start supporting the Arm architecture. Similarly, having a family of processors that could execute the same instructions enabled the software developers to propose many operating systems, libraries, frameworks or various elements that could easily run or be adapted to several components. Finally, this allowed engineers to avoid having to learn about a new processor every time they changed their chip, which allowed them to build strong expertise and become more efficient.

All of these factors meant that Arm could add several additional partners in the ecosystem, bringing even greater value to every participant and making Arm-based solutions even more attractive. This virtuous circle has significantly contributed to the success of the Arm ecosystem.

Softbank Acquisition

Even if the IP model has been duplicated many times, no other company has managed to be as successful. This propelled Arm into a very special position in the industry. Its long-term success required fairness with each member of the industry, and careful management to keep the balance between all partners of the ecosystem.

2016 marked a significant milestone in Arm's history: Softbank group agreed with Arm management to acquire the company with the promise to continue promoting the same values of fairness and partnership while accelerating its development.

Market and Applications

Arm-based processors are used in virtually all applications requiring processing capability: as the company says, "wherever computing happens." Over the years, the company has developed a range of products that address very different needs, from the tiniest processors for embedded applications (the Arm Cortex-M processor portfolio) to the largest application processors that are used in high-performance servers or that power 95% of the mobile phones in the world (the Cortex-A processor portfolio). There is more than a factor of 100 in complexity and size between the smallest and the highest performing cores.

However, central processing units are not the only IP offered by Arm: a diverse range of IP has been developed or acquired by the company to address the needs of many applications. This is the case of what is called 'System IP': all the elements that enable processors to connect to the rest of the system, transfer or store data between those elements, manage security, enable the debug of the software, and manage power. Another very important line of products relates to media processing, and the Arm Mali series is now the world's 'most shipped' commercial GPU IP.

Enabling Future Technology Today

Even if the core business of Arm remains semiconductor IP, more and more software is being developed to complement hardware designs. This can be seen, for example, in products for IoT applications. With the Mbed software platform, Arm not only brings the software that is closest to the hardware elements but also provides many standard functions needed in these devices: to manage security, connectivity, firmware updates or association to the Cloud services.

An entire division in Arm is now focusing on building this embedded software foundation, and also creating a Cloud platform, called Pelion, to connect and manage to all these embedded devices, and to integrate the associated data into enterprise systems.

From providing the IP for the chip to delivering the Cloud services that allow organizations to manage the deployment of products throughout their lifecycle securely, Arm delivers a pre-integrated IoT solution for its partners, rooted in its deep understanding of the future of compute and security.

Arm technologies continuously evolve to ensure that intelligence is at the core of a secure and connected digital world. With a range of licensing options, such as Arm DesignStart and Arm Flexible Access, it's now never been easier or faster to start working with Arm IP. Developed to facilitate the design of modern innovations—from the sensor to the smartphone to the supercomputer—Arm technologies are making smart possible.

Mike Eftimakis
Director of Business Innovation Strategy, Arm

Preface

In the past, apart from microprocessors and microcontrollers, not many chip designs had internal embedded processors. This has changed significantly since Arm Cortex-M processors were released, and many more device types have emerged that are part of the rapidly growing Internet of Things (IoT). Today, Arm processors are being used in smart sensors, smart batteries (e.g., for battery health monitor systems), wireless communication chipsets, power electronics controllers, etc. This trend is driven by the need for tighter system integration, additional functional features, better system reliability, and reduction of supply chain dependency.

SoC design is an exciting industry with plenty of opportunities – the applications of Cortex-M based SoCs ranges from consumer products, industrial and automotive applications, communications, agriculture, transportation, healthcare/medical, etc. With the expanding IoT device market, the need for embedding processors into SoC designs continues to increase.

Cortex-M processors, like Cortex-M0, Cortex-M0+, and Cortex-M3, are very small and can integrate into a range of SoC designs easily. With Arm DesignStart lowering the cost barrier, many small businesses and start-ups are taking advantage of this to develop their own SoC solutions to offer better product differentiation. All of these developments have resulted in significant demand for SoC designers with Arm DesignStart. Arm DesignStart has also received strong interest from academia, where we see some universities interested in introducing SoC design topics into their courses.

In addition to the popular Armv6-M and Armv7-M processors, newly available SoCs/microcontrollers based on the Armv8-M processors such as Cortex-M23 and Cortex-M33 processors, deliver enhanced security solution with Arm TrustZone technology. In February 2019, Arm announced the new Armv8.1-M architecture with Arm Helium technology, which brings vector processing capability to Arm Cortex-M devices. These technology enhancements continue to enable the Cortex-M processors to be used in an even wider range of applications.

While there are many technical resources on the internet on Arm software development, very limited information was available for Arm-based SoC design, particularly on topics about integrating Arm processors and on-chip bus protocols. This book is written to fill this gap to enable beginners in the field to understand a range of technical concepts on SoC design, and also provide detailed descriptions of design integration with several of the Arm Cortex-M processors. A range of other topics, including system component design, SoC design flow, and software development, are also covered.

If you are a beginner in SoC design, I hope that this book will enable you to gain SoC design knowledge and help you to kickstart your SoC or FPGA design projects. For those of you who are experienced chip designers, I hope that you find this a useful reference source. Enjoy the book - and let your SoC design creativity go wild! There are always opportunities for new and fascinating Arm-based SoCs on the market.

Example Codes and Projects – Free to Download!

For readers of this book, Joseph Yiu has prepared a package of example codes and projects to download that includes:

- An example Cortex-M3 system design based on Arm Cortex-M3 DesignStart Eval.

- A simulation setup for the example system.

- An FPGA project setup for the example system, for Digilent Arty-S7-50T FPGA board and Xilinx Vivado 2019.1.

The package can be downloaded from the book section of Arm Education Media's website at https://pages.arm.com/socrefbook.html

Disclaimer

The Verilog design examples and related software files included in this book are created for educational purposes and are not validated to the same quality level as Arm IP products. Arm Education Media and the author do not make any warranties of these designs.

A note about the scope of this book

This book focuses on the concepts of system designs based on Cortex-M0 and Cortex-M3 processors. Since the product offering DesignStart and DesignStart FPGA will change over time, the full details of using those packages will not be covered here. However, the system design concepts and some of the technical details in this document are relevant to most of the Cortex-M system designs.

About the Author

Joseph Yiu
Distinguished Engineer, Embedded Technology at Arm

Joseph is a distinguished engineer in the Arm IoT/Embedded processors product marketing team. His role is focused on technologies and products for embedded applications, including areas such as:

- Cortex-M processor products technical development

- Embedded product roadmaps

- Technical marketing

- Technical advisory for various internal and external projects, as well as Arm's product support team

He also works with EEMBC (www.eembc.org) on benchmark development – for example, ULPMark.

Joseph started as an IP designer on accelerated 8-bit processors in 1998 before joining Arm in 2001, where he worked on some of the first Arm-based SoC projects in the emerging System-on-Chip group. In 2005, he moved to the processor division and worked on a range of Cortex-M processor and design kit projects. After over 10 years in various senior engineering roles, he moved into the product management team, while continuing his involvement in Arm embedded technology projects. His technical specialisms include microcontroller and SoC system-level design with Arm Cortex-M processors, applications and programming, ASIC/SoC designs, verifications, FPGA prototyping and implementation areas such as low-power design and production tests (DFT), and RF circuit design.

Authorship
Joseph's previous book titles include:

The Definitive Guide to ARM Cortex-M3 and Cortex-M4 Processors, 1st to 3rd edition
(Elsevier, October 2013)

The Definitive Guide to the ARM Cortex-M3, 1st and 2nd edition
(Elsevier, January 2010)

Acknowledgments

A big thank you to the editor, Michael Shuff, for his efforts in proofreading and various useful suggestions. I would also like to thank Christopher Seidl, Chris Shore, and Jon Marsh for contributing materials, and the Arm marketing team for their support on this project.

CHAPTER 1

Introduction to
Arm Cortex-M

1.1 Why learn Cortex-M system design?

1.1.1 Starting Cortex-M system design is easy

Arm Cortex-M processors represent one of the most popular architectures used today for Internet of Things (IoT) and embedded applications. For many digital system designers, the digital blocks they design need to interface with processors in some ways, for example, using a processor for operation flow control. Having a small, easy-to-use Cortex-M processor integrated into the design makes it easier for them to provide a total solution.

You may wonder, 'Why not use a state machine to handle the control function?' In the simplest digital applications, a finite state machine (FSM) implemented in Verilog or VHDL could handle all the required control functions, and in those cases, there is indeed no need to have a processor in the system. However, when the application gets more complex, the number of states in the control function FSM increases, or when the system's behavior needs to be more flexible, the inclusion of a processor in the system is unavoidable. To enable better flexibility, complex control flows are handled by a processor running control software, which can be easily modified and debugged. As a result, embedded processors are being increasingly embedded in FPGA designs. Although it is possible to use a separate microcontroller to control an FPGA-based digital system, this will result in an increased component count in the completed system, as well as potential issues with signal routing between the processor and the FPGA-like timing, PCB signals routing, noise, and reliability problems.

In general, the advantages of including a processor in the FPGA are:

- Ability to handle complex tasks like Graphical User Interface (GUI) and data storage management (e.g., file system);

- Application programs can be developed and updated separately from the hardware design, allowing better flexibility in product development;

- Reduces the total number of components in the system because there is no need for a separated processor chip;

- Signal routing between the processor and the functional logic is handled automatically by FPGA design tools;

- Debugging software on a well-established processor is much easier than debugging a complex state machine;

- Little limitation on the interface between the processor and the user-defined logic blocks;

- In comparison, the use of separated processor chips can have limitations on the interface like the number of pins, selection of protocol and electrical characteristics;

- Program code can be stored on configuration flash for the FPGA, allowing firmware update to the hardware design and the application code to be carried out at the same time;

- Processor implementation features are now becoming part of the FPGA development tools, making integration of the processor into FPGA easier than using separate processor chip.

There are other intellectual property (IP) products available in the market, of course. However, the designs of the Cortex-M processors provide:

- Good performance with a small area/power budget,

- Easy software development, and

- Well-proven technology.

Products based on Arm Cortex-M processors have been around since 2005. In recent years, Arm has made Cortex processor IP more accessible to cost-constrained companies through easy to arrange, fast, no/low-cost licensing. For example, Arm Flexible Access introduced in 2019 offers a simple way to evaluate and fully design system-on-chip (SoC) solutions with a wide-ranging mix of Arm IP before committing to production, paying only for what is used at manufacture. There are also Arm DesignStart programs that assist designers who are new to Cortex-M technology with a range of Arm IP to help them get started on their designs instantly and risk-free. You can source various FPGA development solutions, like affordable FPGA development boards, that can save you both time and money. Through partnerships with FPGA vendors, Arm also offers DesignStart FPGA, which includes instant and free access to Cortex-M1 and Cortex-M3 soft CPU IP Cortex-M processors for use on selected FPGA platforms. Together with an industry-leading ecosystem of tools, software, and services, the Arm Cortex-M processor portfolio offers some of the best embedded processors for digital system designs.

1.1.2 Cortex-M processor systems on FPGA
Since there are so many ready-to-use Cortex-M based microcontrollers and SoCs, why should someone spend their time to create their own Cortex-M based systems in FPGA? There can be many different reasons:

- Education – for many universities teaching digital system design, FPGAs are perfect platforms. Universities had been interested in using Arm processors in their teaching of digital design courses, like how to create a typical SoC design with a processor and develop applications for it. However, doing real chip design is costly and takes a long time, making the FPGA platform much more suitable.

- Commercial product development – many digital designers are creating custom digital systems with FPGA and need a processor to control the operations of the digital systems they design. In some other applications, the digital functions needed are not available in off-the-shelf microcontroller products, and therefore using the Cortex-M processors in FPGA enables alternate solutions.

- Prototyping for chip/SoC designs – many ASIC designers use FPGA for prototyping their designs and their chip/SoC designs that contain the Cortex-M processors. It is also a useful way to prototype new product ideas, and to provide demonstrations/proof of concepts. With these systems, software developers can reuse their Cortex-M programming knowledge to program such devices.

While there have been several FPGA vendor-specific processors available, most of those architectures are proprietary and could be restricted to certain FPGA architectures. In contrast, the Cortex-M processors are much more generic. Most of the Cortex-M processors (e.g., Cortex-M0 and Cortex-M3) are optimized for ASIC/SoC applications. The Cortex-M1 processor was designed to be optimized for most of the FPGA devices (it is small and allows high operation frequency), and at the same time can be portable between different FPGA types and is upward-compatible to other Cortex-M processors. For example, from a software point of view, the architecture used in Cortex-M1 is based on the same instruction set used by the popular Cortex-M0, Cortex-M0+ processors. Designers can also upgrade to a Cortex-M3 or other Cortex-M processor if more instruction features are needed.

Since the recent availability of the Cortex-M processor IP in FPGA design tools, Cortex-M system designs are no longer restricted to SoC design professionals. Even students, academic researchers, and electronics enthusiasts now have access to the world of Cortex-M system design.

1.1.3 Security by design is made easier with Arm architecture
Securing connected devices requires a step-by-step approach to building in the right level of device security, reducing risk around data reliability, and allowing businesses to innovate on new ideas to reap the benefits of digital transformation. Arm has started an industry-wide initiative called **Platform Security Architecture** (PSA) that is supported by a range of silicon vendors and ecosystem partners who are seeking better collaboration and alignment of security standards.

Although the PSA framework was devised by Arm, it is 'architecture agnostic' in that it requires that all compliant devices, regardless of architecture, are designed to meet a set of defined security objectives. PSA resources include programming interfaces (APIs), best practices, threat models to consider, and open-source reference firmware. You can find out more by visiting: https://developer. arm.com/architectures/security-architectures/platform-security-architecture

1.2 Understanding different types of Arm processors
Arm processors are deployed in many different applications, with very different needs - and to support that, Arm has developed a broad portfolio of processors to help designers select the best-fit compute for their device. For example, the application requirements for a smartphone are very different from the requirement of a motor controller. To address the wide variety of application requirements, Arm provides a range of processor products in different profiles belonging to the Cortex processor families:

- The Cortex-A portfolio – Application processors for complex systems. An example of the processors in this class is the Cortex-A53. It is developed to support applications like smartphones, PDAs, set-top boxes, which need high-performance processing and require OS support like Linux, Android, Microsoft Windows, etc.

- The Cortex-R portfolio – Processors for real-time, high-performance systems. An example of a processor in this class is the Cortex-R52. It is developed to provide high performance, low latency, and robust characteristics. Typical applications include hard disk controllers and baseband processing in communication devices.

- The Cortex-M portfolio – Processors for microcontroller applications. An example of a processor in this class is the Cortex-M3 processor. It has been developed for deeply embedded, and cost-sensitive applications, and yet provides good performance and rapid interrupt response. Typical applications include industrial controls, consumer products, like portable audio devices, and digital cameras.

Key characteristics of these processors are summarized in Table 1.1.

	Cortex-A	Cortex-R	Cortex-M
Architecture type	Support both 64 and 32-bit from Armv8-A, 32-bit in Armv7-A and older architecture	Support both 64 and 32-bit from Armv8-R, 32-bit in Armv7-R and older architecture	32-bit only
Clock frequency range and pipeline	Longer pipeline optimized for high clock frequency range	Medium-length pipeline (e.g., 8-stage in Cortex-R5)	Short to medium length pipeline (2 to 6 stages) for low-power systems
Virtual memory support (required for Linux)	Yes	No (it is permitted in Armv8-R, but not supported in current Cortex-R processors)	No
Virtualization support	Yes	Yes, from Armv8-R (e.g., Cortex-R52)	No
Arm TrustZone security extension	Yes	No	Yes, from Armv8-M, but not in Armv6-M and Armv7-M architectures
Interrupt handling	Based on Generic Interrupt Controller (GIC) with multi-core and virtualization support. Non-deterministic interrupt response speed.	Based on Generic Interrupt Controller with multi-core and virtualization support, or Vectored Interrupt Controller in older Cortex-R. Fast interrupt response.	Based on Nested Vectored Interrupt Controller (NVIC) internal to the processor. Low interrupt latency and easy to use.
ISA for DSP acceleration	Neon Advanced SIMD (128-bit vectored processing). Latest architecture from Armv8.3-A supports Scalable Vector Extension (SVE).	Neon Advanced SIMD support on Armv8-R. Also, support legacy SIMD (32-bit vector processing).	Support legacy SIMD (32-bit vector processing) in Cortex-M4, Cortex-M7, Cortex-M33, and Cortex-M35P

Table 1.1: Key characteristics of different Cortex processors.

If you are planning to use Linux in your applications, a Cortex-A processor would be needed. Both Xilinx and Intel (previously Altera) have FPGA products with built-in Cortex-A processor subsystems. On the other hand, the Cortex-M processors are ideal for smaller embedded systems, often with real-time requirements.

There are different types of the Cortex-M processors, too. We can classify them into three product ranges:

	Armv6-M and Armv7-M architecture	Armv8-M architecture (supports TrustZone security extension)
High performance	Cortex-M7 (Armv7-M)	Coming soon
Mainstream processor	Cortex-M3 and Cortex-M4 processors (Armv7-M)	Cortex-M33 and Cortex-M35P processors
Processors for constrained systems	Cortex-M0, Cortex-M0+, and Cortex-M1 (all Armv6-M architecture)	Cortex-M23 processor

Table 1.2: Different Cortex-M processors.

For general data processing and control applications, Armv6-M processors are more than capable of handling these requirements:

- Cortex-M0 processor: the smallest Arm processor (only 12K gates in minimum configuration) with a simple 3-stage pipeline, based on Von-Neumann bus architecture. No privilege level separation and no memory protection unit (MPU).

- Cortex-M1 processor: similar to the Cortex-M0 processor, but optimized for FPGA applications. It provides Tightly-Coupled-Memory (TCM) interface to simplify memory integration on FPGA and delivers higher clock frequency for FPGA implementations.

- Cortex-M0+ processor: also based on Armv6-M architecture, with privilege level separation and an optional memory protection unit (MPU). It also has an optional single-cycle I/O interface for connecting peripheral registers that need low latency accesses, and a low-cost instruction trace feature called Micro Trace Buffer (MTB).

- Cortex-M23 processor: For constrained embedded systems that need advanced security, the Cortex-M23 processor with the Arm TrustZone security extension is more suitable. In addition to TrustZone support, the Cortex-M23 processor has many other enhancements compared to Armv6-M processors:

  □ Additional instructions (e.g., hardware divide, compare, and branches);

  □ Supports more interrupts (up to 240);

  □ Real-time instruction trace using Embedded Trace Macrocell (ETM);

  □ More configurability options.

- Cortex-M3 processor: For applications that need more complicated data processing, Armv7-M processors could be more suitable. The instruction set in Armv7-M provides support for more addressing modes, conditional execution, bit field processing, multiply, and accumulate (MAC). So even with a relatively small Cortex-M3 processor, you can have a relatively high-performance system.

- Cortex-M4 processor: If DSP-intensive processing or single-precision floating-point processing are needed, the Cortex-M4 processor is more suitable than Cortex-M3 because it supports 32-bit SIMD operations and an optional single-precision floating-point unit (FPU).

- Cortex-M7 processor: the highest performance Cortex-M processor today with a six-stage pipeline and superscalar design, allowing execution of up to two instructions per cycle. Similar to the Cortex-M4, it supports 32-bit SIMD operations and an optional FPU. The FPU in Cortex-M7 can be configured to support single-precision or both single and double-precision floating-point operations. It is also designed to work with high performance and complex memory system by supporting instruction and data caches and TCM.

- Cortex-M33 processor: a mid-range Armv8-M processor at similar footprint to Cortex-M4, adding TrustZone security extension support, co-processor interface and a newer pipeline design to enable higher performance.

- Cortex-M35P processor: similar to the Cortex-M33 processor, but with the enhancement of anti-tampering features to prevent physical security attacks (e.g., side-channel and fault injection attacks). It also includes an optional instruction cache.

For beginners, Cortex-M0, Cortex-M1, and Cortex-M3 are good starting points for most projects.

1.3 Cortex-M deliverables

1.3.1 Licensing through Arm Flexible Access and Arm DesignStart

When this chapter was written, the following licensing options were available from Arm:

Find out more about various Arm licensing options

Arm provides a range of licensing options, including no or low upfront fees and free access for academic purposes. Visit www.arm.com/licensing for more information.

Arm DesignStart

- Cortex-M0 and Cortex-M3 processors are available via DesignStart program (Note: The Cortex-A5 processor is also available, but this book is not intended to cover this).

- Cortex-M1 and Cortex-M3 processors are available at no cost as soft CPU IP optimized for easy integration with FPGA partners.

The Cortex-M33 processor is available as DesignStart FPGA on Cloud: (https://developer.arm.com/docs/101505/latest/designstart-fpga-on-cloud-cortex-m33-based-platform-technical-reference-manual)

There are different types of deliverables for each of these DesignStart programs. Currently, Cortex-M DesignStart is divided into several types:

- DesignStart Eval(ulation) – delivered as obfuscated Verilog with fixed configuration. Instant access and free. Suitable for evaluation, research, and teaching.

- DesignStart Pro – delivered as full RTL source, configurable and requires a simple license; Zero license fee and success–based royalty model.

- DesignStart for University - delivered as full RTL source, configurable and requires a simple license. Zero license fee.

- DesignStart FPGA – delivered as packages for FPGA development tools. Instant access and free. Suitable for evaluation, research, teaching, and commercial use.

For the latest information and details of DesignStart (including licensing conditions), please visit the Arm website: https://developer.arm.com/products/designstart

Cortex-M0 and Cortex-M3 DesignStart Eval and Pro contains the following offerings:

Cortex-M0 DesignStart Eval	Cortex-M3 DesignStart Eval	Cortex-M0 DesignStart Pro	Cortex-M3 DesignStart Pro
Cortex-M0 obfuscated model	Cortex-M3 obfuscated model	Full version of Cortex-M0 deliverable	Full version of Cortex-M3 deliverable
Cortex-M0 System Design Kit (CM0SDK)	Corstone-100 foundation IP including SSE-050 subsystem	Cortex-M0 System Design Kit (CM0SDK)	Cortex-M System Design Kit (CMSDK), Corstone-100 foundation IP including SSE-050 subsystem and several IP blocks including TRNG (True Random Number Generator) for security
	Cortex-M3 Cycle Model (1-year license)		Cortex-M3 Cycle Model (1-year license)
FPGA project for MPS2 FPGA board	FPGA project for MPS2 FPGA board	FPGA project for MPS2 FPGA board	FPGA project for MPS2 FPGA board
Trial license of Keil MDK (time-limited license)	Trial license of Keil MDK (time-limited license)	Trial license of Keil MDK (time-limited license)	Trial license of Keil MDK (time-limited license)
		DesignStart RTL Review	DesignStart RTL Review

Table 1.3: Offerings from Arm Cortex-M DesignStart Eval and Pro.

Trial license for IAR Embedded Workbench for Arm is also available from IAR Systems (https://www.iar.com/designstart).

You can find out more about Flexible Access and DesignStart on the Arm website and request more information: https://arm.com/why-arm/how-licensing-works

Disclaimer: The IP offering and commercial terms available through Arm DesignStart and Flexible Access above are accurate as of July 2019 and are subject to change.

1.3.2 Obfuscated Verilog – DesignStart Eval

The Cortex-M0 and Cortex-M3 DesignStart Eval deliver the processors as obfuscated Verilog files. These RTL files are not encrypted, but the internal logic is flattened, and the signal names replaced with random names. You can simulate it with standard Verilog simulators and synthesize it for FPGA testing (but the synthesis outcome will not be optimized due to the nature of the code). The top-level signals of the processors are retained as clear un-obfuscated text. DesignStart Eval can be implemented using any FPGA fabric.

The Cortex-M0 DesignStart Eval includes an example system based on the Cortex-M System Design Kit (CMSDK) product. The example system is delivered as RTL sources, with example test codes and simulation scripts. A FPGA prototyping project for MPS2 (Microcontroller Prototyping System 2) is also included.

The Cortex-M3 DesignStart Eval includes a system design based on the CoreLink System Design Kit SDK-100 (a successor of CMSDK). It also has examples, simulation scripts, and FPGA projects for MPS2.

1.3.3 Verilog RTL sources – DesignStart Pro

The Cortex-M0 and Cortex-M3 DesignStart Pro deliver the RTL source code of the processor (not obfuscated). These provide configuration options in the form of Verilog parameters, allowing designers to select the features they need. Since the design is delivered as RTL source, the synthesis tools can provide the best optimization in synthesis.

The DesignStart Pro also includes the deliverable for the full CoreLink subsystem products.

1.3.4 FPGA Packages - DesignStart FPGA

Cortex-M1 and Cortex-M3 can be integrated into an FPGA vendor's toolchain as an encrypted component. The components will typically allow some configuration and already include TCM integration. Some packages will convert the native AHB interface of the processor to an AXI bus. These packages can only be used with the toolchain from the specific FPGA vendor, but support a range of devices.

1.3.5 Documentation

There are several types of documents that you will come across when working on Arm system designs:

Architecture reference manuals: these documents specify the behavior of the architecture (e.g., instruction set, programmer's model) but not the processor-specific implementation details (e.g., pipeline and interface). There are separated architecture reference manuals for Armv6-M, Armv7-M, and Armv8-M, and you can download them from https://developer.arm.com (Please refer to Table 1.2 to see which architecture is for which processors).

Technical reference manuals: Often known as TRM, they describe the specification of the processors or other system IPs. These documents are public and can be found on https://developer.arm.com

Integration and Implementation manuals: Also known as IIM, they describe the interface, configuration options and explain how to use the deliverables like the execution testbenches. These documents are confidential and are inside product bundles.

User guides: The details of the FPGA examples are documented in user guides notes.

Release notes: All of the deliverables from ARM are provided with a release note which identifies the versions of parts within a bundle, any known issues and any changes since a previous release. The release note will also describe how to install and test the deliverable. These documents are confidential and are inside product bundles.

Errata: The errata document describes known issues with ARM products, together with workarounds if applicable.

CHAPTER

2

Introduction to system design with Cortex-M processors

2.1 Overview

One of the key advantages of using the Cortex-M processor is that, for small system designs, in particular, it is not that difficult to get the system to work in a Verilog simulation or on FPGA. You will, of course, need to acquire some knowledge beforehand, like a basic overview of the architecture used in the Cortex-M processors. Also, if you are using a Verilog RTL version of the design, you will need an understanding of the bus protocols used in the Cortex-M processors, such as AHB and APB protocols.

The first step of the project is to understand the requirements of the applications. For example, you will need to know:

▧ Which Cortex-M processor is the best fit for your needs?

▧ How much memory (ROM and SRAM) is needed?

▧ How fast the system runs (i.e., clock speed)?

▧ What peripherals are needed?

For ASIC designs, many additional areas should be investigated. For example, the following are generic chip design considerations:

▧ What semiconductor process node should be used?

▧ What types of memory technologies are available (e.g., embedded flash memories are not available for many small geometry process nodes)?

▧ How should non-volatile memory (NVM) programming be handled?

▧ What type of power management features should be used?

▧ What type of chip packaging should be used?

▧ What type of Design-for-Test (DFT) features are needed for device manufacturing testing?

For the era of IoT, designers should also investigate security aspects and many other challenging areas of integrating wireless communication interfaces inside SoC designs.

To keep this document manageable, let us look into the processor system design areas only. To get a simple Cortex-M processor system to work, typically we need to consider and, where appropriate, define, the following (this is not a definitive list):

▧ Memory blocks – what type of memories are needed, and memory sizes?

▧ Peripherals – what peripherals are needed, and creation of peripherals if needed?

- Memory map.

- Bus system design.

- Processor configuration options.

- Interrupt assignments and interrupt types.

- Event interface integration.

- Clock and reset generation.

- Debug integration.

- Power management features of the system.

- Top-level pin assignment and pin multiplexing.

In the rest of this chapter, you can read an overview of some of these areas.

2.2 What memories are needed?

2.2.1 Overview of memories

In a typical Cortex-M based system, there are at least two types of memories:

- Non-volatile memory (NVM), typically using embedded flash technologies or masked ROM, for program storage;

- RAM, for read-write data including stack and heap.

In some systems, there can be additional memories for bootloader and other preloaded firmware. Some low-power devices also have special retention static RAM (SRAM) for holding small amounts of data while the rest of the device is shut down during sleep modes.

Most of the Cortex-M processors use 32-bit AHB for memory interfacing (except Cortex-M1 which uses Tightly Coupled Memory (TCM) interfaces for connecting memories, and Cortex-M7 which supports both Tightly-Coupled-Memory (TCM) and AXI bus interfaces). Therefore, the memory system designs are normally 32-bit wide, but they also need to be byte-addressable – it means the RAM must support byte (8-bit), half-word (16-bit) and word (32-bit) write operations.

For FPGA-based projects, the SRAM inside the FPGA can be used for both program storage (most FPGA initialization sequences can initialize SRAM contents at the same time) and read-write data.

Therefore, in theory, you could use just one SRAM block for a Cortex-M based FPGA system design.

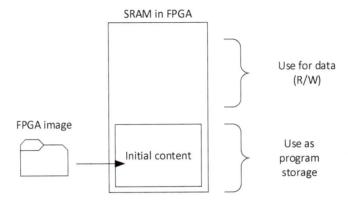

Figure 2.1: SRAM in FPGA can have initial values so that a single SRAM block can be used as both program ROM and RAM.

However, such an arrangement differs from ASIC/SoC system designs where SRAM cannot be initialized in the same way. Also, doing so will impact performance on a Cortex-M3/M4-based system as it will no longer be using a Harvard bus architecture. To avoid confusion, the rest of the examples in this book use two memory blocks for separating program storage and data read-writes.

2.2.2 Memory declarations in FPGA design tools

If you are using FPGA DesignStart, the memory system for the Cortex-M1 or Cortex-M3 could be generated for you by the FPGA design tools, so it is easy to do. However, if you are not using FPGA DesignStart, you might need to handle the memory integration manually.

A long time ago, FPGA tools could not generate RAM blocks using behavioral Verilog codes and declaration of memories in FPGA projects required instantiation of memory macros manually. This was changed a few years ago, but such a capability might require the RAM declarations to be written in a specific way to allow the FPGA design tools to recognize it correctly.

In the Cortex-M0 & Cortex-M3 DesignStart Eval, the file "logical\cmsdk_fpga_sram\verilog\cmsdk_fpga_sram.v" provides a synthesizable SRAM model that works with most FPGA flows. You can attach this SRAM model to an AHB bus using a bus wrapper("cmsdk_ahb_to_sram.v"), as shown in "logical\models\memories\cmsdk_ahb_ram.v" or "logical\models\memories\cmsdk_ahb_rom.v".

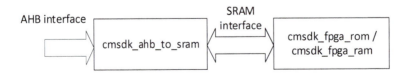

Figure 2.2: FPGA SRAM instantiation with an AHB interface.

This arrangement allows you to swap over the FPGA ROM/RAM with other memories easily (e.g., when migrating to ASIC).

If you would like to simplify the design, it is possible to use a simple AHB block SRAM design (from my paper in Embedded World 2014 – "Arm Cortex-M Processor-based System Prototyping on FPGA" https://community.arm.com/processors/b/blog/posts/embedded-world-2014---arm-cortex--m-processor-based-system-prototyping-on-fpga

```verilog
module AHBBlockRam #(
// ------------------------------------
// Parameter Declarations
// ------------------------------------
parameter AWIDTH = 12
)
(
// ------------------------------------
// Port Definitions
// ------------------------------------
input HCLK, // system bus clock
input HRESETn, // system bus reset
input HSEL, // AHB peripheral select
input HREADY, // AHB ready input
input [1:0] HTRANS, // AHB transfer type
input [1:0] HSIZE, // AHB hsize
input HWRITE, // AHB hwrite
input [AWIDTH-1:0] HADDR, // AHB address bus
input [31:0] HWDATA, // AHB write data bus
output HREADYOUT, // AHB ready output to S->M mux
output HRESP, // AHB response
output [31:0] HRDATA // AHB read data bus
);
parameter AWT = ((1<<(AWIDTH-2))-1); // index max value
// --- Memory Array ---
reg [7:0] BRAM0 [0:AWT];
reg [7:0] BRAM1 [0:AWT];
reg [7:0] BRAM2 [0:AWT];
reg [7:0] BRAM3 [0:AWT];
// --- Internal signals ---
reg [AWIDTH-2:0] haddrQ;
wire Valid;
reg [3:0] WrEnQ;
wire [3:0] WrEnD;
wire WrEn;
// ------------------------------------
// Main body of code
// ------------------------------------
assign Valid = HSEL & HREADY & HTRANS[1];
// --- RAM Write Interface ---
assign WrEn = (Valid & HWRITE) | (|WrEnQ);
assign WrEnD[0] = (((HADDR[1:0]==2'b00) && (HSIZE[1:0]==2'b00)) ||
                   ((HADDR[1]==1'b0) && (HSIZE[1:0]==2'b01)) ||
                   ((HSIZE[1:0]==2'b10))) ? Valid & HWRITE : 1'b0;
assign WrEnD[1] = (((HADDR[1:0]==2'b01) && (HSIZE[1:0]==2'b00)) ||
                   ((HADDR[1]==1'b0) && (HSIZE[1:0]==2'b01)) ||
                   ((HSIZE[1:0]==2'b10))) ? Valid & HWRITE : 1'b0;
assign WrEnD[2] = (((HADDR[1:0]==2'b10) && (HSIZE[1:0]==2'b00)) ||
                   ((HADDR[1]==1'b1) && (HSIZE[1:0]==2'b01)) ||
                   ((HSIZE[1:0]==2'b10))) ? Valid & HWRITE : 1'b0;
assign WrEnD[3] = (((HADDR[1:0]==2'b11) && (HSIZE[1:0]==2'b00)) ||
                   ((HADDR[1]==1'b1) && (HSIZE[1:0]==2'b01)) ||
                   ((HSIZE[1:0]==2'b10))) ? Valid & HWRITE : 1'b0;

always @ (negedge HRESETn or posedge HCLK)
if (~HRESETn)
```

```
  WrEnQ <= 4'b0000;
else if (WrEn)
  WrEnQ <= WrEnD;

// --- Infer RAM ---
always @ (posedge HCLK)
  begin
  if (WrEnQ[0])
    BRAM0[haddrQ] <= HWDATA[7:0];
  if (WrEnQ[1])
    BRAM1[haddrQ] <= HWDATA[15:8];
  if (WrEnQ[2])
    BRAM2[haddrQ] <= HWDATA[23:16];
  if (WrEnQ[3])
    BRAM3[haddrQ] <= HWDATA[31:24];
  // do not use enable on read interface.
  haddrQ <= HADDR[AWIDTH-1:2];
  end
`ifdef CM_SRAM_INIT
initial begin
  $readmemh("itcm3", BRAM3);
  $readmemh("itcm2", BRAM2);
  $readmemh("itcm1", BRAM1);
  $readmemh("itcm0", BRAM0);
  end
`endif
// --- AHB Outputs ---
assign HRESP     = 1'b0; // OKAY
assign HREADYOUT = 1'b1; // always ready
assign HRDATA    = {BRAM3[haddrQ],BRAM2[haddrQ],BRAM1[haddrQ],BRAM0[haddrQ]};
endmodule
```

Using an Arm toolchain such as Keil MDK (Microcontroller Development Kit) or DS-5, we can create a hex file that can be read by $readmemh for SRAM initialization, using the fromelf utility with the following command-line:

$> fromelf --vhx --8x4 image.elf –output itcm

This generates four hex files (itcm0, itcm1, itcm2 and itcm3), one for each byte lane, which need to be available during the FPGA synthesis. The tool merges the data into the FPGA bitstream so that the SRAM content can be set up during FPGA configuration stage.

2.2.3 Memory handling in ASIC designs
In ASIC designs, SRAM and NVM blocks cannot be generated from Verilog RTL in behavioral synthesis. Typically, you need a specific memory generation tool (SRAM compiler) to create the SRAM, and for embedded flash, you need to instantiate the flash macro manually.

In most cases, to connect a SRAM block to AHB, you can use the "cmsdk_ahb_to_sram" block, possibly with a little bit of glue logic for signal protocol conversion. Additional considerations apply when low-power support is a requirement, as SRAM macros usually have some low-power modes or even state retention modes.

To connect embedded flash macros to AHB, you need a flash interface controller. The interface on the flash macros is vendor and process node-specific. However, Arm has worked with multiple embedded flash vendors to define a Generic Flash Bus protocol (GFB, https://developer.arm.com/docs/ihi0083/a), so most parts of the flash controller are generic; only a smaller part of the interface is process-dependent. Arm provides generic flash controller IP, which is licensable as a part of the Corstone-101 product.

Since embedded flash macros are often relatively slow (e.g., around 30MHz to 50MHz access speed) and many Cortex-M designs run at over 100MHz, cache systems are often required to reach desired performance levels. To address this need, Arm also offers cache units such as the AHB flash cache, which is part of the Cortex-M3 DesignStart Pro.

2.2.4 Memory endianness

When designing memory systems, one of the considerations is endianness. Most Cortex-M systems today are based on little-endian memory systems. However, it is possible to create big-endian Cortex-M systems as these processors support big-endian configuration options. When doing this, it is important to make sure that the software developers of the product are aware so that they can use correct compilation switches in their software projects.

Bits	[31:24]	[23:16]	[15:8]	[7:0]
0x00000008	Byte 0xB	Byte 0xA	Byte 9	Byte 8
0x00000004	Byte 7	Byte 6	Byte 5	Byte 4
0x00000000	Byte 3	Byte 2	Byte 1	Byte 0

Figure 2.3: Data arrangement in a Little-Endian system.

Bits	[31:24]	[23:16]	[15:8]	[7:0]
0x00000008	Byte 8	Byte 9	Byte 0xA	Byte 0xB
0x00000004	Byte 4	Byte 5	Byte 6	Byte 7
0x00000000	Byte 0	Byte 1	Byte 2	Byte 3

Figure 2.4: Data arrangement in a Big-Endian system.

Please note that the endiann configuration only affect data accesses (including read-only data). Instructions are always encoding as little endian. Also, access to the Private Peripheral Bus (PPB) is always in little endian.

2.3 Defining the peripherals

A microcontroller is not complete without a range of peripherals for various input/output and hardware control functions such as timers. For the most basic Cortex-M based systems, we would expect to find digital peripherals like:

▣ General-purpose input/output (GPIO);

▣ Timers;

▣ Pulse Width Modulator (PWM) – usually for motor or power electronic system control;

▣ UART for serial communication;

▣ SPI (Serial Peripheral Interface) for external hardware modules such as LCDs;

▣ I2C / I3C – commonly used for sensors.

In addition to these basic peripherals, a simple system might also integrate a group of registers for various system control functions (e.g., clock source control, selection of low-power modes). This could be integrated as part of the peripheral system, but additional care must be taken for system security reasons. Typically, system management functions need to be restricted to privilege accesses only.

More information on digital peripheral designs is covered in Chapter 8 (page 171).

Microcontrollers also have analog interfaces like ADC (Analog to Digital Converter) and DAC (Digital to Analog Converter). However, many FPGA devices do not support such peripherals. For ASIC designs, typically the ADC and DAC IP need to be sourced from specialist IP providers.

2.4 Memory map definition

The architectures used in the Cortex-M processors define a memory map that allocates address ranges into regions. This allows the built-in peripherals like the interrupt controller and debug components to be accessed by simple memory access instructions, thus allowing system features to be accessible in C program code. Having a predefined memory map also allows the Cortex-M processors to be optimized for performance. For example, a memory region called CODE at the beginning of the memory is dedicated to program memory, and a memory region called SRAM starting from 0x20000000 is dedicated to data memory. In the Cortex-M3 processor, CODE and SRAM regions use separated buses to allow the system to utilize the performance benefits of a Harvard bus architecture. It is possible to use the memory regions differently, but it may not be able to get the best performance by doing so.

The general layout of the memory map is shown in the diagram below (Figure 2.5).

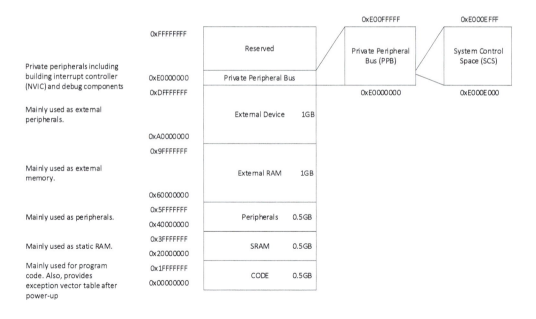

Figure 2.5: Memory map overview.

The top 512Mb of the System Level Memory contains a region for system control and reserved areas. This bus provides access to the built-in interrupt controller and various debug components. Within the PPB memory range, a special range of memory is defined as System Control Space (SCS). It contains the interrupt control registers, system control registers, debug control registers, and so on. The remaining system-level memory space from address 0xE0100000 is reserved.

By having a predefined memory map, it makes porting of applications easier as all of the Cortex-M systems have a similar look and feel, and an identical address range for NVIC and SysTick timer, etc. It also simplifies the boot code as there is no need to program the system to define the memory attributes for different memory/device types.

There are some restrictions concerning what the memory maps look like:

1. In many Cortex-M processors, including Cortex-M0, Cortex-M0+, Cortex-M1, Cortex-M3, and Cortex-M4, the initial vector table address must be zero after reset.

2. In Cortex-M3 and Cortex-M4 processors, there is an optional bit band feature that allows the first 1MB of SRAM and the first 1MB of Peripheral region to be bit addressable. When this feature is enabled, the bit-band alias region is remapped to bit band address range, and therefore the bit-band alias address range cannot be used for data memory or peripherals.

3. In Cortex-M1 and Cortex-M7 processors, the instruction TCM and data TCM has fixed memory addresses (TCM sizes are configurable). Both of these TCMs are optional.

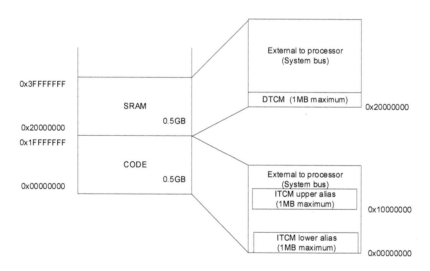

Figure 2.6: TCM memory map in Cortex-M1.

For example, in the Cortex-M1 processor, there are two TCM interfaces: the ITCM interface is primarily for instruction memory (including literal data access inside a program), and the DTCM is primarily for data transfers. If the TCM size is set to 0, the TCM interface is not used, and the transfers are carried out on the system bus. The maximum size of the TCM supported on Cortex-M1 is 1MB for each TCM interface.

The TCM interfaces on the Cortex-M1 processor are designed to be used with typical RAM blocks in modern FPGA architecture. The accesses are single-cycles (i.e., have no wait state) and are limited to a maximum size of 1MB each.

It is possible to add additional memory blocks on the system bus of the Cortex-M1 processor. The original design of the Cortex-M1 system bus is based on AHB Lite protocol (AMBA version 3), it is generic and allows wait state and error response. Please note that the Cortex-M1 design integrated with the FPGA design tool might have been customized for a specific FPGA design environment and might, therefore, have some cycle timing differences as a result.

The TCM interfaces on the Cortex-M7 processor are designed to be used with RAM blocks for ASIC designs and support wait states. The maximum TCM size is 16MB each, but in practice, the TCM sizes used in Cortex-M7 based microcontrollers are likely to be in the range of 64KB to 512KB. A large TCM can increase the cost of the silicon due to the size of the area used and can have an impact on the maximum clock frequency that can be achieved. For Cortex-M7, you can also add additional memories on the AXI master interface.

Peripherals are typically placed in the Peripheral region of the memory map (0x40000000 to 0x5FFFFFFF). In most designs, peripherals are grouped into address ranges based on the bus segment that they are placed in. For example, a Cortex-M based system can have multiple AHB and APB peripheral buses. Bus bridges can be used to allow these buses to run at different clock frequencies.

When using Cortex-M3 and Cortex-M4 processors, if the designer would like to take advantage of the bit-band feature which allows peripheral registers to be bit addressable (using bit-band alias), then the peripherals that use this feature need to be in the first 1MB of the peripheral region. Similarly, when supporting the bit-band feature for SRAM, the SRAM must be placed in the 1MB of the SRAM region.

When using Cortex-M23 and Cortex-M33 processors with TrustZone security extension enabled, the memory map design needs to divide memory spaces into Secure and Non-secure ranges. More details on this topic are covered in Section 3.5 AHB5 TrustZone support.

2.5 Bus and memory system design

When designing the bus system for a Cortex-M processor system, many factors need to be considered:

- The bus interface on the Cortex-M processor being used – different Cortex-M processors can have different bus interfaces (e.g., Harvard versus Von Neumann bus architecture).

- The performance of memory blocks (e.g., if embedded flash memories are used for program storage and the design need to provide high performance, then a cache unit should be considered).

- The bus bandwidth of other bus masters in the system. For example, a USB controller is likely to have a bus master interface and needs high data bandwidth to SRAM. In such cases, you might need to have multiple blocks of SRAM and design the bus system to allow the processor and the

USB controller to have concurrent access to SRAM blocks. Another type of common bus master is DMA controller – DMA operations enable high-performance data transfers and device-driven data transfers without software intervention.

- The clock speed of peripheral buses – your designs might have multiple peripheral buses with multiple clock speeds to enable low-power operations for some peripherals and higher performance for peripherals that can benefit from lower access latency.

- Security – with TrustZone based systems for Cortex-M23 and Cortex-M33 processors, security management in bus system design is an important area to ensure that security measures cannot be compromised. For some of the other Cortex-M systems without TrustZone, you might still want to have some levels of security level management to handle the separation of privileged and unprivileged software components.

Later on in this book, we cover some of the processor-specific bus system design concepts in Chapter 4.

2.6 TCM integration

In the case of system designs for Cortex-M1 and Cortex-M7 processors, memory blocks can be connected to the processor using the TCM (Tightly Coupled Memory) interfaces. In most designs, SRAM macros generated by SRAM can be connected to the processor via simple glue logic.

For microcontroller designs with the Cortex-M7 processor, it is unlikely that you will connect slow memory blocks like an embedded flash to instruction TCM because accesses to TCM memories bypass the caches. Therefore, for Cortex-M7 system designs, slow program memories are expected to be connected via the AXI master interface.

For details of TCM integration, please refers to the Integration and Implementation Manual (IIM) in the product bundle.

2.7 Cache integration

Another type of memory that needs to be integrated is caches. Currently, these Cortex-M processor products support cache(s):

- The Cortex-M7 processor supports optional built-in instructions and data caches (they are optional).

- The Cortex-M35P processor supports an optional built-in program cache (sometimes referred to as instruction cache but technically it is a unified cache that can cache both instruction and read-only data).

For details of cache RAM integration on these processors, please refers to the IIM in the product bundles.

2.8 Defining the processor's configuration options

The source codes of the Cortex-M processors are highly configurable. You can configure the options using Verilog parameters in the module instantiation. Also, some of the newer Cortex-M processors have configuration scripts to help set up configurations of the product bundle.

System designers using the Cortex-M processor source code need to study the configuration options documented in the Integration and Implementation Manual (IIM) carefully to select the right options for their applications. Some other parts of the product bundles also need to be configured with matching options. If the options of some parts of the deliverable are not configured correctly, items like the execution testbench might not work correctly.

2.9 Interrupt signals and related areas

Assigning interrupt numbers and connecting interrupt signals from peripherals to the processor is possibly one of the easiest parts of the system design task. Normally you have several interrupt signals from peripherals to be connected to the processor. The allocation of interrupt signals affects the C head files for software development, including the vector table definitions and interrupt numbers, which are both visible to the software.

The maximum number of interrupts supported by the Cortex-M processors are listed in Table 2.1:

Processor	Maximum number of interrupts
Cortex-M0, Cortex-M0+, Cortex-M1	32
Cortex-M3, Cortex-M4, Cortex-M7, Cortex-M23	240
Cortex-M33, Cortex-M35P	480

Table 2.1: Maximum number of interrupts in the Cortex-M processors.

If the number of interrupt signals exceeds the maximum number support, it is possible to merge multiple interrupt lines and share one interrupt service routine (ISR) and determine which interrupt to be serviced in the ISR by software.

On all current Cortex-M processors, the interrupt signals:

- Are active high and must be synchronous to the processor's system clock signal;

- Can be level triggered or pulse triggered. If using pulse triggered, the duration of the pulse must be at least one clock cycle.

The unused or not implemented interrupt input pins should be tied to 0 and must not be allowed to enter unknown state 'X.' (e.g., if a peripheral outputs X in its interrupt line when the peripheral is powered down, the signal level must be clamped to 0 before the power down happened). Issues with unknown or 'X' signal values generally affect simulation but represent possible unexpected values when using ASIC or FPGA.

If the peripheral interrupt is generated at a different clock domain, a synchronization circuit (such as the example in Figure 2.7) is needed to remove potential metastability issue and to prevent transients from forming unexpected pulses.

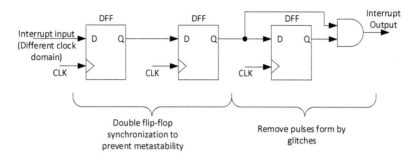

Figure 2.7: Interrupt synchronizer to convert interrupt signal from one clock domain to processor's clock domain.

Cortex-M processors have a Non-Maskable Interrupt (NMI) input. In common embedded systems the NMI could be connected to:

- Voltage monitoring logic (also known as brownout detector) to ensure that the system is shut down correctly when support voltage drops to a certain value or

- The NMI could be connected to a watchdog timer to carry out remedial actions if the system has stopped normal operation.

NMI is unlikely to be used as the interrupt for normal peripherals. This is because the built-in interrupt controller NVIC already provides interrupt prioritization, so each peripheral can already be programmed as the highest priority by just using the normal IRQ connection. Also, a fault generated within the NMI handler can cause the processor to enter lockup state, which can be problematic for some applications. Faults in normal interrupt handlers allow the Hard Fault handler (or other configurable fault handlers) to be triggered and executed.

Another characteristic of the NVIC is that it can handle interrupt requests in the form of pulse as well as level signal. If a peripheral generates an interrupt request in the form of a pulse signal, the request is held by pending status within the NVIC until the interrupt request is processed, or when the pending status is cleared manually. If a peripheral generates an interrupt request in the form of a level signal, the interrupt handler must clear the request at the peripheral.

The key advantage of a pulsed interrupt is that it saves a few clock cycles in the ISR that there is no need to clear the interrupt requests at the peripherals. However, in many cases, a level-triggered interrupt is preferred because:

- Cross clock domain synchronization of level-triggered interrupts is simpler than pulsed interrupts. In the case where pulse interrupt synchronization logic is used, two successive interrupt request pulses could be merged into one after the synchronizer due to the latency of the synchronization, which can be confusing.

- If the interrupt event occurred when the processor is reset, the interrupt event could be lost.

- Level trigger interrupts can remain at a high level to indicate an additional service is needed by the peripheral (e.g., when additional data is available in a receiver's FIFO).

- Easier for debugging (e.g., in Verilog simulation, where it is hard to tell if there has been an interrupt event unless the event information is kept by, for example, a waveform database).

- The peripheral design can be reused for other processors that do not support pulsed trigger interrupts.

In addition to the number of interrupts, there are other configuration options related to interrupt handling:

Number of interrupt priority levels – In Armv7-M and Armv8-M Mainline processors, the programmable interrupt priority level registers has configurable width from 3-bits to 8-bits. Typically, the options of 3-bit to 4-bit are used, and some devices do support 5-bit. Most applications do not need many interrupt priority levels, so eight levels (3-bit) is likely to be sufficient.

Wakeup Interrupt Controller (WIC) – An optional block to handle interrupt detection while the processor is in-state retention power gating (SRPG) or when the processor's clock is completely stopped. If the WIC feature is implemented and enabled, the interrupt masking information is transferred from NVIC to WIC automatically before entering sleep mode. The WIC then takes over the role of interrupt event detection and can generate a wakeup request to power management blocks in the system when an enabled interrupt event is detected. The interrupt pending status is held in the WIC when the processor is waking up and transfers the interrupt request to NVIC when the processor is back up. At the same time, the masking information inside the WIC is cleared automatically by hardware as the NVIC is back running.

2.10 Event interface

Apart from the Cortex-M1 processor, all other Cortex-M processors have an event input (typically named RXEV – receive event) and an event output (typically named TXEV – transmit event). The RXEV input is used to wake up a processor from Wait-For-Event (WFE) sleep operation, and TXEV output allows a processor to send an event to another processor in WFE sleep using the SEV (Send event) instruction. These signals are active high single-cycle pulse.

The event interface is typically used in multi-core systems to allow one processor to wake up another during spinlocks. In RTOS semaphores, if a processor is waiting for a spinlock, it can enter sleep mode using WFE to save power and wakes up if there is an interrupt to serve or if there is an event from another processor. By crossing over the event interface signal (as shown in Figure 2.8), processors in a dual-core system can wake up each other from WFE sleeps using the SEV (send event) instruction.

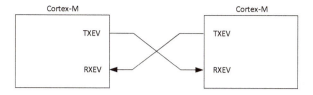

Figure 2.8: Example connection of event interface in a dual-core system.

Events could also be generated from peripherals or DMA controller, but normally interrupts are more suitable for that purpose as we need software to react to those hardware events vis ISRs. For single-processor systems, it is fine to tie RXEV to 0 and leave TXEV unconnected.

Please note: The event interface on the Cortex-M processor is unrelated to the definition of events in RTOS. In RTOS, an application thread waiting for a certain operation X to be carried out can call an OS API that waits for an event Y. This API call also takes the thread out of the ready task queue. When the specified operation X has been carried out (e.g., in another thread or an ISR), the other thread or ISR that carried out the operation X can call another OS API to set the OS event Y. This puts all the waiting threads that were waiting for the operation X to be put back in the ready task queue to resume operation.

2.11 Clock generation

There are several clock signals on the Cortex-M processors. Over the years there have been different design approaches and therefore the clock and reset signal names vary between different processors.

Most of the existing Cortex-M processors provide:

▪ Free-running clock (if gated, all logic in the processor stopped and needs external logic blocks such as WIC to handle interrupt detection and wakeup);

▪ System clock (can be gated during sleep mode);

▪ Debug clock(s) – this includes the JTAG or Serial Wire debug clock signals for debug interface, and also a clock signal for internal debug components which can be gated if there is no active debug connection.

The free running clock, system clock and debug clock (except the clock for the debug interface and DAP interface on Cortex-M3/M4 processors) must be synchronous and in the same phase. The separation of clock signals is to allow the system power to be reduced by gating off some of the clock signals when they are not needed.

▪ In Cortex-M0 and Cortex-M3 processors, the design exported GATEHCLK signal is asserted when the processor is in sleep mode, and there is no debug connection. This signal can be used to gate off the system clock.

▪ In some of the Cortex-M processors, the clock gating logic is done internally and so might not have all these clock signals visible on the top-level.

It is important not to gate off the system clock when the processor is running. In system-level designs, there can be multiple clock sources, and a glitch-less clock switching circuit would be needed. The clock switching circuit is outside of the processor and is normally application and process node dependent. In FPGA designs, you can design an FSM that controls the PLLs (Phase-Locked Loops) and gate-off the clock signals to the processor subsystem during PLL configuration changes.

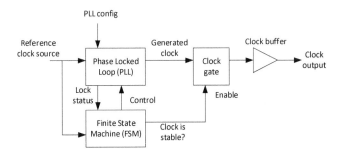

Figure 2.9: Example clock generation arrangement in a FPGA system design.

Depending on the FPGA design tool being used, the system clock generation/control logic might be generated by the tools. In this case, there is no need to develop your own clock generation/control logic.

In ASIC designs, you might have the following clock sources:

▨ External crystal oscillator for medium speed (e.g., 1MHz to 12MHz) – this might be turned off by default after a reset to save power. Instead of using a higher frequency crystal to generate higher frequency clocks, it is more common to use a PLL to generate a high clock speed when needed to avoid having a high-frequency clock running all the time to save power.

▨ Internal RC oscillator for medium speed (e.g., 1MHz to 12MHz). This will use less power than a crystal oscillator, but will not provide an accurate frequency reference for timing or peripheral interfaces.

▨ External 32KHz oscillator for real-time clock (might also be used for system management).

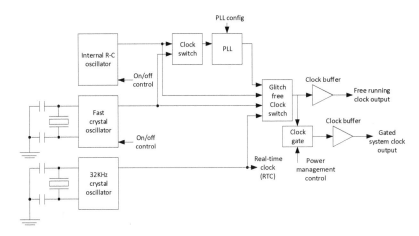

Figure 2.10: Example clock generation arrangement in an ASIC system design.

In ASIC/SoC implementations, the system can boot-up from the internal RC oscillator and switch over to external crystal oscillator or PLL for clock source when needed. PLL can provide higher clock frequency for high-performance operations.

2.12 Reset generation

In the Cortex-M processors there are usually at least two reset signals, in some cases three signals:

- System reset;

- Debug reset;

- Debug interface reset (e.g., nTRST) for JTAG interface;

- Optionally you might find a power-on reset, which resets both the system and debug logic.

If power-on reset is present, it resets both the system and debug system. The reason that we separate the reset into two signals is to allow the processor to be reset without affecting the debug system. Otherwise, the debug settings like breakpoints, watchpoints, and the debug connection from the debugger to the core, would be lost each time the processor core is reset.

The processor also outputs a reset request signal called SYSRESETREQ. This is controlled by a register bit in the Application Interrupt and Reset Control Register (AIRCR) inside System Control Space. This allows:

- Software to request a system reset, for example, in the case of fault error handling;

- Debugger to request a system reset. This is essential to allow the debugger to request a reset of the targeted processor.

Designers must make sure that:

- SYSRESETREQ only generates a system reset but not debug reset or power-on reset;

- SYSRESETREQ does not generate a system reset in a combinatorial path (in other words – it must be registered by registers that are not affected by the system reset), as the SYSRESETREQ output is affected by a system reset and the use of a combinatorial path for reset generation causes a reset glitch.

All of the Cortex-M processors use an asynchronous active-low reset signal and must be de-asserted synchronously to the system and debug clock to prevent timing violations. This ensures that most of the registers can be reset when the clock is not running. However, most of the Cortex-M processors require the reset to last at least two clock cycles. This arrangement has the following benefits:

- Enables synchronization flip-flops, which present in double DFF synchronizers to be reset.

■ In the case where the assertion of reset causes timing violations and leads to metastability, the multi-cycle nature of reset ensures the metastability is cleared up. To ensure reset de-assert occurs at the correct time, a simple reset generator could be used for a Cortex-M0/M0+/M1/M3/M4 processor. Figure 2.11 shows such an example.

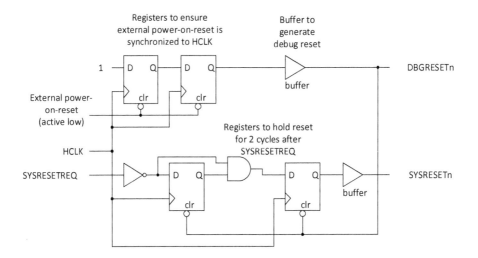

Figure 2.11: A simple reset generator for the Cortex-M processors.

Assuming the Cortex-M1 is used (some other Cortex-M processors have different signal names for reset signals): The Cortex-M1 processor generates the SYSRESETREQ signal. Since the Cortex-M1 processor can be reset by SYSRESETn, the SYSRESETREQ signal must not drive SYSRESETn in a combinatorial path. Otherwise, it could result in a race condition where SYSRESETREQ gets cleared in a very short time after assert, as it gets cleared by its output. This could result in some parts of the processor getting reset and other parts not. For this reason, the SYSRESETREQ signal must be registered by a separated flip-flop that is not affected by SYSRESETn before being used to generate SYSRESETn. In the example above (Figure 2.11), the reset request from the SYSRESETREQ is held in two registers that are reset by DBGRESETn, or if using Cortex-M3/M4, you can use power-on reset in Cortex-M3/M4 processor.

We can also design the reset generator so that it can optionally reset the system if it enters lock-up state. To make this behavior controllable, a programmable register would be needed in your FPGA/system design to specify if a lock-up state can cause a reset. This register is not provided in the Cortex-M processor core as such requirement is application dependent. During software development, the control signal at this external reset control register can be set to 0 to disable the automatic reset. In a production system, the reset control register can be set to 1 so that when the system enters lock-up state, the SYSRESETn is activated automatically.

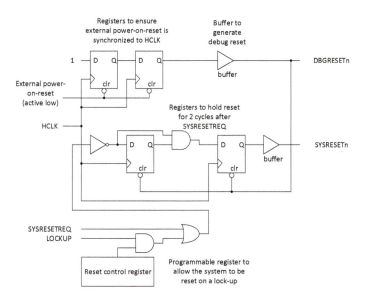

Figure 2.12: A reset generator to allow automatic reset at lockup state.

Depending on the FPGA design tool being used, the system reset controller might already be included. In this case, there is no need to develop your own reset controller.

2.13 SysTick

The SysTick timers in the Cortex-M processors support external reference "clock." Technically the reference "clock" is not a clock signal, as it is sampled by D-flip flops inside the SysTick at the processor's clock speed.

The SysTick interface also provides a calibration input, which is fed to the SysTick calibration value register:

Signal	SysTick calibration value register	
STCALIB[25]	NOREF (bit 31)	0 – reference clock is implemented 1- reference clock is not implemented
STCALIB[24]	SKEW	0 – TENMS calibration value is exact 1 – TENMS calibration value is skewed (inexact)
STCALIB[23:0]	TENMS	SysTick reload value for 10ms (100Hz)

Table 2.2: Signals for SysTick calibration value register.

The support for SysTick reference clock and calibration value are optional.

- If no reference clock is provided, STCALIB[25] needs to tied high.

- If TENMS is not used, STCALIB[23:0] should be tied low, and STCALIB[24] needs to tied high.

In CMSIS-CORE, an alternate way for software to determine system clock speed is provided that uses a software approach: the SystemCoreClock variable should provide the clock frequency information, and that is initialized and updated by the software when the clock settings are updated.

2.14 Debug integration

Debug integration typically involves several interfaces:

- **Interface for debug connection** (JTAG or Serial Wire Debug) – for connecting a debugger to the hardware target to carry out halting, stepping, restart, resume, setting breakpoints/watchpoints, access to memories and peripherals. Debug connection is also used for downloading code and flash programming.

- **Interface for trace data** (connecting ATB from the processor and ETM to trace port) – enables the debugger to obtain real-time trace information, either using trace port protocol which contains multiple data bits (usually 4-bit) and a clock signal or using a single pin trace output protocol for trace with lower bandwidth (e.g., instrumentation trace, event trace). The trace interface is optional and is not available on Cortex-M1, Cortex-M0 and Cortex-M0+ processors.

- **CoreSight timestamp generation** – CoreSight timestamp feature integrates timing information into the trace package. Real-time trace operation can take advantage of this to allow the debugger to restructure timing information. To allow this to work, some Cortex-M processors and ETM (Embedded Trace Buffer) have a timestamp interface. Typically, a simple counter is used to generate the timestamp value.

- **Debug authentication control** – Cortex-M processors provide hardware interface signals to allow other hardware blocks in the system to control whether debug and trace operations are allowed. Typically, debug authentication is controlled by security management IP blocks based on certificate-based authentication methods. For Armv8-M processor systems, there are separate debug authentication signals to define debug access permissions for Secure and Non-secure environments.

- **Debug system clock and reset generation, and power management** – depending on which processor is used, the debug system can have its own clock and reset signals, and in some designs, debug logic can be powered down or clock gated if not being used.

More details on the debug interface are covered in Chapter 5. Please note, here we only cover single-core designs. In the case of multi-core designs, the debug integration should be handled by Arm CoreSight SoC-400/600 products.

2.15 Power management features

Cortex-M processors (except Cortex-M1 which is designed for FPGA) support a range of low-power features.

- **Sleep modes** – architecturally, the processor can have sleep and deep sleep, but these sleep modes could be extended with additional system-specific registers to have addition granularity of sleep characteristics. The processors have sleep mode status output signals so that system designers can use these signals to control clock gating and other power management hardware.

- **Sleep hold interface** – in the case where a system designer utilizes sleep mode signals to turn off hardware resources (e.g., program ROM), the wake-up process can take a while (e.g., hundreds to thousands of clock cycles). In such cases, it is essential to be able to hold off the processor's program execution, and the sleep hold interface is designed exactly for this purpose. To use this feature, the system designer needs to design a simple Finite State Machine (FSM) to handle the handshaking with the sleep hold interface.

- **Wakeup Interrupt Controller (WIC)** – explained in this chapter earlier, the WIC is an optional feature that allows interrupts or other wakeup events to be detected when the processor is in a powered-down state, retention state, or if the clock to the processor is gated off. The system designer can customize the example WIC design if needed.

- **Debug power management** – the debug interface modules provides handshaking signals to indicate whether there is a debugger connection, which allows system designers to implement power management for the debug system of the processors if needed. For example, in Cortex-M0, Cortex-M0+, Cortex-M7, Cortex-M23, Cortex-M33, and Cortex-M35P processors, there is a separate debug power domain that can be powered down if there is no debug connection.

System designers are also likely to integrate additional power management features for memory blocks, clock generation and distribution systems, and some of the peripherals.

2.16 Top-level pin assignment and pin multiplexing

One of the tasks that chip designers need to do is to define the top-level signals of the devices. Often, many of the pins on the chips carry multiple functions. For example, a pin might be configurable to work as a GPIO pin, a communication interface pin, or a debug/trace pin. You can find examples of pin multiplexing in Cortex-M3 DesignStart Eval.

Apart from the debug and trace signals, normally there is no need to expose other interfaces of the Cortex-M processors directly to the top-level of the devices. For external interrupt generation, usually, that is handled by GPIO blocks so that external hardware can trigger interrupts via GPIO. In some cases, chip designers can also implement a signal path to allow off-chip hardware to generate an event pulse to the Cortex-M processor so that it can wake up from WFE (Wait-for-event) instruction; however, this is not essential for many systems.

When designing top-level pins, several areas related to the Cortex-M processors should be considered:

■ In most cases, the debug interface pins (JTAG or Serial Wire Debug) need to be accessible at the device's top-level by default. For Cortex-M3, Cortex-M4 and Cortex-M33 processors, the debug interface module supports dynamic protocol switching, so it is possible to expose just two pins of the SWD debug by default. If there is a need to switch over to JTAG, then you can program a device-specific pin multiplexer (mux) control register to expose the other pins for JTAG, and then apply a switchover sequence to start JTAG operations.

■ The SWD interface requires a tristate pin for the data connection (SWDIO), which is enabled when SWDIEN is high.

■ If the debug interface is multiplexed with other peripheral I/O pins, the peripheral I/O operations can cause a debug connection to be disconnected.

■ The debug and trace interface provides a range of status signals to allow some of the signals to be multiplexed with functional pins. It is also possible to use device-specific programmable registers to help control the pin multiplexing. However, in such cases, the device vendor needs to provide the details of the setup sequence for various debug tools to allow them to work correctly with the device.

■ When creating systems using Armv8-M processors with TrustZone, the debug connection might contain Secure information, and therefore the pin multiplexing logic needs to prevent Non-secure software from seeing activities in the debug connection.

2.17 Miscellaneous signals

Cortex-M processors provide various status signals that can be used by system designers. For example, in Figure 2.12, we show that the LOCKUP status could be used to generate system resets automatically. The availability of other status signals depends on the processor you use. Please refer to documentation in the product bundle for more information.

Newer Cortex-M processors support a CPUWAIT signal. This is used to delay the start-up of the processor after releasing from reset. In most single-core systems, this pin can be tied low. In multi-core SoC designs when the Cortex-M subsystem is running a program in SRAM, the CPUWAIT signal can be used to delay the boot-up so that a different bus master can transfer the program image into the SRAM. After the program image is loaded, the CPUWAIT signal can be released, and the Cortex-M processor can start executing the program.

2.18 Sign off requirements

For designers using the Cortex-M processors for ASIC/SoC design projects, please note that the Cortex-M family of products have some sign-off requirements documented in the IIM of the product bundle. This contains a checklist to help designers to minimize the risk of incorrect implementations.

CHAPTER 3

AMBA, AHB, and APB

3.1 What is AMBA?

3.1.1 Introduction to Advanced Microcontroller Bus Architecture

Advanced Microcontroller Bus Architecture (AMBA) is a collection of on-chip bus protocol specifications used by Arm processors as well as a wide range of on-chip digital components such as memory interfaces, peripherals and debug components. The specification is developed by Arm and is an open standard available to the chip design industry. It means that companies do not need to pay license or royalty fees for using the bus protocol spec in their designs. AMBA is widely supported, and many companies develop AMBA-compatible system IP.

Unlike most other bus protocols such as PCI, AMBA bus protocols are designed for on-chip communications. To enable easier system integration inside chip designs, almost all the AMBA specifications have the following characteristics:

- Synchronous operations – use only clock rising edge for flip-flops, friendly to common synthesis flow;

- No on-chip bi-directional signals – avoiding the need for tri-state buffers.

The most common AMBA bus protocols used in microcontrollers include:

- **AHB** (Advanced High-performance Bus) – a lightweight pipelined bus protocol used in the majority of the Arm Cortex-M processors.

- **APB** (Advanced Peripheral Bus) – a simple bus protocol for connecting general simple peripherals with low data bandwidth requirements.

- **AXI** (Advanced eXtensible Interface) – a high-performance bus protocol for efficient, high-performance processors including the Cortex-M7 processor, Cortex-R processors and the majority of the Arm Cortex-A processors. The AXI protocol:

  - Provides multiple data channels running concurrently at high clock frequency.

  - Allows new transfers to be issued and take place even with previous transfers still outstanding.

  - Supports unaligned data and provides data security based on TrustZone technology.

3.1.2 History of AMBA

The AMBA standard was developed by Arm and became an open standard from version 2 in 1996. The version 2.0 of AMBA specification consists of three bus types: AHB, ASB and APB. Both AHB (Advanced High-Performance Bus) and APB (Advanced Peripheral Bus) are popular choices in system-on-chip designs, and both have been extended in newer AMBA versions. The ASB (Advanced System Bus) is obsolete and was only used in older generation Arm cores.

You might wonder why the AMBA standard was developed? Although there are many bus standards in existence, they mainly focus on circuit board level connections. These types of interface standards contain overhead for supporting signal multiplexing, configuration detection, and electrical characteristics handling (e.g., turn-around time when signals switch direction). Overheads of this kind do not apply to system-on-chip environments. At the same time, there is a need to have an open standard to allow better design reusability and enable Intellectual Properties (IP) providers to develop peripherals for the Arm platform. As a result, Arm published the AMBA 2 specification as an open standard (royalty-free), and this has become the most popular processor interface standard for embedded 32-bit processors. Due to its open nature and simplicity, AMBA has been for some time a de-facto standard for bus interface in system-on-chip architectures. The low overhead and low latency characteristics are often necessary for high speed embedded systems. The AHB protocol also supports pipelined operation, which is important to most designs.

3.1.3 Various versions of AMBA specification
The AMBA specification family has evolved over the years. Some of the protocols were introduced in later releases, and not all were updated in more recent AMBA versions.

	Notes	AMBA 2	AMBA 3	AMBA 4	AMBA 5
ASB (Advanced System Bus)	Used on ARM7TDMI, obsoleted	ASB			
AHB (Advanced High-performance Bus)	Used on the Cortex-M processors	AHB	AHB-Lite		AHB5
APB (Advanced Peripheral Bus)	Used on almost all Arm processor systems	APB2	APB3	APB4	
AXI (Advanced eXtensible Interface)	Used on high-performance processors		AXI3	AXI4 AXI4-Lite AXI4-Stream	AXI5
ACE (AXI Coherency Extension)	Used on high-performance processors with cache coherency requirements			ACE ACE-Lite	ACE5 ACE5-Lite
CHI (Coherent Hub Interface)	Advanced coherency management				CHI
DTI (Distributed Translation Interface)	Used with system-level Memory Management Unit (MMU)				DTI
Low-power Interface specification	For power management			Q channel and P channel	
ATB (Advanced Trace Bus)	For transferring trace data during debugging		ATB		

Table 3.1: Bus protocols in the AMBA specification family.

In this chapter, we will only cover the AHB and APB protocols as they are the most commonly used in simple embedded microcontrollers and SoC designs. For other protocols, the specifications can be downloaded from the Arm website. Additional reference materials are also available:

	Web page address
AMBA	https://developer.arm.com/architectures/system-architectures/amba
ACE	https://www.arm.com/files/pdf/CacheCoherencyWhitepaper_6June2011.pdf
CHI	https://community.arm.com/processors/b/blog/posts/what-is-amba-5-chi-and-how-does-it-help

Table 3.2: Reference sources for some of the bus protocols that are out of scope for this document.

3.2 Overview of AHB

3.2.1 Various versions of AHB

The AHB specification was first released as a part of the AMBA 2 Specification. It is a multi-master, multi-slave bus protocol designed to support embedded processors with very low silicon overhead and low latency. Most of the AHB based systems are 32-bit, but the protocol is designed to support different bus sizes. The typical bus width for AHB systems is 32 or 64-bit.

The AHB standard has gone through multiple releases and phases:

- AMBA 2 AHB – first release. This specification release uses a pair of handshaking signals (Bus Request and Bus Granted) for arbitration between multiple bus masters.

- Multi-layer AHB designs – The AMBA Design Kit product from Arm introduced an AHB interconnect component called AHB Bus Matrix. This enables concurrent bus transfers in multi-master systems for higher bandwidth, avoids the need for the Bus Request and Bus Granted signals, and was unofficially called 'AHB Lite.'

- In the AMBA 3 Specification, AHB Lite became the official name. It removed Bus Request and Bus Granted signals and simplified several other aspects of the AHB protocol. It is used on many Arm processor systems.

- In the AMBA 5 specification, AHB has been updated to support TrustZone for Armv8-M and add official support for exclusive access sideband signals. It also introduced several improvements including additional cache attribute support and clarifications.

AMBA 5 AHB (also known as AHB5) is the most recent release of the AHB specification. In many ways it is highly compatible with its predecessor and existing bus slaves designed for AHB Lite can be reused in AHB5 systems.

3.2.2 AHB signals

An AHB system operates with a clock signal called HCLK. This signal is common to all bus masters, bus slaves, and the bus infrastructure blocks in a bus segment. All registers on the AHB trigger at rising edges of HCLK. There is also an active-low reset signal called HRESETn. When this signal is low, it resets the AHB system immediately (asynchronous reset). This allows a system to be reset even if the clock is stopped. For correct operation, the HRESETn signal itself should be synchronized to HCLK so that race conditions can be avoided. Otherwise, if the HRESETn de-asserts about the same time as HCLK rising edge, you might find that parts of the registers are still reset at the clock edge and some are not.

For a typical AHB system, you can find most of the following signals:

Signals	Direction	Descriptions
HCLK	Clock source → all AHB blocks	Common clock signal
HRESETn	Reset source → all AHB blocks	Common active-low reset signal
HSEL	Address decoder → Slave	Device select
HADDR[31:0]	Master → Slave	Address bus
HTRANS[1:0]	Master → Slave	Transfer control
HWRITE	Master → Slave	Write control (1=Write, 0=Read)
HSIZE[2:0]	Master → Slave	Transfer Size control
HBURST[2:0]	Master → Slave	Transfer Burst Type control
HPROT[3:0]/[6:0]	Master → Slave	Transfer Protection control. 4 bits in AHB Lite, extended to 7 bits in AHB5
HMASTLOCK	Master → Slave	Transfer Lock control
HMASTER[3:0]	Bus components → Bus slave	Indicates current bus master identity[1]
HWDATA[31:0]	Master → Slave	Write data (typically 32-bit, but it can be 64-bit wide on 64-bit systems)
HRDATA[31:0]	Master ← Slave	Read Data (typically 32-bit, but it can be 64-bit wide on 64-bit systems)
HRESP[1:0] / HRESP	Master ← Slave	Slave response (2 bit wide in AMBA 2, 1 bit wide in AHB Lite and AHB5)
HREADY (HREADYOUT)	Master ← Slave (HREADYOUT), Bus component → other slaves (HREADY)	Slave ready (transfer completed). The HREADY signal goes two ways. The currently selected slave drives the HREADY to bus master as well as all other AHB slaves. As a result, an AHB slave has HREADY input and HREADYOUT output.

Table 3.3: Typical AHB signals.

AMBA 5 AHB introduced additional signals:

Signals	Direction	Descriptions
HNONSEC	Master → Slave	Security attribute of the transfer (TrustZone support)
HEXCL	Master → Slave	Indicates the transfer is Exclusive access
HEXOKAY	Master ← Slave	Exclusive access success response
HAUSER	Master → Slave	Optional user sideband for address phase signals (the actual definition of this signal is system-specific)
HWUSER	Master → Slave	Optional user sideband for data phase signals (the actual definition of this signal is system-specific)
HRUSER	Master ← Slave	Optional user sideband for data phase signals (the actual definition of this signal is system-specific)

Table 3.4: Additional signals defined in AHB5.

[1] AHB3 does not have HMASTER though most Cortex-M processors using AHB-Lite have an HMASTER signal provided.

For older AHB systems (AMBA 2) that use AHB Arbiter to handle multiple master accesses, you can also see the following signals:

Signals	Direction	Descriptions
HBUSREQ	Master → Arbiter	Bus access request
HGRANT	Master ← Arbiter	Bus granted
HLOCK	Master → Arbiter	Lock transfer control
HMASTLOCK	Arbiter ← Slave	Transfer Lock control In newer AHB systems Arbiter is not used and HMASTLOCK is generated by the bus master or bus interconnect

Table 3.5: AMBA 2 AHB signals for arbiter connections.

Many of the signals are optional. For a minimal AHB system with a single Arm Cortex-M0 processor, it is possible to create a working system using:

- HCLK, HRESETn, HADDR, HTRANS, HSIZE, HWRITE, HSEL, HWDATA, HRDATA, HRESP, and HREADY signals.

3.2.3 Basic operations

In a simple design with just one bus master (e.g., a Cortex-M processor) and multiple bus slaves, the design can be arranged as follows:

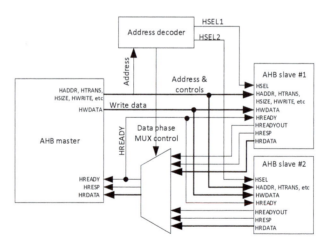

Figure 3.1: Simple AHB system with one AHB master and two AHB slaves.

The connections between AHB masters and AHB slaves based on the AMBA 5 Specification can be viewed in the following diagram: multiple bus masters share the same bus using a master multiplexer, controlled by a bus arbiter. The return data and responses from bus slaves are also multiplexed using a slave multiplexer and feedback to the bus masters.

The signals are grouped into "address phase" signals and "data phase" signals.

The **address phase** signals include:

▪ HADDR, HTRANS, HSEL, HWRITE, HSIZE.
▪ Optional: HPROT, HBURST, HMASTLOCK, HEXCL, HAUSER.

The **data phase** signals include:

▪ HWDATA, HRDATA, HRESP, HREADY (and HREADYOUT).
▪ Optional: HEXOKAY, HWUSER, HRUSER.

Each transfer is composed of an address phase and data phase. The transfers are pipelined. The address phase of a transfer can be overlapped with the data phase of the previous transfer.

Figure 3.2: Splitting of a transfer into address phase and data phase.

Each phase is terminated by the assertion of HREADYOUT (HREADY) from the currently activated AHB slave in the data phase. The HREADYOUT from the AHB slaves are multiplexed by the slave multiplexer, forming the system-wide HREADY signal. The multiplexer is operating at the data phase of each transfer. Control of the multiplexer can be generated from the AHB decoder, or the HSEL signals and the HREADY signal.

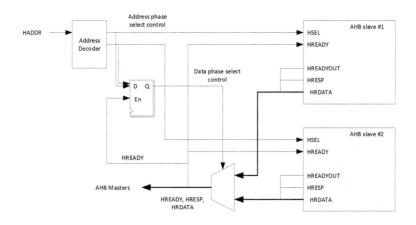

Figure 3.3: HREADYOUT route from AHB slave output to HREADY inputs of AHB slaves and AHB masters.

If an AHB slave is not currently selected, its HREADYOUT should be high to indicate it is ready. However, it can only accept a transfer from the bus master when the previous transfer is completed, indicated by a high level in the system-wide HREADY. For example, if transfer N selects AHB slave A, transfer N+1 selects AHB slave B, and transfer N+2 selects AHB slave C, the waveform can be like:

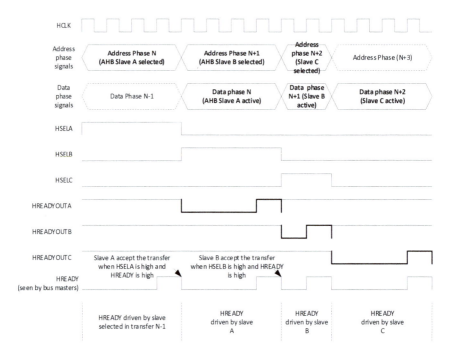

Figure 3.4: AHB transfer can only be accepted when the previous transfer is completed, indicated by HREADY being high.

3.2.4 Minimal AHB systems

In a minimal AHB system with a single bus master (e.g., a Cortex-M processor) and bus slaves, we would expect to find the following components:

Components	Descriptions
Address decoder	Based on HADDR input, generates HSEL signals to bus slaves and AHB slave multiplexer
AHB slave multiplexer	Connect multiple bus slaves to a single AHB segment
Default slave	This is a special type of AHB bus slave, which is selected when the transfer address (HADDR) does not match the address range of other AHB slaves. This only happens when something has gone wrong (e.g., the software attempts to access an invalid memory location due to an error in C pointer processing). This bus slave only returns an ERROR response when accessed, write data is ignored by the default slave, and it returns 0 for read accesses. Default slave is optional - If the address space is fully-utilized by other bus slaves, then there is no default slave.

Table 3.6: AHB infrastructure components needed in a minimal AHB system.

The design of the address decoder is system-specific – each system has its memory map, and the chip designers need to create the address decoder for each bus slave accordingly. The HSEL signal is an address phase signal generated by decoding the HADDR signal. Since the HSEL generation process is combinatorial, the design of memory maps needs to avoid complex decoding of HADDR. Otherwise, the synthesis timing could be affected.

The design of AHB slave multiplexer can be much more generic and is available in various Arm AHB based system IP bundles. Since each AHB slave has their own read data output and response outputs, an AHB slave multiplexor is needed to select the return data and response from the current active slave.

The slave multiplexer is controlled by a data phase version of the HSEL signal (delayed by one pipeline stage). This can be generated by registering the HSEL with system-wide HREADY as the enable signal, as shown in Figure 3.3. In most cases, the functionality of delaying the HSEL is included within the AHB slave multiplexor, so the system integrator only needs to connect the address phase HSEL to the AHB slave multiplexor.

There can be more than one address decoder and slave multiplexer in an AHB system. For example, an AHB system design can be divided into two or more subsystems, and each AHB subsystem can contain only a part of the memory space. In this case, the address decoders in the subsystems also need to take account of the HSEL signals from the top-level address decoder.

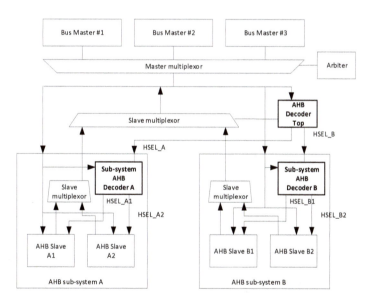

Figure 3.5: Multiple AHB decoders could be needed if the AHB system is divided into multiple subsystems.

3.2.5 Handling of multiple bus masters

The connections between AHB masters and AHB slaves based on the AMBA 2 Specification can be viewed as the following diagram: multiple bus masters share the same bus using a master multiplexer, controlled by a bus arbiter. The return data and responses from bus slaves are also multiplexed using a slave multiplexer, and feedback to the bus masters.

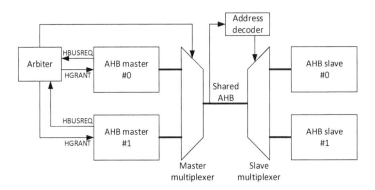

Figure 3.6: AMBA 2 AHB system with two AHB masters and two AHB slaves.

The HBUSREQ (Bus Request) and HGRANT (Bus Granted) handshaking take place before the bus master is allowed to issue any transfers:

▨ A bus master must first assert a bus request (HBUSREQ) to the arbiter, then

▨ After arbitration, the arbiter returns the bus granted signal (HGRANT) to one of the bus masters, then

▨ The bus master can then generate transfers on the bus.

▨ If the HGRANT signal is de-asserted, the bus master must stop issuing new transfers.

This arrangement works for simple systems, but the maximum bus bandwidth is limited. When the AMBA Design Kit (ADK) product was launched, a new approach called multi-layer AHB was used to support multiple bus masters.

The AHB Bus Matrix component in the ADK is an AHB interconnect component with multiple bus ports for connections to bus masters and multiple bus ports for connection to AHB slaves. Potentially, each bus port for bus slave connection could have multiple bus slaves connected to it by having additional bus slave multiplexer.

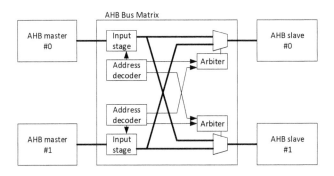

Figure 3.7: System with multiple bus masters using AHB Bus Matrix.

To resolve the bus access conflict when multiple bus masters try to access to the same bus slave at the same time, each master port (the port that connects to AHB slaves) has an arbiter. If a transfer from a bus master is targeting a bus slave, which is accessing by a different bus master, the incoming transfer is held in the input stage with a buffer. With this arrangement, the HBUSREQ and HGRANT signals are no longer needed.

The bus matrix design allows different bus masters to access to different bus slaves at the same time, hence enhance the system bandwidth.

The bus matrix component in AMBA Design Kit is configurable and was enhanced when the Arm Cortex-M System Design Kit (CMSDK) was developed. In newer IP product development, the AHB Bus Matrix is now part of the Corstone foundation IP / CoreLink SDK (System Design Kit).

For systems that do not require high data bandwidth, a simplified arrangement similar to the AHB in AMBA 2 can be used with the AHB Master Multiplexer. The redesigned AHB master multiplexer component has its internal input stage and arbiter, just like the AHB bus matrix. However, since there is one downstream AHB, there is no need for an internal address decoder.

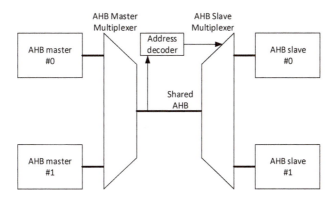

Figure 3.8: System with multiple bus masters using AHB Master Multiplexer.

3.3 More details on the AHB protocol

3.3.1 Address phase signals

There are several essential transfer control signals in the address phase. These are HTRANS, HADDR, HWRITE, and HSIZE.

The HTRANS signal is used to indicate transfer types. Most AHB systems do not need to handle data transfers 100% of the time. When a bus master does not need to start another transfer immediately, it can issue an idle transfer. The HTRANS signal in the AHB is used to indicate if the current transfer is an active transfer or in idle state.

HTRANS[1:0]	Descriptions
00	IDLE (non-active)
01	BUSY (non-active)
10	Non-Sequential (active)
11	Sequential (active)

Table 3.7: HTRANS encoding.

When a data transfer is needed, the AHB master generates a Non-sequential (NSEQ) or a Sequential (SEQ) transfer. NSEQ is used in normal transfers or at the beginning of a burst transfer, and SEQ is used for the remaining part of a burst transfer, indicating that the transfer is a continuation of the previous one.

Both IDLE and BUSY are non-active transfers. It means that no real data transfer takes place. BUSY is only used when the bus master has started a burst transfer but is not ready to handle the next data transfer. In this case, it issues the BUSY transfer between the burst transfers to keep the burst sequence going, and continues with the next sequential transfer when it is ready.

The HADDR signal is usually 32-bit and specifies the address of the transfer. HWRITE signal indicates that the transfer is a write transfer if it is set to 1, or if it is set to 0, then the transfer is a read operation.

HWRITE	Descriptions
0	Read operation
1	Write operation

Table 3.8: HWRITE encoding.

The HSIZE signal is used to indicate the data size to be transferred. Typically, the HSIZE signal is 3-bit wide, but in most AHB systems only the lowest two bits are used so that you might find some systems or AHB components with HSIZE of only two bits.

HSIZE[2:0]	Size of transfer
000	Byte
001	Half-word
010	Word
011	Double word (64-bit)
100	128-bit
101	256-bit
110	512-bit
111	1024-bit

Table 3.9: HSIZE encoding.

When a bus master generates a transfer, the bus master should ensure that the data being transferred is aligned. In other words, a half-word transfer should only take place in even memory addresses, and a word transfer should only take place in addresses divisible by 4. The AHB interface does not support unaligned transfers; if a bus master needs to access unaligned data, it should split the transfer into multiple aligned AHB transfers of smaller size.

The Cortex-M processors can generate read and write transfers of byte, half-word, or word size. In some of the Cortex-M processors like the Cortex-M3 and Cortex-M4, Instruction fetches are always in word size. For some others like the Cortex-M0+ and Cortex-M23 processors, instruction fetch of a branch target could be in word or half-word size, depending on the instruction address alignment.

Besides the crucial AHB control signals, there are also optional sideband signals in the AHB interface. They are helpful for processor systems, for example, providing privilege level information and supporting burst transfers. However, they might not be present in some AHB systems.

Signals	Descriptions
HPROT[3:0]/[6:0]	Protection information (AHB5 has 7 bits of HPROT, and previous versions of AHB has 4-bits)
HNONSEC	Security attribute (available in AHB5 only. This is needed for TrustZone security extension)
HBURST[2:0]	Burst transfer information
HMASTLOCK	Indicate the transfer sequence is atomic, so bus ownership is locked until this signal is released
HMASTER[3:0]	Indicates which bus master issued the current transfer. In some Cortex-M processors, this signal is used to indicate the transfer types (e.g., whether the transfer is generated by the debugger). The width of this signal can be customized to fit the system requirement.
HEXCL	Exclusive access indication signal. This signal is introduced in AHB5 to support exclusive accesses in Arm processors. The bus slave response to exclusive access with HEXOKAY, a data phase signal.
HAUSER[x-1:0]	This is a user-defined address phase signal introduced in AHB5. Potentially it could be used for the following: propagation of additional information about the transfer; parity bits for address phase control signals.

Table 3.10: Additional AHB control signals in the address phase.

In AMBA 2 AHB and AHB Lite, the HPROT signal contains 4 bits, each of them has a different function:

Signal	Function	When equal 0	When equal 1
HPROT[0]	Data/Opcode	Instruction fetch	Data Access
HPROT[1]	Privileged	Non-privileged (user)	Privileged
HPROT[2]	Bufferable	The transfer must complete before a new transfer is issued	Write transfer can be buffered
HPROT[3]	Cacheable	Data cannot be cached	Data can be cached

Table 3.11: HPROT encoding.

When accessing to normal memories (not peripherals), the encoding of the HPROT[3:2] can be used to indicate cache types:

HPROT[3:2]

2'b00	Device (non-bufferable)
2'b01	Device (bufferable)
2'b10	Cacheable memory with Write Through
2'b11	Cacheable memory with Write Back

Table 3.12: Cache type indication with AMBA 2 AHB / AHB Lite.

In AMBA 5 AHB, the cache attribute information is extended, and as a result, the HPROT signal becomes:

Signal	Function	When equal 0	When equal 1
HPROT[0]	Data/Opcode	Instruction fetch	Data Access
HPROT[1]	Privileged	Non-privileged (user)	Privileged
HPROT[2]	Bufferable	The transfer must complete before a new transfer is issued	Write transfer can be buffered
HPROT[3]	Modifiable	Data cannot be cached	Data can be cached
HPROT[4]	Lookup	The transfer is not cached	The transfer must be looked up in the cache
HPROT[5]	Allocate	No need for cache line allocation	Allocate cacheline on cache miss
HPROT[6]	Sharable	Data is not shared (no need to maintain data coherency) or transfer is to a Device (Non-cacheable)	Bus interconnect needs to ensure data coherency

Table 3.13: HPROT encoding in AHB5.

The cache type indication with AMBA 5 AHB is shown below:

HPROT[6] Sharable	HPROT[5] Allocate	HPROT[4] Lookup	HPROT[3] Modifiable	HPROT[2] Bufferable	Memory Type
0	0	0	0	0	Non bufferable Devices
0	0	0	0	1	Bufferable Device
0	0	0	1	0	Normal Non-cacheable, Non-shareable memory
0	0 or 1	1	1	0	Write Through, Non-shareable memory
0	0 or 1	1	1	1	Write-Back, Non-shareable memory
1	0	0	1	0	Normal Non-cacheable, shareable memory
1	0 or 1	1	1	0	Write Through, shareable memory
1	0 or 1	1	1	1	Write-Back, shareable memory

Table 3.14: Cache type indication with AMBA 5 AHB.

The Cortex-M0 processor does not have a user access level, so HPROT[1] is always 1. Since Cortex-M0/M0+/M3/M4/M23/M33 processors do not support internal cache, the cacheability information is often not used.

Another address phase signal is HBURST, which indicates a burst transfer type. Burst transfer can often improve system performance if the memory device can access data quicker when the accesses are in sequential orders. If a burst transfer is used, the HBURST signal will indicate the burst transfer type. AHB supports several types of burst transfers:

▪ Single. (Not burst transfer. Each transfer is separated from each other.)

▪ Incrementing burst transfer. (The address is incremented by the size of the transfer.)

▪ Wrapping burst transfer. For each transfer, the address increments as in an incrementing burst except when the address reaches the block size boundary of the burst. In this case, the address wraps round to the beginning of the block size boundary. The block size of the burst can be determined from the number of beats times the size of each transfer.

Burst transfer sequence is composed of multiple "beats." Each beat is an AHB transfer with addresses linked to others inside the burst. Within a burst, the transfer size, direction, and control information of each transfer must be the same-. Both incrementing and wrapping bursts are supported for 4-beats, 8-beats, and 16-beats transfers. Incremental bursts can also be of unspecified length.

HBURST[2:0]	Burst Type	Descriptions
000	Single	Single transfer (not burst)
001	INCR	Incrementing burst of unspecified length
010	WRAP4	Wrapping burst with 4 beats
011	INCR4	Incrementing burst with 4 beats
100	WRAP8	Wrapping burst with 8 beats
101	INCR8	Incrementing burst with 8 beats
110	WRAP16	Wrapping burst with 16 beats
110	INCR16	Incrementing burst with 16 beats

Table 3.15: HBURST encoding.

Wrapping burst is useful in cache controller designs. For example, when a processor requests to read word data in address 0x1008, a cache controller for cache line size of 4 words might want to fetch address 0x1000, 0x1004, 0x1008 and 0x100C into the cache memory. In this case, it can use a 4-beats incrementing burst from address 0x1000, or a wrapping burst from address 0x1008. If wrapping burst is used, the address wraps around in a block size boundary, which is four times word size, or four words. Therefore, the address wraps around to 0x1000 after the transfer to 0x100C.

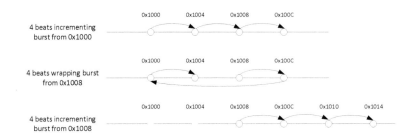

Figure 3.9: Incrementing burst versus wrapping burst (word size).

The wrapping burst transfers the same data as the incrementing burst, but it has the additional advantage that the data needed by the processor can be transferred first, hence, reducing the waiting time in the processor. Wrapping burst is commonly used by cache memory line fill. It allows the processor core to access the required data as soon as possible while allowing the rest of the data in the cache line to be cached. Unlike wrapping burst, an incrementing burst from address 0x1008 will not fetch the data in 0x1000 and 0x1004, so it is not suitable for caching because the data for the cache line is not complete.

Burst transfers can be carried out in different data sizes (e.g., byte, halfword, word, etc.). For each beat, the address calculation should be adjusted by the size of the transfer data. There is a restriction in burst generation: An AHB burst must not cross a 1K byte address boundary. This is because:

▓ Easier design of AHB device: to optimize the performance for burst transfers, both AHB masters and AHB slaves might need to have internal counters to monitor the burst operation and possibly for advance address generation. By limiting the burst transfers to within a 1K byte address boundary, a 10-bit counter will be sufficient for all possible burst transfers, even if third parties develop some of the blocks in the system.

▓ It prevents a burst from going across multiple AHB slaves. If a burst crosses a device memory boundary, the second device receiving the burst will have a SEQ transfer as its first transfer, which violates the AHB protocol.

HMASTLOCK is used to indicate the bus ownership should be locked for an atomic access sequence. When HMASTLOCK is set, the bus infrastructure (e.g., arbiter) must not switch the bus ownership until the HMASTLOCK is released. This is commonly used for semaphore operations, where a memory location (lock flag) is used to indicate a resource is locked by a process or processor. When a processor needs to lock a resource, it carries out a locked transfer sequence that reads the lock flag and then updates it. Since the read-modify-write transfers are locked (atomic), another bus master cannot change the lock flag between the two transfers, and hence this prevents race conditions.

Apart from the Cortex-M3 and Cortex-M4 processors, most of the Cortex-M processors do not use HMASTLOCK signal. In Cortex-M3 and Cortex-M4 processors, HMASTLOCK is used for atomic read-modify-write when a bit-band write operation take place. For other Cortex-M processors, if the processor top-level does not have HMASTLOCK and connects to a standard AHB component that has HMASTLOCK. The unused signal can be tied to 0.

In a system with multiple bus masters, the arbiter or master multiplexer can output a signal called HMASTER. This is used as an ID value for AHB slaves. In most cases, the AHB slave does not need to know which bus master is accessing it. However, in a few cases, a peripheral might need to have different behaviors when accessed by different bus masters. In the Cortex-M processors, often the HMASTER signal is used to indicate if the transfer is generated by software running on the processor or by debugger connected to the processor.

3.3.2 Data phase signals
There are several AHB data phase signals. For signals from bus masters to bus slaves:

Signals	Descriptions
HWDATA[n-1:0]	Write data. Data bus width "n" is typically 32, but can also be 64-bit.
HWUSER[x-1:0]	This is a user-defined data phase signal introduced in AHB5 connecting from the bus master to bus slaves. Potentially this can be used for: Parity bits for write data.

Table 3.16: Additional AHB data phase signals from bus masters to bus slaves.

Signals	Descriptions
HRDATA[n-1:0]	Read data. Data bus width "n" is typically 32, but can also be 64-bit
HRUSER[x-1:0]	This is a user-defined data phase signal introduced in AHB5 connect from bus slaves to bus masters. Potentially this can be used for: - Parity bits for read data.
HRESP / HRESP[1:0]	Bus response type. In AHB Lite and AHB5, this signal is single bit. In AMBA 2 AHB, this is two bits
HREADY / HREADYOUT	HREADYOUT signals are generated from bus slaves. After the AHB slave multiplexer merges the responses from bus slaves, the result HREADY is returned to all the bus slaves in the same AHB segment to indicate the end of the current bus phase.
HEXOKAY	Exclusive access is okay. This was introduced in AHB5. If the bus transfer is indicated as exclusive access.

Table 3.17: Additional AHB data phase signals from bus slaves to bus masters.

HRDATA and HWDATA
Data buses on AHB systems are usually 32-bit or 64-bit. For Cortex-M processors with AHB interface, the data connections on the AHB are 32-bit only. Aside from word transfers, AHB also allows transfers of byte and half-word data. The position of the data on the bus depends on the transfer size as well as the address. For example, for byte transfers, the data position on the bus is:

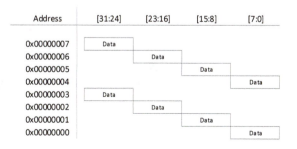

Figure 3.10: Data position in HWDATA/HRDATA during byte transfers.

Similarly, if the transfer is in half-word size, the data appears on the data bus as:

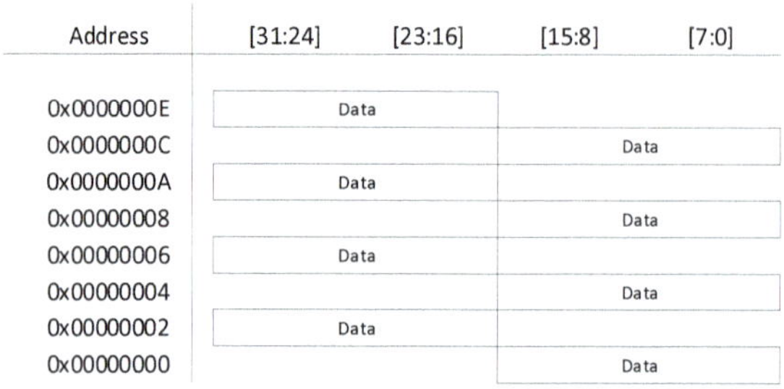

Address	[31:24]	[23:16]	[15:8]	[7:0]
0x0000000E		Data		
0x0000000C			Data	
0x0000000A		Data		
0x00000008			Data	
0x00000006		Data		
0x00000004			Data	
0x00000002		Data		
0x00000000			Data	

Figure 3.11: Data position in HWDATA/HRDATA during halfword transfers.

For word transfers, the whole 32-bit is used.

AMBA 2 AHB, AHB LITE and AHB 5 support aligned transfers only. Unaligned transfers are not supported (except for the ARM1136 processor, which has extra sideband signals to support unaligned transfers). Aligned transfers have address values which are a multiple of the transfer size. For example, word transfer addresses have address values that are multiples of 4, and half-word transfers have address values that are multiples of 2. Byte transfers are always aligned.

HRESP

The HRESP signals are responses from the AHB slaves. In AHB for AMBA 2, these can be OKAY, ERROR, RETRY, or SPLIT. Hence the HRESP is two-bit wide. For AHB LITE and AHB5, they can only be OKAY or ERROR and are one bit wide.

When an AHB slave receives a transfer, it should carry out the transfer as requested by the AHB master. If needed, it can insert wait states during the data phase. In normal circumstances, an AHB slave should generate an OKAY response status, indicated by zeros in HRESP[1:0].

HRESP[1:0]	Response	Description
00	OKAY	Transfer carried out successfully
01	ERROR	An error occurred
10	RETRY	The AHB slave cannot carry out the transfer immediately. The AHB master should retry the transfer.
11	SPLIT	The AHB slave cannot carry out the transfer immediately. The AHB master can drop bus ownership, and when the AHB slave is ready, it can request bus ownership to complete the transfer.

Table 3.18: HRESP encoding.

The OKAY response can be a single-cycle (no wait state is needed), but other responses are two cycles, with the possibility of additional wait states before the response is asserted. For a simple case of an AHB slave read, followed by a write, and then idle, it can look like:

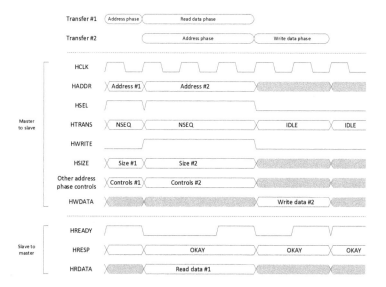

Figure 3.12: AHB Slave interface – a read with 2 wait states, followed by a write with 1 wait state.

Note that the AHB slave should not start to process a transfer on the AHB until it sees that HREADY is high. In the Figure 3.12, the AHB slave does not start to process the transfer request of a second transfer until HREADY is high (fourth cycle), and starts the data phase of the second transfer from the fifth cycle.

In case the slave cannot handle the transfer due to an error condition, it can respond with ERROR on the HRESP signal. The error response must be two cycles wide. Using the previous example, if both transfers reply with error response, the waveform will look like:

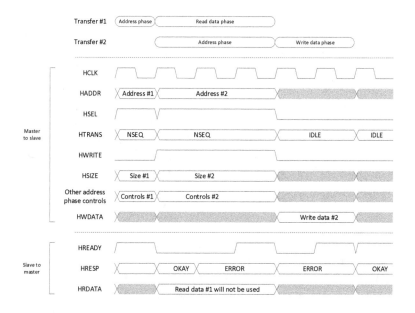

Figure 3.13: AHB Slave interface – a read with 2 wait states with error response, followed by a write with 1 wait state and error response.

An error response must be two cycles, but additional wait states with OKAY responses can be added before the error response. The minimum data phase for an error response is two cycles. Having a single-cycle error response is illegal.

Upon receiving the first cycle of the error responses (when HREADY is still low), the bus master can choose to continue the announced transfer in the next cycle, or cancel the announced transfer by putting HTRANS as IDLE. The behavior might depend on which processor you are using.

An AHB slave must respond OKAY in the next cycle with no wait state if the HTRANS is IDLE or BUSY, or if HSEL is not active.

RETRY and SPLIT responses have the same waveform as an ERROR response. However, they are used when the AHB slave is not ready to complete the transfer in a short time. They ask the bus master to drop the current transfer and retry it later. By doing this, and if the system contains multiple bus masters, they provide a chance for other bus masters to take ownership of the bus to prevent bandwidth from being wasted.

On the bus master side, RETRY and SPLIT are handled differently. When a bus master receives the first cycle RETRY response, it will cancel the current announced transfer by replacing it with an IDLE transfer, and then retry the transfer that the slave could not process from the last attempt.

On the other hand, when a bus master receives the first cycle of a SPLIT response, it cancels the currently announced transfer by replacing it with an IDLE transfer, at the same time dropping the HBUSREQ to bus arbiter to allow the bus ownership to be switched over. When the AHB slave is ready to receive the transfer, it uses a separate sideband signal called HSPLIT to alert the arbiter to restore bus ownership to the bus master, which can then issue the transfer again.

Due to the complexity of the operation, SPLIT response and HSPLIT signals are rarely used. Starting from 2001, the multi-layer AHB approach was developed and effectively made SPLIT and RETRY mechanisms obsolete because the new solution is easier to use and can prevent a single transfer from slowing down the rest of the system, while at the same time allowing a higher system bandwidth to be achieved.

Some Cortex-M processors like Cortex-M3 and Cortex-M4 have two-bits wide HRESP but are designed for AHB Lite. This is because the processor was released before the AHB Lite specification was officialized. When the AHB LITE system is connected to such a bus master, for example, the Cortex-M3 processor, it is possible that the HRESP from the AHB slave is only 1-bit wide (the HRESP[1] signal is not implemented). In this case, only the HRESP[0] needs to be connected, and HRESP[1] can be tied 0 since HRESP[1] should never be asserted in an AHB LITE system.

HEXOKAY
HEXOKAY is designed to support exclusive access operations. It was introduced in AMBA 5 AHB and is generated by a global exclusive access monitor in the bus system. Exclusive access sequences contain an exclusive load and an exclusive store of the same data. The exclusive access monitor detects if the same data might have been modified by another bus master between the load and store. If there is a potential access conflict, the monitor blocks the store operation and returns an exclusive fail status using HEXOKAY.

When an exclusive store occurs, HEXOKAY is asserted at the same cycle as HREADY if the global exclusive access monitor does not detect an access conflict. Otherwise, the HEXOKAY remains low (an exclusive access conflict might result if the bus slave does not support exclusive accesses).

HEXOKAY must not be asserted in the same cycle as HRESP is asserted (i.e., ERROR response). More information on exclusive accesses is contained in Section 3.4.

3.3.3 Legacy arbiter handshake signals

If using AMBA 2 AHB with multiple AHB masters, you might need to deal with the legacy arbiter handshaking signals. (In general, multi-layer AHB is preferred for performance reasons and can be used with AHB bus masters with AMBA 2 AHB interface).

The bus arbiter solution requires each bus master to have a HBUSREQ (Bus Request) output and a HGRANT (Bus Granted) signal. Optionally the bus masters can also provide a HLOCK signal to indicate they need to carry out a locked transfer. All these signals are connected to the bus arbiter.

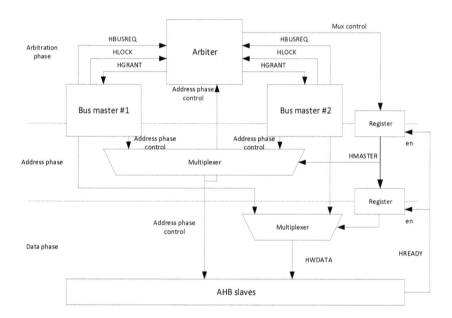

Figure 3.14: Example of arbiter with two bus masters.

Basically, the arbitration phase is a step ahead of the address phase. If the address phase is multi-cycled, the arbiter updates the arbitration continuously. At the end of a transfer phase, the arbitration result is captured by the register and becomes the HMASTER signal, which indicates which bus master is the current owner of the bus. Since the bus masters will know the arbitration result one cycle earlier based on HGRANT, they can prepare for the switching and start outputting their transfers on the AHB as soon as HMASTER switch to route the bus master's outputs to the AHB slaves.

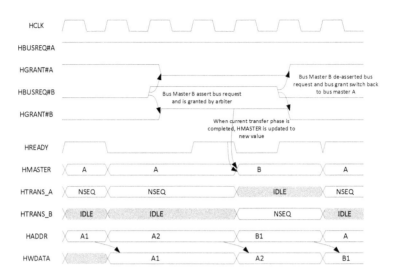

Figure 3.15: Example waveform of bus ownership switching.

In the example in Figure 3.15, two bus masters share one AHB. In the waveform, bus master #A continuously requests bus accesses, and during transfer accesses from master A, master B requests the bus as well. In this example, bus master B has higher priority, so the arbiter switches the bus grant signal to allow bus master B to gain access to the bus when the current transfer phase is completed. When HREADY goes high, and HGRANT #B is high, this indicates that the current transfer phase has been completed and the bus master is given bus ownership; bus master B can then output its transfer control signals to the bus in the next cycle.

The control signals generated from the bus masters can be multiplexed to AHB slaves using the HMASTER signal. The only signal that must be handled differently is the HWDATA. This is a data phase signal; as a result, a further registration of HMASTER is needed to control the multiplexing of HWDATA.

Various arbitration schemes can be used for the arbiter. The most common arrangements are 'fix priority' or 'round robin.' More complex arrangements which support a mixture of multiple schemes can also be found. The arbitration process should usually also consider the type of transfer currently being applied to the AHB slave. If a burst transfer is taking place, the arbiter should wait until the burst is completed before switching the bus ownership. In addition, if one of the bus masters supports locked transfers (e.g., the ARM7TDMI processor generates lock transfers when a SWAP instruction is executed), the bus arbiter must also support the HLOCK signals from the bus master and must not switch the bus ownership if the processor is generating a locked transfer.

With bus arbiter solutions, if a bus slave needs a longer time to process a transfer, the bandwidth of the system can be badly impacted if the bus slave generates a long wait state. To solve this problem, the AHB slave can generate a RETRY response. When the bus master receives such response, it will retry the same transfer again. The retry process can repeat several times before the bus slave is finally able to complete the transfer. During this process, if another bus master requires bus access, the bus arbiter can switch the bus ownership so that the other transfer can be carried out.

The SPLIT response is very similar to the RETRY response, except that the bus master should drop the bus request and wait until the AHB slave responds with another signal HSPLIT.

3.4 Exclusive access operations

3.4.1 Introduction to exclusive accesses

Exclusive accesses are important for OS semaphore operations because they can detect access conflicts in the handling of read-modify-right (RMW) sequences. RMW access conflicts can happen when:

- A processor system is running an OS, and a context switch happened at the middle of a RMW sequence;

- One of the processors in a multiple processor system executes the RMW sequence, and another processor accesses the same memory location.

To handle exclusive accesses, several areas of support are needed:

1. Exclusive access instructions - In Cortex processors (except Armv6-M processors), exclusive access instructions (e.g., LDREX, STREX) are available to support exclusive accesses.

2. Exclusive access signals on the bus interface – exclusive access signals are introduced in AHB5. Previous Cortex-M processors (Cortex-M3/M4/M7) use non-standardized exclusive access sideband signals to support exclusive accesses.

3. System-level – for multi-processor systems, a bus-level global exclusive access monitor is needed to detect access conflicts between multiple bus masters. Potentially, multiple global exclusive access monitors could be used to detect access conflicts for different address ranges.

First, let us look at the access conflicts issue. Semaphores are needed in resource management in OS, for example, to ensure that different application threads/tasks won't try to access the same hardware resource (e.g., a DMA channel) at the same time. The OS uses data variables (e.g., a data variable can be used to indicate if a resource is locked) in memory to keep track of resource allocation, and the application thread can request the resource by calling APIs which have access to the semaphore data.

Take the case of semaphore data (P), which indicates that a DMA channel is allocated. An application task X calls an API to set this data to 1:

- Read P to see if the value is 0. If the value is 1, then the DMA channel is already allocated and return with fail status;

- Value of P is 0 (resource is free), write 1 to it to lock the resource ownership.

If the OS context switch happens between the read and the write operation, then another task Y can execute the same RMW sequence to set P to 1, and when the OS returns to task X, it resumes the RMW operation and writes 1 to the semaphore data. Now both task X and Y think that they have allocated the DMA channel resource.

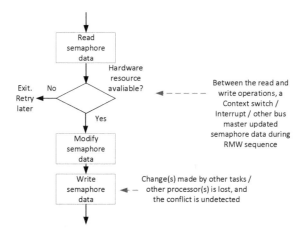

Figure 3.16: Semaphore access conflict with a simple read-modify-write sequence.

The same problem can happen between an application thread and an interrupt handler, or between two different processors. In the case of two processors, the following sequence can occur:

- Processor X read semaphore data P, got 0

- Processor Y read semaphore data P, got 0

- Processor X write 1 to P

- Processor Y write 1 to P

Now both threads running on processor X and Y believe that they have secured the DMA channel resource.

To solve this problem, legacy processors like Arm7TDMI use locked transfers to ensure that bus interconnect does not switch bus ownership in the middle of RMW. However, lock transfers cannot be implemented in high-speed bus protocols that use separated read and write bus channels. As a result, exclusive accesses were introduced in Armv6 architecture.

A simple exclusive access sequence is as follows:

- Processor X read semaphore data P with an exclusive load instruction;

- If the value of P is 0, Processor X write 1 to P with an exclusive store instruction;

- The exclusive store instruction returns a success or fail status. If the status is success, then the application task can continue the operation. If the status is fail, then it means there is a potential access conflict, and it needs to restart the RMW sequence. The store operation is blocked if the exclusive store returns fail status.

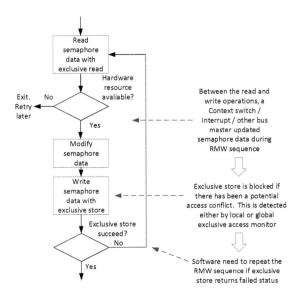

Figure 3.17: Concept of exclusive accesses.

To determine the return status, the system contains two exclusive access monitors:

- Local exclusive access monitor – This hardware is inside the processor, and it triggers exclusive fail if there has been a context switch (including exception entry/exit);

- Global exclusive access monitor – This hardware is at the bus level, and it triggers exclusive fail if another bus master has access to the address which is marked for exclusive access (when exclusive load is made).

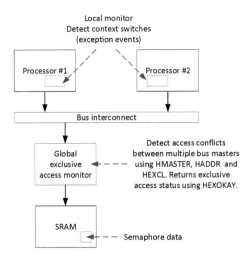

Figure 3.18: Local and global exclusive access monitors.

When the processor executes an exclusive store:

- If the local exclusive access monitor returns fail status – the exclusive store is blocked before it gets to the bus interface level, so it won't be carried out.

- If the global exclusive access monitor returns fail status - the exclusive store is blocked by the global exclusive store monitor, so the memory won't get updated.

- If either local or global exclusive access monitor return fail status, the write operation will not be carried out, and the processor should retry the RMW sequence.

3.4.2 AHB5 exclusive access support

To support exclusive access in AHB5, the following signals are needed by the global exclusive access monitor in addition to standard AHB Lite signals:

- HEXCL

- HEXOKAY

- HMASTER

To generate exclusive access responses, the global exclusive access monitor contains at least one Finite State Machine (FSM) and one tag register (it can contain multiples of these components).

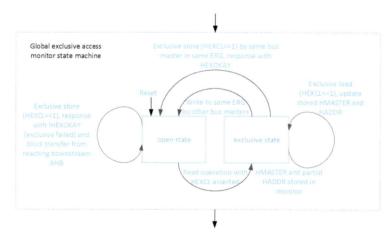

Figure 3.19: Global Exclusive Access Monitor.

The address tag in the monitor does not necessarily record all bits of the address value. Typically, the monitor can drop the lowest bits of the address as the exclusive fail information can be speculative:

- The data might be written with the same value.

- Nearby data could have been accessed by a different bus master.

There is no harm (except the cost of extra execution cycles and power) if the global exclusive access monitor returns exclusive fail status in these cases as the software just needs to repeat the RMW sequence.

The minimum region that can be tagged for exclusive access is called the Exclusive Reservation Granule (ERG). There can be different ERG sizes in different platforms, ranging from 8-bytes to 2048-bytes. It is common for Arm systems to use a 128 bytes ERG, it means bit 6 down to 0 are not stored in the address tags in the global exclusive access monitors.

3.4.3 Mapping of Cortex-M3/M4/M7 exclusive access signals to AHB5

The Cortex-M3, Cortex-M4 and Cortex-M7[1] processors support exclusive access instructions but are designed before AHB5 specification was available. As a result, these processors use a non-standard exclusive access signal definition for exclusive access operations:

▪ EXREQ – same as HEXCL, an address phase signal to indicate exclusive load/store accesses.

▪ EXRESP – exclusive fail status in the data phase (assert at the end of the data phase - opposite polarity compared to HEXOKAY).

To use Cortex-M3/M4/M7 processor with AHB5 system, simple glue logic is needed to convert between EXRESP and HEXOKAY:

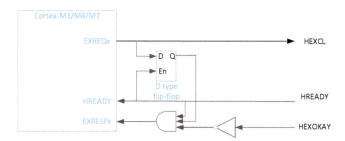

Figure 3.20: Glue logic for using Cortex-M3/M4/M7 processors exclusive access signals with AHB5.

Similarly, glue logic is needed when connecting Cortex-M23/M33 processors to bus slaves that use EXREQ and EXRESP.

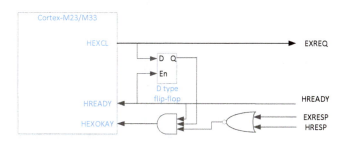

Figure 3.21: Glue logic for using bus slaves with legacy exclusive access signals in AHB5 systems.

[1] Note: The Cortex-M7 processor uses AHB Lite for an optional peripheral AHB part of the peripheral region.

3.5 AHB5 TrustZone support

TrustZone support is one of the key new features of AMBA 5 AHB. The HNONSEC signal is an address phase signal that indicates the security attribute of the transfer:

▪ If HNONSEC is 1 (Non-secure), the bus interconnect must block the transfer if the address of the transfer is pointing to a Secure location.

▪ If HNONSEC is 0 (Secure), the bus master has Secure access privilege.

Please note that in Armv8-M, when a processor is in Secure state, access to Non-secure address is indicated as Non-secure (HNONSEC==1).

A TrustZone capable Cortex-M23/M33 processor system should have:

▪ Secure and Non-secure program spaces.

▪ Secure and Non-secure RAM spaces.

▪ Secure and Non-secure peripherals.

The definitions of Secure and Non-secure address ranges are handled by a Security Attribution Unit (SAU) inside the processor and Implementation Defined Attribution Unit (IDAU) which is tightly coupled to the processor(s). SAU is programmable, and IDAU is system-specific, in some cases, even the IDAU could be programmable.

To enable a high level of flexibility, Arm Corstone foundation IP / CoreLink SDK-200 included several bus components for TrustZone security management:

▪ Memory Protection Controller (MPC): for the partitioning of a memory block into Secure and Non-secure address spaces.

▪ Peripheral Protection Controller (PPC): for assigning bus peripherals into Secure and Non-secure domains.

▪ Master security controller: An AHB5 bus wrapper for legacy bus masters that do not support TrustZone. This handles the blocking of Non-secure transfers to Secure addresses and generation of correct HNONSEC signals.

The details of the TrustZone system design is beyond the scope of this book. To help system designers, Arm provides a document called Trusted Based System Architecture for Armv8-M (TBSA-M) which include guidelines on best practices, including many areas beyond bus system designs. This document is a part of the Arm Platform Security Architecture (PSA). For more information, please visit: https://developer.arm.com/products/architecture/platform-security-architecture

Please note that TrustZone support is optional on the Cortex-M23 and Cortex-M33 processors. So, it is perfectly fine to use Cortex-M23 and Cortex-M33 on a system without TrustZone.

3.6 Overview of APB

3.6.1 Introduction to the APB bus system

APB is a simple bus mainly targeted for peripherals connections. It was introduced as part of the AMBA 2 specification, and the functionalities have been extended in AMBA 3 and AMBA 4 to allow wait states, error responses and additional transfer attributes (including TrustZone support). Most APB systems are 32-bit. Although the bus protocol does not have a bus width limitation, the common practice for Arm-based systems is to use a 32-bit peripheral bus.

Although it is possible to directly connect a peripheral to the AHB, separating peripheral connections using APB has various advantages:

1. Many system-on-chip designs contain large numbers of peripherals. If they are connected to the AHB system bus, they could reduce the maximum frequency of the system due to high signal fan out and complex address decoding logic. Grouping peripheral connections in the APB can reduce the performance impact on the AHB.

2. A peripheral subsystem can run at a different clock frequency, or be powered down without affecting AHB.

3. APB interfaces use a simpler bus protocol, which simplifies the peripheral designs as well as reducing the verification effort.

4. Most peripherals designed for traditional processors can be connected to APB easily as APB transfers are not pipelined.

An APB system operates with a clock signal called PCLK. This signal is common to bus master (usually an AHB to APB Bridge), bus slaves and the bus infrastructure blocks. All registers on the APB trigger at rising edges of PCLK. There is also an active-low reset signal called PRESETn. When this signal is low, it resets the APB system immediately (asynchronous reset). This allows a system to be reset even if the clock is stopped. Like the reset signal in AHB (HRESETn), the PRESETn signal itself should be synchronized to PCLK so that race conditions can be avoided.

In most simple systems with both AHB and APB, PCLK is from the same clock source as HCLK, and PRESETn is from the same reset source as HRESETn. However, there are also systems that use separate HCLK and PCLK frequencies. In that case, the AHB to APB bus bridge design will need to be able to handle the data transfers across different clock frequencies or different clock domains.

3.6.2 APB signals and connection

For a typical APB system, you can find most of the following signals:

Signals	Direction	Descriptions
PCLK	Clock source → all APB blocks	Common clock signal
PRESETn	Reset source → all APB blocks	Common active-low reset signal
PSEL	Address decoder → Slave	Device select
PADDR[n:0]	Master → Slave	Address bus (see text below regarding bus width)
PENABLE	Master → Slave	Transfer control
PWRITE	Master → Slave	Write control (1=Write, 0=Read)
PPROT[2:0]	Master → Slave	Transfer Protection control (AMBA 4)
PSTRB[n-1:0]	Master → Slave	Byte strobe for write operations (AMBA 4)
PWDATA[31:0]	Master → Slave	Write data
PRDATA[31:0]	Master ← Slave	Read Data
PSLVERR	Master ← Slave	Slave response (AMBA 3 and onwards)
PREADY	Master ← Slave	Slave ready (transfer completed, AMBA 3 and onwards)

Table 3.19: Typical APB signals.

There are different versions of APB specification:

AMBA version	Document	Features and enhancements
AMBA 2	AMBA Specification 2.0	32-bit read/write operations
AMBA 3	AMBA APB Protocol version 1.0	Added waitstate (PREADY) and error response (PSLVERR)
AMBA 4	AMBA APB Protocol version 2.0	Added Protection information (PPROT[2:0] and write byte strobe (PSTRB)

Table 3.20: Various versions of APB specification.

Normally, the APB only occupies a small part of the memory space. As a result, the address bus of the APB system is normally less than 32-bit. There is no transfer size control on APB. All transfers are assumed to be 32-bit, and usually, the two LSB (bit 1 and bit 0) of the PADDR are not used because a word transfer on APB must be aligned.

In most cases, an APB system has a bus bridge as the bus master that connects the APB to the main processor bus. In addition, an APB slave multiplexer and an address decoder are needed, which is sometimes a combined unit.

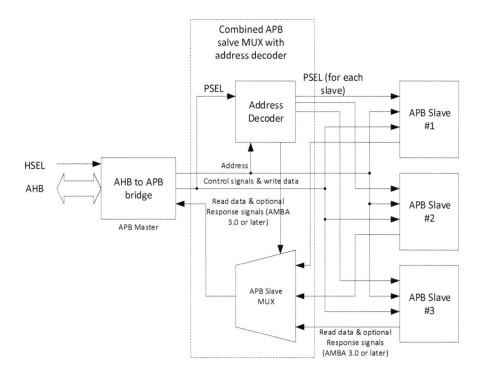

Figure 3.22: An example APB subsystem.

Unlike AHB, APB operations are not pipelined. In AMBA 2, APB transfers must be two cycles. For read operations, the read data needs to be valid - at least at the end of the second clock cycle.

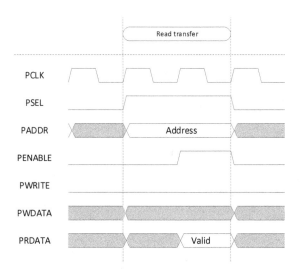

Figure 3.23: Simple APB read for AMBA 2.

For write transfers in APB for AMBA 2, the write data from APB master must be valid for the two clock cycles off the transfer.

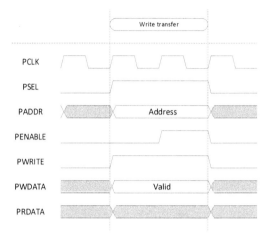

Figure 3.24: Simple APB write for AMBA 2.

During a write transfer on APB, the actual write operation in the slave could happen either in the first clock cycle or in the second cycle. This is implementation-defined. Therefore, the APB master must ensure that the write data is valid for both clock cycles. There can be any number of clock cycles between two transfers on APB.

With AMBA 3, each APB slave can extend a transfer by de-asserting the PREADY output signal or feedback with an error response by the PSLVERR (Peripheral Slave Error) signal. For example, if an APB slave needs 4 clock cycles to complete a read transfer (3 wait states), the read operation waveform will be like:

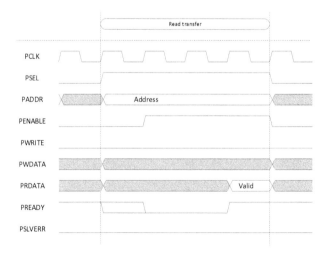

Figure 3.25: APB read for AMBA 3 with 3 wait states.

The end of the read transfer is indicated by the assertion of PREADY. The minimum number of cycles for the APB transfer is two cycles (same as AMBA 2), and the value of PREADY is ignored in the first cycle of the transfer so that even if its value is logic 1, the transfer still takes at least two cycles. In the previous example, the AHB slave responds with OKAY (indicated by logic zero on PSLVERR when PREADY is one). If an APB slave response with an error response, the waveform would be:

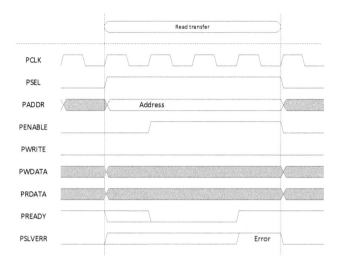

Figure 3.26: APB read for AMBA 3 with 3 wait states and error response.

When an error response is generated, the read data from the AHB slave might not contain any useful information and could be discarded. The value of PSLVERR is only valid when PREADY is high and not in the first cycle of the transfer. For example, if PSLVERR and PREADY are both high in the first cycle of the transfer, it is not considered as an error response as an APB transfer must be at least two clock cycles.

The waveform for APB writes in AMBA 3 are very similar. For write operations with an okay response, the waveform would be like:

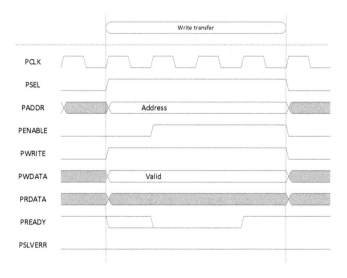

Figure 3.27: APB write for AMBA 3 with 3 wait states.

And for write with error response, the waveform would be like:

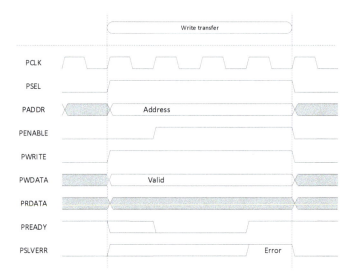

Figure 3.28: APB write for AMBA 3 with 3 wait states and error response.

3.6.3 Additional signals in APB protocol v2.0
The APB v2 in AMBA 4 added the PPROT and PSTRB signals.

PPROT is similar to HPROT in AHB and is asserted throughout the whole transfer. However, it is only 3-bits wide.

Signal	Function	When equal 0	When equal 1
PPROT[0]	Privileged	Non-privileged (user)	Privileged
PPROT[1]	Non-secure	Secure access	Non-secure access
PPROT[2]	Data	Data access	Instruction access

Table 3.21: PPROT encoding.

Please note, unlike AHB5, the TrustZone security attribute is part of PPROT instead of a separate signal.

AMBA 4 APBv2 also introduces byte strobe signals for write operations. For a 32-bit APB, the PSTRB signal is 4 bits – one bit per byte lane. It is also asserted for the whole transfer.

Figure 3.29: Byte lane mapping of PSTRB signal.

The PSTRB signal is active high and is used for write-operations only. During read operations, the PSTRB signal is ignored by the bus slave, and the whole 32-bit word is read.

3.6.4 Data values on APB

Most APB systems are 32-bit. Since the bus protocol does not include transfer size, all transfers are assumed to be the maximum size (i.e., 32-bit) except when PSTRB signals are used during write operations; even sometimes only a small part of the data bus is actually used (e.g., when accessing a peripheral with 8-bit data port). The transfer address should also be aligned to word size boundaries.

During write transfers, an APB slave can sample and register the write data at any cycle within the transfer. It is common for APB slaves to sample the write data at the last cycle of the transfer, especially in APB devices for AMBA 2. However, it is also perfectly acceptable to sample the write data at the first cycle of the write transfer because the APB master must provide valid write data to APB slaves in even in the first clock cycle.

For read transfer, the APB master should only read the return read data value at the last cycle or (when PREADY is 1). If an APB slave returns an error response, the bus master should discard the read data.

3.6.5 Mixing different versions of APB components

It is possible to connect APB slave designed for AMBA 2 to an APB master for AMBA 3. In this case, the PREADY can be tied to one and PSLVERR tied to zero. However, if an APB slave is designed for AMBA 3 and requires wait state or error response support, it cannot be used with an APB master designed with the AMBA 2 specification.

If an AMBA 4 APB master (APBv2) is used, then the suitability of using AMBA 2/3 slaves is dependent on application – if there is a need to support protection information or byte strobe, then AMBA 2/3 APB slaves must be modified to support AMBA 4 APB functionality.

An AMBA 2 APB master (e.g., an AHB to APB bridge) cannot support APB slaves designed for AMBA 3/4 as it cannot handle wait states.

An AMBA 3 APB master might be able to support an APB slave designed for AMBA 4 (APBv2), providing that the bus slave only needs 32-bit write operations (no need to support byte strobe signals). In this case, the PSTRB signals can be tied to PWRITE so that all byte strobes are asserted for all write operations.

CHAPTER 4

Building simple bus systems for Cortex-M processors

4.1 Introduction to the basics of bus design

In this chapter, we will look into the basics of bus system designs for the Cortex-M0, Cortex-M0+, Cortex-M1, and Cortex-M3/M4 processors. The bus system links the processor to the rest of the system design, and there are several general principles to be aware of:

- For processors that support the Harvard bus architecture, design the bus system to enable concurrent instruction and data accesses.

- Use default slaves to detect access to invalid addresses – this enables bus error to be triggered, and software to handle it when something has gone wrong.

- In most of the earlier Cortex-M processor designs, the initial address for vector tables is fixed in address 0x00000000. Therefore, the program image needs to be visible in this address at startup.

- Minimize the number of wait states in the memories – in processors that don't have caches, having wait states in the memory system directly impacts the performance, energy efficiency, and interrupt latency. In general, wait states in peripheral accesses are less of a problem as those accesses happen less frequently.

- Try to keep to a minimum the number of bus slaves on the main system bus.

Separating the peripheral bus from the system bus has a number of advantages:

- A high number of bus slaves in the main system bus could reduce the maximum clock frequency and can also increase the area and power of the bus interconnect. By separating peripheral connections in different buses, address decoding and bus switching logic on the system bus can be optimized for speed because most peripherals are grouped as one item via the bus bridge.

- By using a bus bridge to separate the peripheral bus from the system bus, it is possible to provide timing isolation between the two bus segments. This allows the peripherals to be operated at different clock speeds, as well as providing a better chance to get a higher maximum clock frequency on the system bus.

- Bus protocol for the peripheral bus is simpler. This reduces the time for peripheral development and testing, as well as reducing complexity and gate counts.

As a result, most of the peripherals that do not need low latency accesses (e.g., SPI, I2C, UART) can be placed in separated peripheral buses. Some peripherals like GPIO can gain the benefit of lower access latency, so some GPIO blocks are placed system AHB or single-cycle I/O port interface (available on Cortex-M0+ and Cortex-M23 processors).

4.2 Building a simple Cortex-M0 system

The Cortex-M0 processor is one of the easiest-to-use Arm processors as it only has one AHB interface for the whole memory system. Typically, a simple Cortex-M0 system design could look like this:

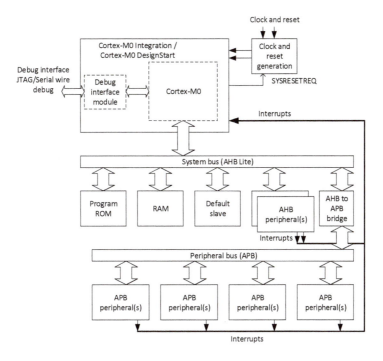

Figure 4.1: Example of Cortex-M0 system design.

In this example design, …

■ The "ROM" (could be embedded flash, or other NVM for holding program image) is placed in address 0x00000000 as the initial vector table address is fixed to this location. For FPGA designs, you can use on-chip SRAM with the initial image. Ideally, use zero wait state for "ROM."

■ The RAM is normally synchronous static RAM with zero wait state to provide the best performance. Usually, we put the RAM in address 0x20000000, the starting address of the SRAM region.

■ Some of the peripherals can be designed with an AHB interface to lower access latency (e.g., GPIO could be designed as an AHB peripheral as some control applications can be I/O intensive).

■ General peripherals that do not need fast access can be designed with an APB interface and connected via an AHB to APB bridge. Potentially, the peripheral bus can run at a lower clock frequency.

■ The address ranges of AHB and APB peripherals are usually within 0x40000000 to 0x5FFFFFFF. The exact arrangement is up to the system designers.

- The default slave is selected when the AHB transaction is targeting an invalid address.

- For minimum requirements, the top-level of the FPGA/SoC design only needs to expose the clock and reset connections, the peripheral interface, and the debug connection.

4.3 Building a simple Cortex-M0+ system

The design of a simple Cortex-M0+ system (Figure 4.2) can be very similar to the Cortex-M0 system. However, there can be two major differences:

1. Optional single-cycle I/O port (IOP) interface for low latency peripheral register accesses;

2. Optional Micro Trace Buffer (MTB).

If a designer decided to use the single-cycle I/O port interface for a peripheral:

- The peripheral might need to be modified to support the single-cycle I/O port interface;

- The system would need to include a simple IOP address decoder to tell the processor which address range should route to the IOP and which should not. This decoder contains simple combinatorial logic that decodes the 32-bit address value, and feedback to the processor that the address belongs to either the IOP or AHB interface.

The MTB feature is used to provide a low-cost instruction trace solution. The MTB is placed between the AHB and SRAM, working as an AHB to SRAM bridge in normal operations. When used for instruction trace, the debugger programs the MTB to allocate a small portion of the SRAM for storing instruction trace information. The MTB has a trace interface to receive instruction trace information from the processor and can also generate a debug event (halting request) to the processor.

Typically, the MTB would be configured in circular buffer mode so that only the recent history is kept. While it doesn't provide the full software execution history, it is still a useful feature in debugging software issues like providing program flow details just before fault exceptions.

The 32-bit SRAM interface can work with most synchronous on-chip SRAM and FPGA block RAM. Please note, it supports zero wait state SRAM only.

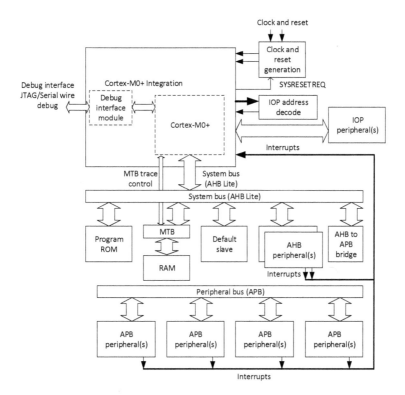

Figure 4.2: Example of the Cortex-M0+ system design.

Since the Cortex-M0+ processor supports the separation of privileged and unprivileged execution levels, you should consider system-level security if this feature is used. To support the separation of privileged and unprivileged levels, a designer should also consider adding the MPU (Memory Protection Unit) option, which can prevent unprivileged codes from accessing privileged memories.

As a part of the security consideration:

- Peripheral registers for system control (e.g., clock, power management, flash programming) should be privileged access only.

- If an AHB access is unprivileged and the address targets a privileged only device, then the address decoder in the system can select the default slave instead of the targeted device to generate a fault exception (bus error).

Similar to the Cortex-M0 processor, the initial vector table address is fixed at address 0x00000000. Therefore, the ROM needs to be visible at the beginning of the memory map after reset.

4.4 Building a simple Cortex-M1 system

If you are using Cortex-M1 FPGA DesignStart, you might not need to study the detailed bus arrangements as the FPGA design environment may be able to handle this for you. However, if you are using Cortex-M1 in Verilog RTL source form, or just interested to know more details, then this section could be useful.

In many aspects, the system-level integration for the Cortex-M1 system is similar to the Cortex-M0 system:

▨ The processor does not have separation of privileged and unprivileged operations;

▨ There is only one AHB interface.

However, there are also some differences:

▨ The Cortex-M1 processor supports optional Instruction TCM (Tightly Coupled Memory) and Data TCM;

▨ There is no sleep mode support on the current Cortex-M1 processor.

Use of Tightly Coupled Memory (TCM) is common in processor systems implemented in FPGA. If this option is implemented, the Cortex-M1 processor provides two TCM interfaces, one for Instruction memory (I-TCM) and the second one for Data (D-TCM). When TCMs are used, the Cortex-M1 processor can execute a program in its best performance. If executing a program from memory blocks connected via AHB, the performance/MHz would be lowered because the AHB interface on the Cortex-M1 has an additional pipeline stage to allow it to reach high clock frequency.

TCM can be implemented with RAM blocks inside the FPGA. The details of implementing RAM blocks inside the FPGA depend on the FPGA type and the FPGA design tools you use. An example is shown in Section 2.2, but you might need to refer to the FPGA vendor's documentation and tools documentation for the correct implementation of the TCMs.

Since the Program "ROM" (it is actually RAMs in the FPGA) and RAM can be connected via the TCM interface, the system AHB connections can be simplified.

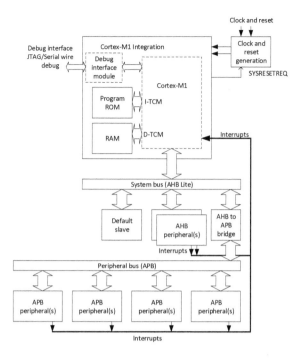

Figure 4.3: Example of Cortex-M1 system design.

The source code of the Cortex-M1 top-level files are available into two versions:

1. With debug interface;

2. Without debug interface.

When the debug features are included, the debug interface has a separate set of TCM interfaces (using the block RAM as dual-port RAM). The reason for having a separated interface for the debugger to access the TCM at maximum speed. In most modern FPGA architectures, the memory blocks can be used as dual-port memory. Therefore, each TCM block can be simultaneously connected to the processor core's TCM interface and the debug TCM interface:

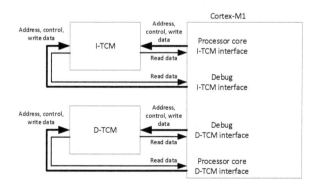

Figure 4.4: The Cortex-M1 TCM connections when the debug option is used.

In most of the modern FPGA architectures, dual-port RAMs are widely supported.

If the debug option is not used in your FPGA design, there is no debug TCM interfaces. Only one interface per TCM is needed. In this case, it does not matter whether the FPGA memory supports dual-port operation or not.

Where the SRAM memory on the FPGA is insufficient for your application, you can add an SRAM interface on the System bus as an AHB bus slave and add external SRAM to extend the total memory size of the system. You can also use SRAM connected to the AHB instead of using I-TCM and D-TCM.

4.5 Building a simple Cortex-M3/Cortex-M4 system

Unlike the previous simple system described in this chapter, the Cortex-M3 and Cortex-M4 processors use the Harvard bus architecture and have three AHB master interfaces and an APB based master interface.

Bus	Types of transfers	Descriptions
I-CODE	Instruction fetches and vector fetches for CODE region (0x00000000 to 0x1FFFFFFF)	Read transfers only
D-CODE	Data and debug read/write for CODE region (0x00000000 to 0x1FFFFFFF)	
System	All accesses not targeting at CODE region, PPB or internal components (SRAM, Peripheral, RAM Devices, and System/Vendor specific address range excluding PPB)	
Private Peripheral Bus (PPB)	All accesses are in external PPB range (0xE0040000 to 0xE00FFFFF) excluding internal components (e.g., ETM, TPIU, ROM table)	Privileged accesses only

Table 4.1: Bus master interface on the Cortex-M3 and Cortex-M4 processors.

The multiple bus interface allows instruction fetches and data accesses to take place at the same time (i.e., Harvard bus architecture) to get better performance. This requires that the program image and data are on different buses.

In a typical Cortex-M3/M4 system design:

- The program image is placed in the CODE region. Similar to the Cortex-M0 processor, the initial vector table address is fixed at address 0x00000000. Therefore, the ROM (which contains the vector table) needs to be visible in this address after a reset.

- SRAM and peripherals are connected via the system bus. Normally in address 0x20000000 (for SRAM) and address 0x40000000 (for peripherals). This arrangement allows software developers to utilize the bit-band feature on SRAM and peripherals.

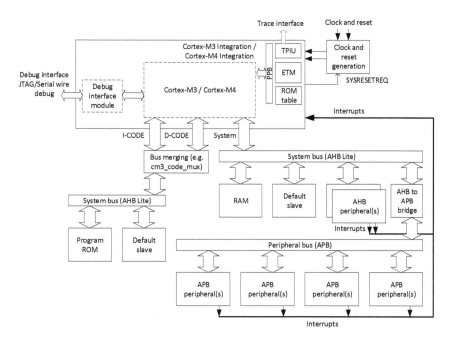

Figure 4.5: Example of Cortex-M3 system design.

Since there are two main AHB bus segments, both having some invalid address ranges, we will need default slaves on each of these buses.

The reason for separating I-CODE and D-CODE in the system is to add a literal data cache (on the D-CODE bus) so that literal data can be read even if the instruction fetch is stalled due to a wait state on flash memory. Typically, flash memories are quite slow (in the range of 30MHz to 50MHz) in comparison to modern microcontrollers, which can run at over 100MHz. When the Cortex-M3 processor was designed, a common approach to overcoming flash performance issues was to use flash memories with a wider bus (e.g., 128-bit) with a prefetch buffer so that sequential instructions could be prefetched while the processor consumed the remaining instructions in the prefetch buffer.

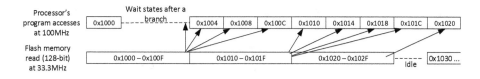

Figure 4.6: Flash prefetching can help eliminate wait states in sequential flash accesses.

However, program operations contain many constant data reads, and these read operations would result in non-sequential accesses, which would be stalled as the data are not available in the buffer. To make matters worse, if the literal access occurred just after the prefetcher started a prefetch, the flash interface needed to wait until the flash read is completed before reading the literal from flash memory. For example, in Figure 4.7, the processor pipeline needs to stall after the literal data read (address 0x1048) until the flash returns the data (end of read operation to 0x1040-0x104F).

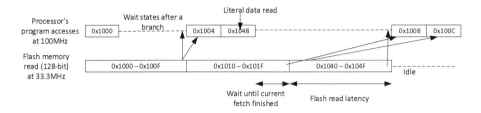

Figure 4.7: Literal data access can reduce the performance of a system with prefetcher.

To help reduce the performance penalty, one solution is to separate the data accesses on a different AHB and put a small literal data cache on it so that literal data used in small loops will not cause latency after the first loop.

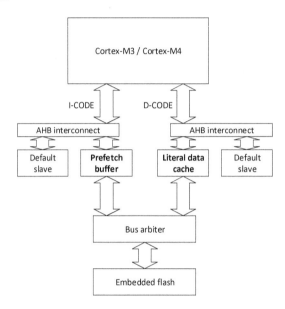

Figure 4.8: Separating I-CODE and D-CODE allows literal data cache to operate in parallel with the prefetcher buffer.

For many simple designs or systems that use system-level caches, there is no need to have such flash access acceleration arrangements. System designers can simply merge the I-CODE and D-CODE buses. The Cortex-M3 and Cortex-M4 product bundles provide two components for this purpose:

1. Code mux component:

This is a simple bus multiplexer with minimal gate count. To use this component, the DNOTITRANS input of the Cortex-M3/Cortex-M4 must be set to 1. This prevents the processor I-CODE interface from generating bus transfers at the same time when D-CODE is used.

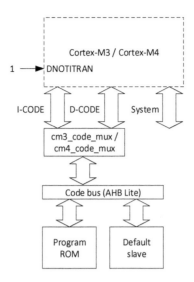

Figure 4.9: Using code mux component to merge I-CODE and D-CODE.

2. Flash mux component:

This component has internal bus arbitration and a register slice to hold I-CODE transfers in a buffer if both I-CODE and D-CODE are active. This can be useful if there are other bus slaves in the CODE region that could be accessed at the same time as instruction fetches.

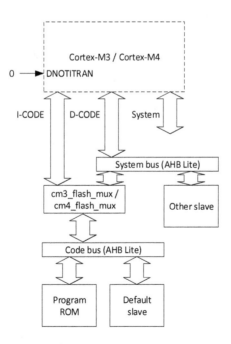

Figure 4.10: Using flash mux component to merge I-CODE and D-CODE.

In newer microcontroller designs, the use of system-level cache for embedded flash is increasingly common. Arm provides the AHB flash cache which can be used with various Cortex-M processors with an AHB interface.

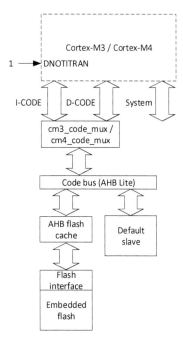

Figure 4.11: Using AHB flash cache in the Cortex-M3/M4 system design.

For such systems, the chance for both instruction accesses and literal data having a cache miss is relatively low (except the first time the code sequence is executed of course), so separating the CODE bus into I-CODE and D-CODE does not bring a lot of benefits. In newer Cortex-M processors like Cortex-M33 and Cortex-M35P, the I-CODE and D-CODE have been merged to reduce system integration complexity and to enable lower power.

Instead of having the cache module closely coupling to the processor, the AHB flash cache arrangement has the following advantages:

▨ The interface between the flash cache and flash interface can be designed as wide bus such as a 128-bit AHB. This enables faster data transfers from flash to the cache, and next flash access (e.g., if there is a cache miss) can start earlier.

▨ If the code bus has another bus master, the flash cache can provide caching to the other bus master.

Please note:

▨ For Cortex-M3 and Cortex-M4 processors, the internal bus interconnect has a registering stage between the instruction fetch interface and the system bus. Therefore, the performance of the system is reduced if the software image is executed from the system bus.

- Peripherals are expected to be connected via the System AHB (or on a peripheral APB via a bus bridge) instead of the Private Peripheral Bus (PPB). The PPB intended for debug components has some limitations; namely:

  - It is accessible in privileged mode only;

  - It is accessed in little-endian fashion irrespective of the processor's data endianness setting;

  - Accesses behave as Strongly Ordered (no other data memory access can start until the current data access finished);

  - No bit-band function is available;

  - Unaligned accesses have unpredictable results;

  - Only 32-bit data accesses are supported;

  - It is accessible from the Debug Port and the local processor, but not from any other agent (processor) in the system.

(Source: http://infocenter.arm.com/help/index.jsp?topic=/com.arm.doc.faqs/ka14334.html)

If needed, it is possible to have an SRAM shared between code and SRAM regions by having bus accesses from both code and system buses (i.e., memory address aliasing). This allows the software to use a single SRAM block and execute code from SRAM without performance loss:

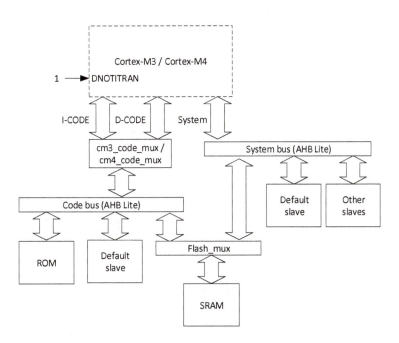

Figure 4.12: Placing a single SRAM into both CODE and SRAM region.

However, from a security point of view, this needs to be handled carefully to prevent vulnerabilities. For example, if a memory region is privileged access only, then the access permission needs to be privileged for both address locations (Alternatively, you can make the RAM visible on only one bus at a time).

4.6 Handling multiple bus masters

In many microcontroller systems, you can find multiple bus masters such as:

▨ Direct Memory Access (DMA) controllers;

▨ Peripherals that need high data bandwidth; for example, USB controllers, ethernet interfaces.

In both cases, these units have bus master interfaces to initiate transfers, as well as bus slave interfaces for configuration. To enable multiple bus masters to access the AHB bus system, Arm provides:

▨ Simple AHB master multiplexers to support two or three bus masters accessing a single AHB bus segment (shared bandwidth);

▨ Configurable AHB Bus Matrix components (allowing concurrent accesses).

The concepts of these components were covered in Chapter 3. For a simple Cortex-M0 based system with a DMA controller, the system design can look like this (Figure 4.13):

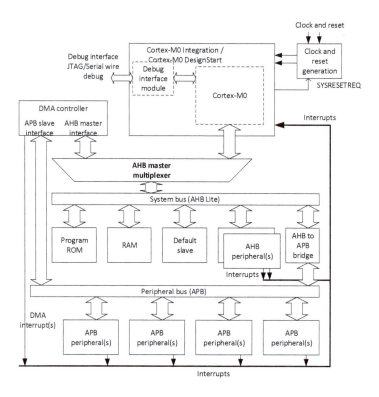

Figure 4.13: Simple Cortex-M0 system design with DMA controller and AHB master multiplexer.

Both the processor and the DMA controller can have a full view of the memory system. The design is simple to create, but the bus bandwidth is shared. As a result, the number of bus masters supported by the AHB master multiplexer component is often limited to 2 or 3. In such systems, it is common to give the DMA controller higher priority as the processor can access the bus very frequently (due to both instruction-fetches and data accesses).

For systems with higher performance needs, the AHB bus matrix component is generally used. In addition, you would also often need multiple banks of SRAM to enable processor and other bus masters to access different banks of SRAM at the same time. Otherwise, the bandwidth of SRAM accesses could become the bottleneck.

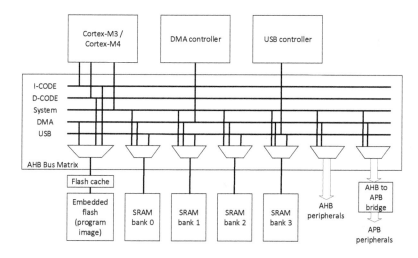

Figure 4.14: A simplified Cortex-M3/Cortex-M4 processor system design with an AHB bus matrix.

In addition, to provide higher total data bandwidth, having multiple banks of SRAM can also allow some banks of SRAM to be powered down when not in use, resulting in lower power consumption in some situations. However, when all banks of SRAM are used, the maximum system power is higher than a single SRAM bank. Of course, the use of multiple SRAM banks has the advantage of higher data bandwidth, which might mean the overall system-level energy efficiency is still better than one SRAM bank.

AHB bus matrix designs have a concept called sparse connectivity, which means some of the AHB bus masters connected to the bus matrix do not need to have access to all of the downstream AHB bus segments. For example:

▓ A USB controller does not need to access to flash program area and peripherals;

▓ The I-CODE and D-CODE bus of the Cortex-M3/Cortex-M4 do not need to access SRAM and peripherals because transfers on these buses are limited to the CODE region (unless the SRAM is mapped into CODE region).

The configurable AHB bus matrix from Arm supports sparse connectivity, which reduces the bus matrix area and potentially helps to improve timing and speed.

Another supported feature in Arm's AHB bus matrix is the internal default slave. Since the AHB bus matrix has an internal address decoder to select which downstream AHB bus segment should be used, it can also detect accesses to invalid address ranges and route them to internal bus matrix, which means that there is no need to add another system-level default slave.

The AHB bus matrix is highly flexible and can bring many advantages to system designs. However, please note that it can also introduce latency cycles when switching a bus segment from one master to another. It is possible to optimize a bus matrix to reduce the chance of unnecessary bus arbiter switching by customizing the logic that defines the default selected bus or forcing the address of the bus to a specific value when the bus is idle.

When designing systems with multiple bus masters, from a security point of view, it is common to make the configuration interface of the bus masters (e.g., DMA controllers) privileged access only. Otherwise, if an unprivileged software component can program a DMA controller, it can use the DMA controller to access privileged-only memories, which means bypassing the memory protection.

4.7 Exclusive access support

Exclusive accesses are supported in Armv7-M and Armv8-M processors. To support exclusive accesses on multiple processor systems, system designers should add global exclusive access monitors to the system. The monitors should be placed downstream of the AHB bus matrix or AHB master multiplexer, which will merge transfers from different bus masters. The bus interconnect must also provide HMASTER signals to allow the global exclusive access monitor to know which bus master the transfer is generated from.

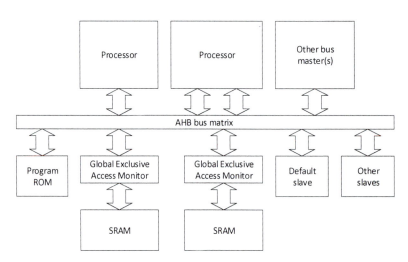

Figure 4.15: Correct location for placing global exclusive access monitors.

In Figure 4.15, there are two banks of SRAM, and each of them needs a global exclusive access monitor because they are on separate AHB bus segments. In system-level designs, you need a global exclusive access monitor for each AHB segment after bus arbitration if:

1. The bus slaves connected to the bus segment can contain semaphore data, and

2. The bus slaves connected to the bus segment can be accessed by more than one bus master that generates access to semaphore data.

Bus segments that only contain general peripherals or flash memories (or other types of NVM) do not require an exclusive access monitor as there is no semaphore data in these buses.

In single-processor systems, it is possible to omit the global exclusive access monitor because even with other bus masters present (e.g., DMA controller, USB controller), the software can ensure that these other bus masters do not access the semaphore data. Therefore, normally, global exclusive access monitors are present only on multi-processor systems.

In single-core systems with Cortex-M3, Cortex-M4 and Cortex-M7 processors, which use proprietary exclusive access handshaking signals (EXREQ and EXRESP), if an AHB bus segment does not have an exclusive access monitor:

■ Where the bus contains SRAM, you can tie EXRESP low (do not tie EXRESP high as OS semaphore functions using exclusive accesses will always fail).

■ Where the bus segment only contains NVM or peripherals that do not contain semaphore data, it is valid to tie EXRESP high to indicate exclusive access to such address range is not supported.

In single-core systems with Cortex-M23, Cortex-M33 and Cortex-M35P processors, which use AHB5 bus protocol with exclusive access support (HEXCL and HEXOKAY):

■ If the bus contains SRAM, you can use a simple glue logic to assert HEXOKAY in data phases of exclusive accesses (do not tie HEXOKAY high as AHB5 protocol requires that HEXOKAY is asserted only when HREADY is asserted and must not be high when HRESP is high).

■ If the bus segment only contains NVM or peripherals which do not contain semaphore data, it is valid to tie HEXOKAY low to indicate exclusive access to such address ranges is not supported.

Additional information related to exclusive access support on Cortex-M3 and Cortex-M4 processor can be found in this knowledge base article:

http://infocenter.arm.com/help/index.jsp?topic=/com.arm.doc.faqs/ka16180.html

4.8 Address remap

Address remap is a common system design technique used in Cortex-M microcontrollers that needs to support multiple boot stages or multiple-boot modes. For example, in a Cortex-M0 design that needs to support a boot loader (which executes before the program in embedded flash is executed), address remap allows the memory map to place the boot loader ROM into address 0x00000000 for startup, and then later maps the embedded flash to 0x00000000 for execution of programs in flash.

To use the address remap function, the system design needs to include a program register to control the behavior of the address decoder. For the use case, we mentioned, this control register only needs 1-bit to switch between two memory maps. However, some other devices support multiple boot arrangements, and this register might have multiple bits.

An example of an address map design with remap is shown in Figure 4.16 below:

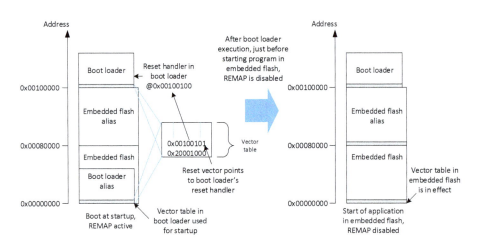

Figure 4.16: An example address map of address remap to support boot loader.

With the arrangement shown in Figure 4.16, the vector table in the boot loader is used for booting up the system. The execution of the boot loader is based on its real address 0x001000000. However, during this period, the vector table in the boot loader alias is still being used. After the boot loader has finished its work, it switches the REMAP off so that the vector table of the program image in embedded flash is used. It can then read the vector table of the application, set up the MSP value, and branch into the reset handler.

Please note the embedded flash might also have an alias address range to allow the boot loader to handle flash programming. Otherwise, the beginning of the embedded flash address range will not be visible as the bootloader alias is placed there during start-up.

In the design of the remap control register, there are several considerations:

- In many system designs, the remap control register needs to be privileged access only for security reasons.

- In some systems, it is desirable to make the remap control register reset by power-on reset so that the bootloader only executes once, and does not get executed again during debugging (the debugger normally resets the target using a system reset, with SYSRESETREQ field in AIRCR).

- In some systems, the remap control register could be designed to only be switched off but cannot be switched back on by software. This arrangement is used by some secure boot systems where the information associated with the security checks are hidden inside the boot loader and are masked out (non-accessible) after REMAP is switched off.

In addition to bootloader use cases, a remap arrangement is also used to allow part of the SRAM to be used as a vector table in systems with Cortex-M0 processors because Cortex-M0 does not have a programmable Vector Table Offset Register (VTOR). In such usage scenarios, a REMAP control register bit is needed and defaults to off (no REMAP). When set to 1, a portion of system SRAM is aliased to the first 192 bytes (maximum vector table size in Cortex-M0) of system memory. Before setting the REMAP control register, software should copy the original vector table to the SRAM that will then be remapped so that exceptions can still work afterward.

The remap feature is supported by the AHB bus matrix designed by Arm. However, for processors with VTOR, there is no need to use REMAP to allow runtime updates of vector tables because you can program VTOR to point to the SRAM area. In newer Cortex-M processors like Cortex-M7, Cortex-M23, Cortex-M33, and Cortex-M35P, the initial address of the vector table for boot-up is configurable and, therefore, there is no need to use REMAP to enable multiple boot options.

4.9 AHB-based memory connection versus TCM

Some embedded processors support Tightly-Coupled Memory (TCM). In some cases, the availability of a TCM interface makes memory integration easier. However, memories like SRAM can also be connected to AHB using AHB SRAM wrappers, such as the one bundled in Cortex-M0/M3 DesignStart (cmsdk_ahb_to_sram.v).

In terms of performance, at the interface level, TCM and AHB provide the same read access latency. Write access timings are different, but at the processor pipeline level, the write could still be a single-cycle, even when using an AHB interface (e.g., when the processor has a write buffer, or when the AHB pipeline is mapped into two stages of the processor's pipeline).

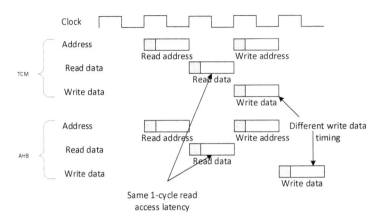

Figure 4.17: Timing characteristics comparison between TCM interface and AHB interface.

Some designers suggest that a dedicated TCM interface could be beneficial if the bus is often occupied by other transactions from other bus masters. In that situation, access to TCM will not be delayed by other bus traffic. However, if using a multi-layer AHB approach, processor access to memories can still be carried out immediately providing that the bus slave segment accessed is not being used by another bus master. Even if a processor supports TCM unless its bus interface supports multiple outstanding transfers, it is impossible to start a new data access while the current memory read/write is on-going.

While having TCM reduces the complexity at the system-level interconnect, the merging of read data from the system bus and TCMs is placed inside the processor, so there is no area saving. Potentially, the TCM design might restrict the address range and size of the memories while connecting memories on the AHB instead could be more flexible, as designers can customize address ranges and memory sizes based on application needs. It is also possible to optimize the AHB bus structure to minimize timing delays between the processor and the memory blocks.

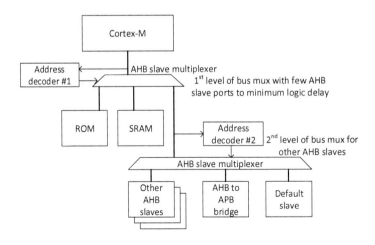

Figure 4.18: AHB path optimized to minimize timing delay between processor and memories.

In some processor designs, the use of TCM is required to allow deterministic interrupt responses. For example, in the Cortex-M7 processor, access to memories on the AXI bus system can have non-deterministic timing due to cache hit/miss scenarios. Having TCM enables interrupt services to be carried out quickly in deterministic manners. But in small processors like Cortex-M0 to Cortex-M33, the omission of a TCM feature is not a real issue.

4.10 Handling of embedded flash memories

4.10.1 IP requirements

Embedded flash memories are widely used in microcontrollers. They are process node-specific, so if you want to use embedded flash in your design, you need to license it from the foundry of your choice (or their partners that offer embedded flash macros that are compatible with the process node).

In addition to the embedded flash memories, you need an embedded flash memory controller IP that links the embedded flash to AMBA buses, and potentially system cache IP. The flash memory controller IP can be flash technology-specific; however, in 2018, Arm announced the Generic Flash Bus (GFB) standard, making it possible to create generic embedded flash controllers and allow embedded flash macros to be connected to those controllers via simple glue logic, which is process technology-specific. Arm also offers embedded flash controllers based on GFB interface. Information about AMBA GFB can be found here: https://developer.arm.com/products/architecture/system-architectures/amba/amba-gfb

Embedded flash memories are usually quite slow (e.g., 30MHz to 50MHz access speed for most of the low-power embedded flash macros). Typically, caches in some form are needed to enable the processor system to run at higher clock speeds. Having caches also enables better energy efficiency by reducing the memory accesses on the embedded flash (which could be relatively power-hungry).

Such cache components are available from Arm and other IP suppliers. For example, the AHB flash cache is part of the Arm Corstone-100 foundation IP (https://developer.arm.com/products/system-design/corstone-foundation-ip/corstone-100).

4.10.2 Flash programming

Normally, embedded flash memories partition the memory spaces into pages. To update flash memories, the update process has to be done on a page-by-page basis; i.e., you cannot update just a few bytes / words of the flash. The flash programming and erase operations are supported by the embedded flash controllers mentioned earlier. For security reasons, the programming interface of the embedded flash controller should be privileged access only. If TrustZone security extensions are used, then it needs to be restricted to secure privileged access only to enable secure firmware updates.

When doing flash programming, instead of using the debug connection to access the flash controller directly, the common approach is to:

■ Download a small piece of code to SRAM called a flash programming algorithm, and

■ Download a block of data for a flash page to be programmed to SRAM, then

▓ Download additional configuration information and set the PC (program counter) to the flash programming algorithm, before executing the code to program the flash page.

Each time a flash page is programmed, optionally, the flash programming algorithm can verify the contents of the page. The debug host can then download another page of data and repeat the process until all the pages are programmed.

If a device contains TrustZone security extensions and the on-chip secure firmware is already loaded to the device, the flash programming algorithm might already be present within the on-chip firmware. In such cases, the flash programming sequence only needs to load the new flash contents and configurations before triggering the flash programming steps.

4.10.3 Bringing up a new device without a valid program image

One of the common questions from new Cortex-M designers is: How can you bring up a microcontroller device first time without any valid program in the embedded flash? The actual sequence is no different from normal flash programming:

▓ When the device starts up for the first time, since the flash does not contain a valid program image, it will quickly enter fault exception and eventually go into LOCKUP state.

▓ Even if the device is in LOCKUP state, the debugger can still establish a debug connection via JTAG/Serial Wire.

▓ The debugger can then enable a reset vector catch (a debug feature in the Cortex-M processors), and use System Reset Request (by programming Application Interrupt and Reset Control Register, AIRCR) to reset the system. When the processor comes out from system reset, it enters halt state immediately because the reset vector catch is enabled.

▓ The debugger can download the flash programming algorithm and pages of program image into SRAM and set the PC (program counter) to launch the flash programming algorithm.

▓ When all the required flash pages are programmed, it can reset the system again to start the application or to debug it.

The same concept can also be applied to devices that run code from external flash (e.g., QSPI flash).

CHAPTER 5

Debug integration with Cortex-M processor systems

5.1 Overview of debug and trace features

In the majority of Cortex-M based systems, the designs need to support debug and trace features. These interfaces are not only needed for software development and troubleshooting, but they are also used for flash programming and the collection of diagnostic data in the field when required.

Debug and trace features are configurable in most of the Cortex-M processors (except DesignStart Eval versions, which provide the processor designs with fixed configurations). In general, the debug features include the following:

- Access to the memory space (including download of program code into SRAM for the FPGA platform. Flash programming is a bit more complex and will be explained later). Memory access can be carried out while the processor is running.

- Breakpoint events can be used to halt the processor, or if using a software debug agent (i.e., using the debug monitor in Armv7-M or Armv8-M Mainline), then the debug monitor exception is triggered. There are two types of breakpoint mechanisms:

  - **Hardware breakpoints** that use hardware comparators to compare the program counter with breakpoint addresses. The number of breakpoint comparators is limited. For example, the Cortex-M0 processor has only up to 4 breakpoint comparators.

  - **Software breakpoints** that use the BKPT (breakpoint) instruction to trigger breakpoint event. There is no limit on the number of breakpoints. It is suitable for creating breakpoints during software development on devices with reprogrammable memory.

- Watchpoints are debug events that are triggered when a specific data address is accessed. They use hardware comparators to compare data read/write addresses with specific values and emit watchpoint events when a match is detected. When a watchpoint event is triggered, the processor can be halted, or a debug monitor exception can be triggered (Armv7-M or Armv8-M Mainline).

- Halt / Resume – software developers can send a command to halt the processor when it is running, and when debug operations are done, they can also send a command to resume the operations.

- Access to processor's registers – registers in the processor's register banks and special registers can be accessed and modified when the processor is halted. Memory-mapped registers can be accessed at any time.

- Reset – debugger can request a reset of the target board, typically a system reset through the SYSRESETREQ feature. It is also possible to have a debugger to trigger the whole device reset if a separated reset connection is provided and the debug probe can support this.

- Debug authentication – from an IP protection and system security point of view, there is a need to disable debug and trace in some parts of the product life cycle. Cortex-M processors provide interface signals for debug authentication hardware so that debug and trace features can be disabled. For Armv8-M processors, the interface can also restrict debug and trace visibility to Non-secure side only.

- Multi-code debug and trace – the debug and trace systems in Arm Cortex processors are based on an architecture developed by Arm called CoreSight Debug Architecture. This debug architecture supports multi-core debug and allows multiple processors to be connected to the debugger with a single debug connection. In addition, debug events (e.g., breakpoint, watchpoint) can propagate between various cores to allow the whole system to halt or resume at the same time. The trace interface also allows trace information from multiple processors to be merged and collected by a single debug probe with a single connection, and then be decoded and separated back into multiple trace streams on the debug host.

The trace features on the Cortex-M processors include:

- Micro Trace Buffer (MTB) – a low-cost instruction trace solution that enables the system to allocate a small part of system SRAM for instruction trace. The trace result can be collected through the debug connection.

- Embedded Trace Macrocell (ETM) – a real-time instruction trace solution that streams instruction execution information to debug host via a trace connection.

- Event trace – Real-time trace of exception events generated by the DWT (Data Watchpoint and Trace unit).

- Profiling trace – trace generation for system performance analysis generated by the DWT.

- Selective data trace – a real-time trace of a small selection of data generated by the DWT. The comparators for data watchpoints are used to detect accesses to the specific address location, and if a transfer to such a monitored location is made, information about it can be exported on the trace interface.

- Full data trace – the ETM on Cortex-M7 processors has an implementation option to support full data trace to provide maximum visibility of the program's operations. However, this requires a much higher trace bandwidth and hardware cost, and is therefore only used in specialized SoC designs.

- Instrumentation trace – a real-time trace that is generated by the software to provide debug messages and OS awareness support. For example, it is possible to direct printf("Hello World") messages to the Instrumentation Trace Macrocell (ITM) to display the message on a debug console on the debug host.

- Timestamp support – most trace sources (except MTB) support timestamp and that allows the debug host to reconstruct the timing of various events.

Due to area and power constraints, not all of the Cortex-M processors support all these features. Table 5.1 lists the debug and trace features supported by current Cortex-M processors.

	Breakpoint comparators	Watchpoint comparators	MTB	ETM	DWT's selective data trace	ITM
Cortex-M0	Up to 4	Up to 2				
Cortex-M1	Up to 4	Up to 2				
Cortex-M0+	Up to 4	Up to 2	Y			
Cortex-M3	Up to 6 (instruction) + 2(literal)	Up to 4		Y	Y	Y
Cortex-M4	Up to 6 (instruction) + 2(literal)	Up to 4		Y	Y	Y
Cortex-M7	Up to 8	Up to 4		Y	Y	Y
Cortex-M23	Up to 4	Up to 4	Y	Y		
Cortex-M33	Up to 8	Up to 4	Y	Y	Y	Y
Cortex-M35P	Up to 8	Up to 4	Y	Y	Y	Y

Table 5.1: Debug and trace features support in the Cortex-M processors.

Since most of the debug features are optional, system designers might need to define the options optimized for their requirements (except when using Cortex-M0/Cortex-M3 DesignStart Eval with fixed configurations).

5.2 CoreSight Debug Architecture

5.2.1 Introduction to Arm CoreSight

The debug systems on the Cortex-M processors are based on the Arm CoreSight Debug Architecture. This architecture covers:

▧ The infrastructure to connect the debug interface to the debug components;

▧ The infrastructure to connect trace sources to the trace interface;

▧ High-level mechanisms for debug power management;

▧ Mechanisms for debug component discovery (ROM table);

▧ Control interface for debug authentication.

Based on this architecture, the debug system is scalable and is consistent with debug systems on other ARM Cortex processors, making it easy for tools developers to adapt their tools to the various Cortex-M products.

The full CoreSight debug architecture specification document is available on the Arm website. The Cortex-M processors listed in Table 5.1 were developed with CoreSight Architecture version 2.0. Please note: The Cortex-M processors utilize a subset of the features in CoreSight.

5.2.2 Debug connection protocols

In order to allow the debug host to connect to the processor, we need debug communication protocol(s). Currently, two debug connection protocols are used:

1. JTAG protocol, created by Joint Test Action Group and originally used for various chip level and PCB level testing. This protocol uses 4 or 5 pins for the debug connection: TDI (test data in), TDO (test data out), TCK (test clock), TMS (test mode select), and optional TRST (test reset).

2. Serial Wire Debug (SWD) protocol, created by Arm, uses only two pins: SWDIO (Serial Wire Data I/O, bidirectional), and SWCLK (Serial Wire Clock).

Since the SWD protocol only needs two pins, it is very popular in microcontrollers. JTAG and SWD can co-exist in a microcontroller device and share the same pins: TMS shares a pin with SWDIO, and TCK and SWCLK share the same pin.

Signal	JTAG Mode	SWD Mode	
SWCLKTCK	TCK (Test clock)	SW Clock	
SWDTMS	TMS (Test mode select)	SW Data	
TDI	TDI (Test Data In)	-	(not used)
TDO	TDO (Test Data Out)	-	(not used / shared with SWO trace output)
nTRST	nTRST (Test Reset, active-low)	-	(not used)

Table 5.2: Pin sharing arrangement between JTAG and Serial Wire Debug.

Please note that there are two releases of SWD protocol:

- SWD v1 is supported by Cortex-M3, Cortex-M4, Cortex-M0, optional in Cortex-M0+, Cortex-M23, and Cortex-M7.

- SWD v2 is supported as an optional feature (when multi-drop SWD is selected) in Cortex-M0+, Cortex-M23, and Cortex-M7. It is always used in Cortex-M33 and Cortex-M35P processors when SWD protocol is selected.

SWDv2 supports an optional feature called multi-drop serial wire debug. When this feature is enabled, it allows multiple multi-drop SWD devices to share an SWD connection in parallel. Not all devices implementing SWDv2 support multi-drop features.

If a debug interface supports both protocols, in most case the device would support dynamic protocol switching, which uses a special sequence of bit patterns on SWDTMS to switch between JTAG and SWD modes. The details of the sequence are documented in the Arm Debug Interface (ADI) specification, which is available on the Arm website. Existing Cortex-M designs are based on ADIv5.

Please note that there are standardized connector arrangements. More details can be found here: http://infocenter.arm.com/help/topic/com.arm.doc.faqs/attached/13634/cortex_debug_connectors.pdf

or CoreSight Architecture specification: http://infocenter.arm.com/help/topic/com.arm.doc.ihi0029e/coresight_v3_0_architecture_specification_IHI0029E.pdf

Some of the debug connectors also support trace connections.

5.2.3 Debug connection concept - Debug Access Port (DAP)

In order to make the debug system scalable, the debug interface in CoreSight architecture decouples the debug protocol interface hardware and debug components. In a generic CoreSight system, a configurable DAP (Debug Access Port) block provides the debug protocol interface and a number of bus interface ports to support various debug components in multiple processor subsystems (Figure 5.1).

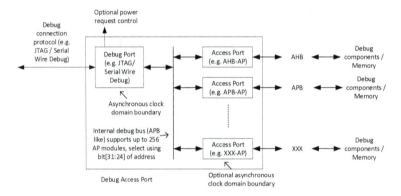

Figure 5.1: Concept of a generic Debug Access Port (DAP).

In a SoC design with a single Cortex-A processor, potentially the DAP can contain two Access Port modules: one for accessing the debug components and one for accessing the memory space. A bus multiplexer is needed if some of the debug components require software accesses.

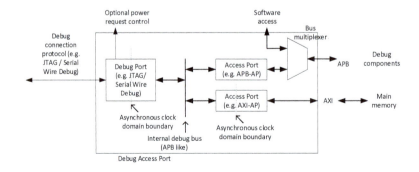

Figure 5.2: Concept of a Debug Access Port (DAP) arrangement for a single-core Cortex-A processor system.

With Cortex-M processors, the debug components are part of the memory map. As a result, the debug connection can be simplified significantly to enable lower power and area. The Cortex-M processor's internal bus interconnect routes the debug accesses to the debug components and memory interfaces, so there is no need to have the bus multiplexer in the DAP.

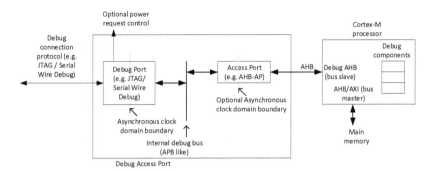

Figure 5.3: Concept of a Debug Access Port (DAP) arrangement for a single-core Cortex-M processor system.

To further reduce silicon area and power consumption, the structure of the DAP can be reduced by removing the optional asynchronous clock domain crossing in the AHB-AP and simplifying the internal debug bus. The result is a very small area in the optimized debug interface design, but the Cortex-M processors can still be connected to a full CoreSight debug system if they are used in a complex SoC design.

5.2.4 Various arrangements of debug interface structure
Over the years, there have been different choices of debug hardware structures used on the Cortex-M processors:

Early Cortex-M processors including Cortex-M3, Cortex-M4, and Cortex-M1, provide an APB-like debug bus interface, and a module called SWJ-DP (Debug Port) that is connected to this bus interface to provide the JTAG or Serial interface. Inside the processor, there is another hardware module called AHB-AP (Access Port) to convert the transfer commands into AHB transactions.

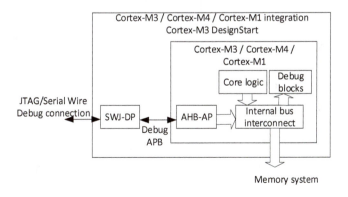

Figure 5.4: Debug connection arrangement in Cortex-M3/M4/M1.

Recent Cortex-M processors deliver a Debug Access Port (DAP) module that is optimized for a smaller silicon area, which combines the functionalities of the Debug Port and Access Port. The processor exposes a debug AHB interface that allows AHB transactions to be routed into the processor's memory system directly.

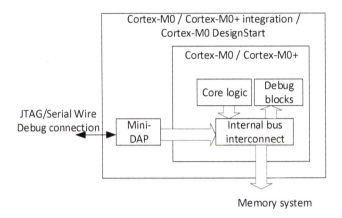

Figure 5.5: Debug connection arrangement in Cortex-M0/M0+.

To simplify integration, in the Cortex-M0 and Cortex-M3 DesignStart Eval versions, the debug interface module is pre-integrated, exposing only the JTAG/SWD interface but not the internal debug buses. However, the designs still support the power request control interface to enable low-power designs.

5.2.5 Trace connection concept
The CoreSight debug architecture also defines a way to support multiple trace sources with a single trace port interface. Each of the trace sources outputs the trace through an Advanced Trace Bus (ATB) interface. The ATB protocol supports an ID value (7-bit) that identifies the trace source, and this ID propagates alongside with the trace data.

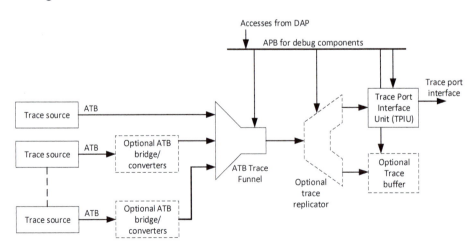

Figure 5.6: Trace system concept.

With various trace bus infrastructure components in CoreSight SoC products, trace sources can be merged, converted between different bus widths, and transferred across different clock / power domains. Most of the trace components are configurable and need to be set up by the debug host through a debug connection (via the DAP that we have already introduced).

Trace data can then be formatted and exported to the trace port interface via a Trace Port Interface Unit (TPIU). The trace port interface (trace data + trace clock) needs to be available at the top-level of the chip (it can be multiplexed with function pins and hidden when trace is not used). The software developer can collect the trace data using a debug probe that supports trace.

In Cortex-A and Cortex-R systems, the trace bandwidth requirements are usually higher (mostly due to the higher clock speed, but potentially with more trace sources when multiple processors are present) so the trace port could have up to 16-bit or 32-bit trace data (plus clock). In some cases, for example, when the trace port does not have sufficient bandwidth, trace data can be stored in a trace buffer instead of streaming out to the trace port immediately.

In most Cortex-M systems, the TPIU included in the IP bundle can support a parallel trace port of up to 4 trace data bits (plus clock), or use an asynchronous single pin trace protocol called SWO (Serial Wire Output) for a low-cost trace arrangement, but with a much lower trace bandwidth. The TPIU used in Cortex-M systems also further reduces the area by merging ATB trace funnel functionality into it, so it can accept trace from the processor (trace generated by DWT and ITM)) as well as from the optional ETM simultaneously.

If needed, the trace buses from a Cortex-M processor can be connected to other CoreSight trace bus infrastructure components and CoreSight TPIU. This is common for complex SoC designs where a number of processors are present including Cortex-A and the Cortex-M processors.

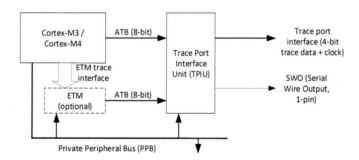

Figure 5.7: Trace system in Cortex-M3/Cortex-M4 processors.

Please note that the MTB instruction trace solutions in Cortex-M0+, Cortex-M23, Cortex-M33, and Cortex-M35P do not use ATB at all. With MTB, trace information is directly stored in SRAM connected to the MTB unit and therefore trace information cannot be collected in real-time. Instead, the debugger can use a standard debug connection to extract trace results when the content of the SRAM is in the memory map. This enables a very low-cost trace solution as software developers do not need to use an expensive trace probe to collect instruction trace information.

5.2.6 Timestamp

In order to allow the debug host to reconstruct event timing from trace data, many trace components support a global timestamp mechanism. To ensure various trace units have the same timestamp source, in small processor systems a single timestamp generator is used. This unit can be a simple binary counter, with the counter value connected to various trace sources. Using this information, trace components can output timestamp packets periodically to provide timing information.

In Cortex-M3 and Cortex-M4 processors, the timestamp interface is 48-bit (input signal). In Cortex-M7 and Armv8-M processors, a 64-bit timestamp interface is used. You can use a simple binary up counter to generate timestamp and enable this counter only when the TRCENA output signal (Trace Enable) from the Cortex-M processor is set.

The timestamp interface also contains an input signal call TSCLKCHANGE. The intention of this signal is to help trace reconstruction software to be aware of clock frequency changes. Since processor systems can switch between different clock sources, and this can affect the timing reconstruction, TSCLKCHANGE was introduced with the intention that it could be pulsed when clock/frequency changes were made. This was to enable the trace components to output new timestamp packets immediately to resynchronize timing information. However, it was found that in some system designs that it was difficult to implement this feature accurately. TSCLKCHANGE has now been removed from the ETMv4.0 specification and can be tied low in system designs if needed. More information on this topic can be found in https://developer.arm.com/docs/300818048/latest/what-is-tsclkchange

5.2.7 Debug components discovery (ROM table and component IDs)

CoreSight architecture has a lookup table mechanism to allow debug components to be discovered automatically by a debug host. Inside each of the bus system connected to the Access Port module, there can be one or more look-up table(s) called ROM table(s) to provide the address information of the debug components, and with ID registers in each of the debug components, the debug host can then detect the debug components connected to each Access Port.

To get the component discovery process working, the AHB-AP component contains a register BASE (address offset 0xF8) that listed the base address – the address of the top-level ROM table component in the AHB memory map. The ROM tables are 4KB in size, and the end address range has ID values that indicate that it is a ROM table.

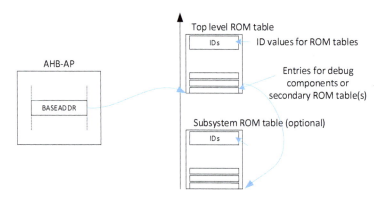

Figure 5.8: Concept of ROM table lookup.

The ROM table entries contain address offsets of the debug components/additional ROM tables. There can be multiple ROM tables in a system, which are arranged in a hierarchical way. The addresses used as table entries are relative - in this way a subsystem can contain its ROM table and does not need to know the absolute address of the debug component inside.

SoC designers should consider customizing the system-level ROM table. The ID values of the ROM table contains a JEP106 Identity Code, and this represents the company's identification. You can register for a JEP106 from www.jedec.org. For more information on this topic, please see: https://developer.arm.com/docs/103489663/latest/peripheralid-values-for-the-coresight-rom-table, and https://www.jedec.org/standards-documents/id-codes-order-form

If additional debug components are added/removed, the ROM table entries need to be updated. Each entry is 32-bit with the following format:

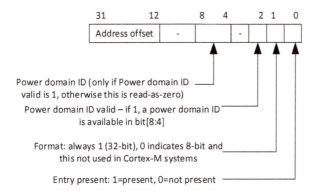

Figure 5.9: ROM table entry format.

The power domain ID field is optional. For most single Cortex-M systems with a single power domain, it is perfectly fine to set power domain ID and power domain ID valid to 0.

The last entry in the ROM table must have the value of 0x00000000, and subsequent locations are also read as zero.

There is an additional read-only register in the ROM table called MEMTYPE, which is in address 0xFCC of the ROM table. If bit 0 (SYSMEM) of this register is 1, it means the system memory is visible on the bus that the ROM table is connected. Otherwise, the bus is for debug components only. For Cortex-M systems, the MEMTYPE of ROM tables is set to 1.

For more information on the ROM table format, please refer to CoreSight Architecture Specification v2.0 section D5: https://static.docs.arm.com/ihi0029/d/IHI0029D_coresight_architecture_spec_v2_0.pdf

Since the current Cortex-M processors listed in Table 5.1 are based on CoreSight architecture specification v2.0, the designs use class 0x1 ROM tables.

5.2.8 Debug authentication

CoreSight debug architecture supports a number of control signals (input of processor or debug/trace components):

Signal	Description
DBGEN	Invasive debug enable
NIDEN	Non-invasive debug enable (for trace components)
SPIDEN	Secure Invasive debug enable (available for systems with TrustZone)
SPNIDEN	Secure Non-invasive debug enable (for trace components, available for systems with TrustZone)

Table 5.3: CoreSight debug authentication signals.

In simplified terms, DBGEN and NIDEN control the Non-secure debug and trace permissions, while SPIDEN and SPNIDEN control the Secure debug and trace permissions. Not all combinations of these signals are valid – if a debug action is allowed for Secure state, it must also be allowed for Non-secure state (i.e., you cannot have SPIDEN set to 1 while DBGEN set to 0, or SPNIDEN set to 1 and NIDEN set to 0).

There is another enable control signal on AHB-AP component which will enable/disable memory accesses of AHB-AP (when disabled, the debugger can still access the AHB-AP registers, but cannot initiate an AHB transfer).

▪ In Cortex-M3/Cortex-M4, this is named as DAPEN (DAPCLK domain).

▪ In newer Cortex-M DAP, this is named DEVICEEN (not available in Cortex-M0 DesignStart Eval as it is obfuscated within the module).

In simple systems that do not need debug authentication support, these signals can be tied high. This enables all the debug functionalities.

In systems that need debug authentication support, the CoreSight debug authentication signals are connected to a debug authentication control unit (not a part of the Cortex-M processor) that authenticates debug connections. The authentication process typically based on the product's life cycle state and user's input such as debug certificate or password. Based on guidelines from Platform Security Architecture (PSA), generally certificated based debug authentication is preferred over password-based authentication for products that can contain sensitive information.

Please note that:

▪ The behavior of debug access control has changed between different versions of Armv7-M architectures. In older Arm Cortex-M processors like Cortex-M3 and Cortex-M4, and Armv6-M processors, the AHB-AP can access to the memory space when DBGEN and NIDEN are 0. Since Cortex-M7 processor (from version E of Armv7-M architecture), DBGEN and NIDEN signals affect the debug access permission.

- Although Cortex-M3 and Cortex-M4 have internal trace sources (ITM, DWT), it does not have a NIDEN signal. It is still possible to disable trace output by disabling the ATB path from the processor's ATB to TPIU, but the masking control has to be a static control signal and cannot be changed during trace operations.

- For all Armv8-M processors, permission for debug to access the memory system depends on the debug authentication status, as describes in the Armv8-M Architecture Reference Manual.

5.2.9 Debug power request

The DAP modules contain simple handshaking for power management. These signals are in SWDCLK or TCK clock domains and must be synchronized before being used for power control or clock gating.

Signal	Direction	Description
CDBGPWRUPREQ	Output from DAP	Power up request for debug
CDBGPWRUPACK	Input to DAP	Acknowledge debug is powered up
CSYSPWRUPREQ	Output from DAP	Power-up request for the system (optional)
CSYSPWRUPACK	Input to DAP	Acknowledge system is powered up (optional)

Table 5.4: CoreSight DAP power request signals.

Some of the DAP modules only have the debug power up handshaking.

The handshaking interface is used at the beginning of a debug connection – the debug host requests the debug system to be powered up and wait for the acknowledgment before proceeding to access debug and system components.

In simple FPGA designs, you can handle these signals with a loopback via a double D flip-flop synchronizer. The synchronized version of the signals could be used for clock gating control.

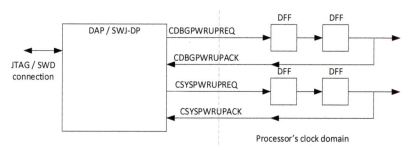

Figure 5.10: DAP power management for simple FPGA designs.

In ASIC designs where multiple power domains are used, the acknowledge signals need to be handled by the power management logic to ensure that the acknowledge is sent only after the power domain is up and running.

A knowledge base article on these signals are available on Arm website:
http://infocenter.arm.com/help/topic/com.arm.doc.faqs/ka14237.html

5.2.10 Debug reset request

Similar to the debug power request handshaking, some of the DAP designs also support an optional debug reset request handshaking signal that allows the debug host to request a reset to the debug and trace system in case the debug/trace system has become unresponsive. Normally this should reset only the debug and trace system, but not the functional logic.

Signal	Direction	Description
CDBGRSTREQ	Output from DAP	Debug reset request (optional)
CDBGRSTACK	Input to DAP	Acknowledge debug reset has been carried out (optional)

Table 5.5: CoreSight debug request handshake signals.

In a few cases, such debug reset also resets functional logic if there is no easy way to isolate the reset. If that is the case, chip designers should document this clearly to avoid confusing tool vendors.

5.2.11 Cross Trigger Interface

The Cross Trigger Interface (CTI) is an optional feature in Cortex-M0+, Cortex-M7 and Armv8-M processors. This unit is useful for multi-processor systems where debug events can distribute to multiple processors to allow multiple processor cores to halt and resume at the same time during a debug session. For designers using Cortex-M3, Cortex-M4 and Cortex-M0 processors, processor wrappers and a separate CTI component are available in CoreSight SoC products.

For single-processor systems, CTI option can be removed, and its signals can be tied off (for inputs) or unused (for outputs).

5.3 Debug integration

5.3.1 JTAG / Serial Wire Debug connections

Since the Cortex-M processors are designed as generic IP, tristate buffers are not used in the design and system designers need to add them (and optionally pin multiplexers) to the top-level design when integrating JTAG or Serial Wire debug connection.

The top debug connections for JTAG / SWD is summarised in Figure 5.11.

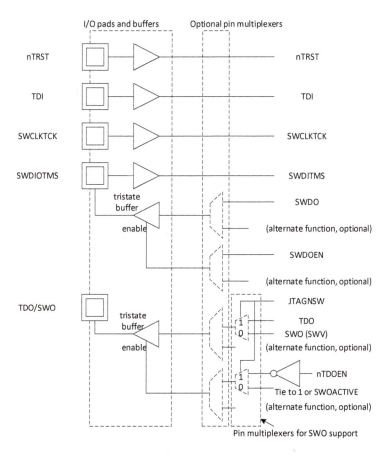

Figure 5.11: Top-level signal handling in for JTAG/SWD debug connection.

Many parts of the logic in Figure 5.11 are optional. For example,

- Some of the JTAG signals like nTRST, TDI, and TDO are not needed if the processor system is configured to support Serial Wire Debug (SWD) only.

- Multiplexing of debug pins and other functional pins this optional – be careful when multiplexing debug pins with functional pins as this could lock out debug connections.

- The use of nTDOEN is optional. Potentially disabling the TDO tristate buffer when it is not used can save power.

- For Armv7-M or Armv8-M Mainline Cortex-M systems that support trace, one integration task required is to multiplex TDO (JTAG's test data out) with SWO (Serial Wire Output). This enables debug tools to support low bandwidth trace operations. Using this arrangement, the SWO is available only when using SWD debug protocol.

- SWO/SWV is not available on Cortex-M0, Cortex-M0+, Cortex-M1, or Cortex-M23, and the associated pin function multiplexers can be removed in those cases.

- When using the SWO/SWV feature, instead of always enabling the output tristate buffer, using SWOACTIVE from the Cortex-M TPIU is also a suitable arrangement. Note: SWOACTIVE signal is not available in Cortex-M3 DesignStart Eval.

In low-power designs, if we need to allow debug connections to be established when the processor is sleeping, the debug interface block (either DAP or SWJ-DP), and the associated logic (including I/O pads and pin multiplexer) should not be powered down.

In addition, the debug power request signals need to be connected as covered in Section 5.2.9 and do not forget to set up the clock and reset timing constraints for JTAG/SWD's signals including clock and reset.

5.3.2 Trace port connections
The trace connections for a common Cortex-M based system might contain:

- SWO (or SWV in Cortex-M3/M4) – already covered in 5.3.1 as it is normally multiplexed with TDO pin;

- TRACEDATA and TRACECLK.

Please note that MTB instruction trace does not require top-level pins because the trace data is extracted via debug connection.

In single-core Cortex-M systems that support trace, the Cortex-M TPIU bundled supports up to 4-bit trace data and a trace clock (all of them are output signals). Optionally, you can multiplex the trace pins with functional inputs/outputs, and use the TRCENA (trace enable) output from the processor and optionally ETMPWRUP (ETM power-up) from the ETM to switch the pins to trace function when trace system is enabled. Note: If using Cortex-M3 DesignStart Eval, SWOACTIVE signal is not available and therefore SWO cannot be multiplexed with TRACEDATA[0]. However, you can still multiplex SWO with TDO as explained in section 5.3.1.

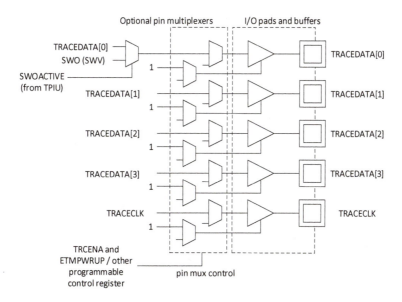

Figure 5.12: Top-level signal handling for trace port connections.

Using TRACENA for pin multiplexing control is easy as it is always set when any of the trace components are enabled, and ETMPWRUP can be used to indicate TPIU need to operate in trace port mode in order to provide enough bandwidth to output ETM trace. Alternatively, it is also possible to use a programmable control register to enable the trace pin functions. This allows software developers to use just SWO trace without forcing other trace pins to trace functions. If you are doing this, you will need debug tools to program this register before using ETM. In most tools, you can set up a debug script to enable this action to take place before the debug session started.

5.3.3 Clocks for the debug and trace system
For the Cortex-M3 and Cortex-M4 processor systems, there can be up to four asynchronous clock domains:

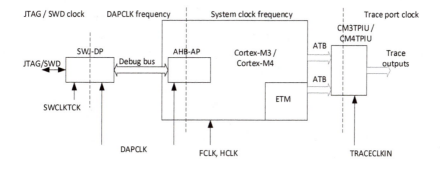

Figure 5.13: Asynchronous clock boundaries in Cortex-M3 and Cortex-M4 processor systems.

Most of the newer Cortex-M processors do not have internal asynchronous clock boundaries apart from the DAP interface modules:

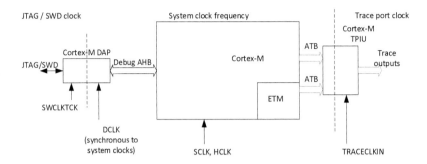

Figure 5.14: Asynchronous clock boundaries in newer Cortex-M systems.

In the case of single-core Cortex-M3 / Cortex-M4 systems, system designers can use the system clock to generate the DAPCLK, with clock gating controlled by synchronized CDBGPWRUPREQ. For multi-core systems, the DAPCLK needs to be the same as the debug APB of the DAP (Debug Access Port).

While technically TRCECLKIN for the TPIU can be completely asynchronous to system clocks, there are some additional considerations when designing the clock systems for TRACECLKIN. From the debug tools point of view, when using SWO (Serial Wire Output), the debug probe expects the data rate to be constant during a debug session.

In an MCU debug use case, potentially you can connect TRACECLKIN to the processor's clock. You can also clock gate TRACECLKIN using TRCENA from the processor. (Please note: the trace system can be enabled using software without a debug connection). For designs using Cortex-M23 and Cortex-M33 processors, the clock gate control should be TRCENA|TPIU_PSEL (clock enabled when either TRCENA or TPIU's PSEL is set).

Considering Serial Wire Output/Serial Wire Viewer user cases, although the processor clock's frequency might change at boot time (as it switches from crystal to PLL), the software trace (i.e., printf via the ITM) normally does not happen until after entering main(), so that will be okay. However, if the application switches clock frequency speed during operations, then connecting TRACECLKIN to the processor's clock would be problematic as the debug probe does not know what the current clock frequency is and therefore cannot extract the serial data.

When using Trace port mode (4-bit data + clock), even if the clock speed changed, the debug probe could recover the data as the reference trace clock is available. Therefore, clock frequency change is not an issue normally. However, for a high-speed trace (if your chip is going to run at >100MHz), some trace probes use PLL/DLL to handle clock recovery and clock frequency changes can cause the PLL/DLL in the debug probe to lose synchronization for a short time.

At the same time, if using a constant but low-frequency clock (e.g., direct from a low-frequency crystal), it might not have sufficient data bandwidth to output an ETM trace when the processor switches to its high-speed clock from PLL. Therefore, in designing of TRACECLKIN source, ideally, use a constant high-speed clock if one is available, providing that it is slower than the frequency limitations of the I/O pins for trace outputs. (Note: this can be completely asynchronous to the processor's clock). In generic MCU designs, it could be desirable to have multiple options (controlled by a programmable register and set up by means of debug configuration script in the debugger). The default setup could use the processor's clock and be changed to other clock sources if needed.

Modern commercial debug and trace probes for Cortex-M support debug connections of maximum 20MHz to 50MHz, and trace port operations at up to 200 to 300MHz. Obviously, connecting debug and trace at lower frequencies is allowed. Please note, the TPIU has an internal programmable pre-scaler to allow the clock speed of SWO to be reduced if needed. The maximum speed of debug and TPIU operations also depends on:

▪ Characteristics of the I/O pads;

▪ PCB designs;

▪ Cable connection between the board and the debug & trace probes;

▪ Stability of the voltage sources and noises in the environment.

Many debug and trace probes might also have their own specific requirements for signal voltage levels. If the debug and trace connection is unstable, it worth trying to reduce the frequency in the connection settings to see if this helps.

5.3.4 Multi-drop serial wire support
Serial Wire Debug protocol v2 optionally supports multi-drop Serial Wire Debug. This feature is optional in the DAP in newer Cortex-M processors and is not available in the SWJ-DP for Cortex-M3 and Cortex-M4 processors, or the DAP module for the Cortex-M0 processor. Even if you are using a more recent processor, support for this feature is optional and therefore might not be included.

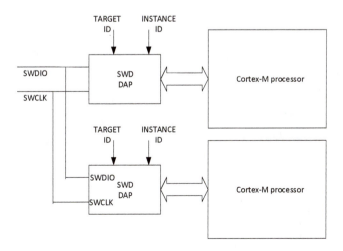

Figure 5.15: Multi-drop Serial Wire Debug.

If using multi-drop SWD, the system designer must provide a target ID and instance ID to the DAP. These ID values are device-specific, where Target ID is unique to a device. Instance ID is needed if a circuit board contains multiple identical devices; in that case, their instance ID needs to be unique.

The use of multi-drop serial wire debug is uncommon in microcontrollers because there is a need to set up target ID and instance ID to ensure that the ID values are unique, and the debug tools know which DAP, is which. Multi-drop Serial Wire is more popular for complex SoC designs that are end-product-specific, as all the target and instance IDs of the end-products can be controlled (e.g., by the OEM). Please also note that some microcontroller debug tools do not have support for multi-drop operations.

5.3.5 Debug authentication

For minimum, a simple debug authentication needs to control the debug authentication signals (see Section 5.2.8), and in the case of Cortex-M0, Cortex-M0+, Cortex-M3, and Cortex-M4 processors, the debug authentication also requires bus level access filtering logic to restrict debug accesses to memories.

To be secure, typically a debug authentication system requires Non-Volatile Memory (NVM) for storage of life cycle state information, secure information for decryption of debug certificates, a communication interface for the authentication process, and, potentially, a crypto accelerator for decryption of the certificates. Often, the debug authentication mechanism is software controlled and integrated into the firmware of the device.

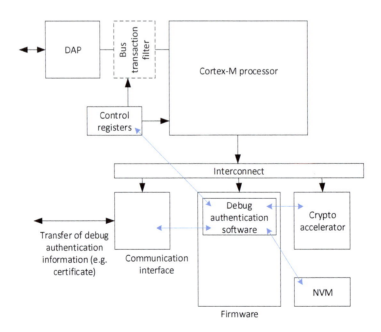

Figure 5.16: Debug authentication system concept.

Note: The bus filtering arrangement in Figure 5.16 cannot be used for Cortex-M3 and Cortex-M4 - in the case of Cortex-M3 and Cortex-M4 processors, the bus connection between AHB-AP and the processor's internal interconnect is not exposed. So, the DAPEN of the AHB-AP (input of Cortex-M3/Cortex-M4 processor) could be used to block all debug accesses until debug connection is authenticated.

The Arm document TBSA-M (Trusted Base System Architecture for Cortex-M) provides comprehensive requirements information about debug authentication. However, occasionally system designers would like to use some simpler designs; for example, by having a passcode mechanism to protect the system, and to allow a full hardware-based approach (since the firmware is not ready). While this is possible, a brute force approach could be used to obtain the passcode, or a replay mechanism employed to reverse engineer the passcode if the attacker has gained access to a working debug session. Unless a system is developed only as a prototype (not for commercial deployment), then a simple passcode approach is not recommended.

If a very simple debug authentication approach is needed, a possible arrangement is to use e-fuse or emulated e-fuse in embedded flash to store debug authentication control information. The information might contain several pieces of information; namely:

■ A NVM location to indicate if the debug authentication feature is enabled;

■ One or more NVM locations to hold passcode(s) – this information must not be readable from software or debugger. If there is a need for multiple levels of debug authentication controls, multiple NVM passcodes could be used.

A separate passcode register (which can be implemented as a memory-mapped register) is needed to allow software development tools to program the passcode, and the value is compared against the passwords stored in NVM by hardware. If using Cortex-M3 or Cortex-M4, this can be implemented as a mirror of the AHB-AP and activates the comparison if the debug tool is writing to a specific address (needed to test the condition of TAR (Target Address Register) and CSW (Control and Status Word) registers):

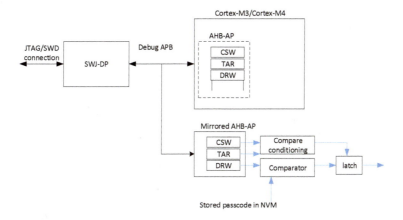

Figure 5.17: Simple debug authentication passcode mechanism for Cortex-M3/Cortex-M4 processor systems (not recommended for general product development).

For other Cortex-M processors, the connection between the DAP and the processor exposes the debug accesses, and therefore, the passcode registers can be memory-mapped registers placed on the debug AHB there.

Please note that such an example scheme only provides limited protection. For stronger protection, debug authentication solutions such as CryptoCell/CryptoIsland could be used. These solutions also offer other security features such as cryptographic accelerators and life cycle state management.

5.4 Other related topics

5.4.1 Other signal connections

HALTED – the HALTED signal is an output status from the processor and can be used for certain peripherals that need to be stopped when the processor is halted and won't be able to serve its interrupt services.

EDBGRQ – external debug request is usually used for systems with multiple processors, to allow the processor to enter halt if there is a debug event in another processor. In single-processor systems, or if multiple core debug events are transferred by built-in CTI, this signal can be tied low.

DBGRESTART and DBGRESTARTED – this is used for systems with multiple processors, to allow multiple processors to be taken out from halted state at the same time. In single-processor systems, or if multi-core debug events are transferred by built-in CTI, the DBGRESTART signal can be tied low and DBGRESTARTED can be left unused.

FIXMASTERTYPE – this signal is available in the Cortex-M3 and Cortex-M4 processors. When this signal is low, it allows the debugger to generate a debug access with the same bus master information (HMASTER) as transfers generated from software running on the processor (this behavior is programmable in the AHB-AP). When this pin is high, an HMASTER signal always indicates the true source of the transfer. This pin should be set to 1 if there are firmware protection mechanisms in the system that needs to know the true generation source of bus transfers. In other Cortex-M processors, the DAP interface does not allow the HMASTER value of debug accesses to be controlled by debug host software and so do not need this pin.

5.4.2 Daisy chain of JTAG connection

In theory, if using the JTAG protocol, it is possible to daisy chain the JTAG connections with another JTAG device. However, some debug tools do not support such arrangements. In addition, daisy-chaining JTAG TAP controllers for device testing and TAP controller for software debug might lead to unexpected conflicts and therefore should be avoided.

CHAPTER
Low-power support

6

6.1 Overview of low-power Cortex-M features

Today's microcontroller designs can be extremely energy efficient. In addition to low-power use during operations, the sleep mode current and additional low-power capabilities (e.g., retention SRAM) can be very impressive. Today, many low-power Cortex-M based microcontrollers can operate at below 50uA/MHz. Together with the ability to run with a lower supply voltage, the battery life of embedded products can be much longer than those designed 10-15 years ago when the Cortex-M processors were just entering the microcontroller market. And with high code density and higher processing performance, the energy efficiencies of Cortex-M based systems are often much better than 8-bit and 16-bit solutions.

To enable low-power capabilities, most of the Cortex-M processors provide various low-power features, including:

- Architecture defined sleep modes: sleep and deep sleep;

- Multiple clock signals for block-level clock gating, and optional support for sub-block level clock gating (sometimes referred to as architectural clock gating);

- State retention power gating (SRPG) support;

- Optional Wake-up Interrupt Controller (WIC);

- Sleep-on-exit – allows interrupt driven applications to enter sleep mode automatically when no interrupt requests are pending.

Newer Cortex-M processors also support multi-power domains and additional pipeline optimizations to enable ultra-low-power designs.

In addition to dedicated low-power features, some of the characteristics of the Cortex-M processors are also helpful for enabling low-power designs:

- High code density – allows applications to fit into smaller program memories;

- Small area – Cortex-M0, Cortex-M0+, and Cortex-M23 processors are designed to meet the power constraints of the most demanding low-power applications;

- High performance – processing tasks can be completed faster, reducing overall energy consumption;

- Low interrupt latency and interrupt handling optimizations – reduce the overhead of interrupt handling.

Additional low-power optimizations can be done at the system-level. For example, in Chapter 4, Figure 4.14, we mentioned the approach of having multiple banks of SRAM. In this chapter, we will also cover some other methods to reduce system-level power.

6.2 Low-power design basics

Clock gating is one of the most basic techniques for lowering power consumptions in digital systems. Typically, a register can have an enable input to reduce unnecessary internal signal toggling. Synthesis tools can transform the logic to gate off the clock to the register using the same enable signal to reduce dynamic power (Figure 6.1) further.

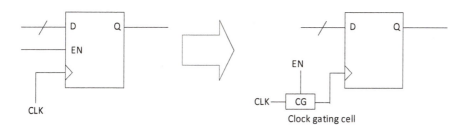

Figure 6.1: Clock gating.

Since all the Cortex-M processors are written in generic Verilog RTL, synthesis tools can handle the clock gating insertion easily.

Another level of clock gating is done inside the processor design where a number of functional units contain instantiations of clock gating cell wrappers (which can be modified to process node-specific clock gating cells). These clock gating wrappers are placed in optimum locations to enable more aggressive clock gating where synthesis tools cannot determine the clock gating opportunities. This technique is referred to as architectural clock gating (ACG) and is optional (enable/disable by a Verilog parameter, usually called ACG).

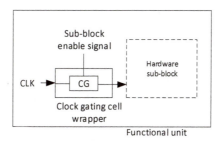

Figure 6.2: Architectural clock gating.

Many Cortex-M processors also have multiple top-level clock signals that enable system designers to place additional clock gating at the clock domain level (Figure 6.3). In some newer processors, this arrangement is handled internally to the processor design.

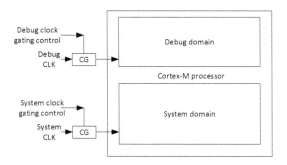

Figure 6.3: Separated clock domains.

In Chapter 5, we have already covered the debug power control signals CDBGPWRUPREQ and CDBGPWRUPACK, which can be used for clock gate control for the debug clock domain. For system clock domain, some of the Cortex-M processors have GATEHCLK signal which can serve the purpose of gating the system clock on/off.

In many cases, just clock gating is not enough, and so power gating is needed. Simple power gating requires power switch transistors and also additional special cells for signal isolation and clamping.

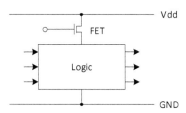

Figure 6.4: Simple power gating.

The most significant disadvantage of simple power gating is that the logic state would be lost and would need to be reset. A newer form of power gating technology is called State Retention Power Gating (SRPG), which introduces state retention elements inside registers and uses separate power rails for state retention. Since the rest of the logic can be powered down, it is still a significant saving for sleep modes. However, the area of state retention registers and their dynamic power are higher than for the standard registers, so such a mechanism is not optimized for systems that are active most of the time.

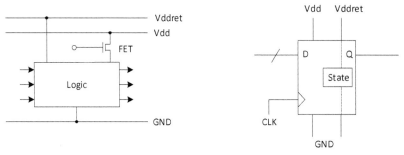

Figure 6.5: State retention power gating.

In addition to digital logic, there are also low-power features in memories (e.g., many SRAM macros support a range of low-power states). A range of peripheral components like ADC (Analog to Digital Converters) can also have their own low-power features.

6.3 Cortex-M low-power interfaces

6.3.1 Sleep status and GATEHCLK output

Most of the Cortex-M processors have the following status output signals:

Signal name	Description
SLEEPING	When it is 1, it indicates the processor is in a sleep state
SLEEPDEEP	When it is 1, it indicates the processor is in a sleep state, and the SLEEPDEEP bit (bit 2) in the System Control Register (SCR) is set
GATEHCLK	When this is 1, it means it is safe to gate off the HCLK signal. (Processor is sleeping, and there are no debug accesses)

Table 6.1: Sleep interface.

Architecturally, the processor supports two sleep modes: sleep and deep sleep. The mechanisms for entering these sleep modes are the same.

■ Execution of WFI or WFE will enter sleep mode conditionally;

■ The sleep-on-exit feature is enabled, and the processor is returning from an exception handler to thread level.

The selection of entering sleep and deep sleep is defined by SLEEPDEEP bit in the System Control Register (SCR). Inside the processor, there is not much difference between the two types of sleep. System designers can make use of the SLEEPING and SLEEPDEEP signals to define power-saving measures on the chip level, and optionally extend the sleep modes with device-specific programmable registers if preferred.

(Please note in Armv7-M and Armv8-M Mainline processors, the WIC is used only in deep sleep).

When the processor is sleeping, it is still possible to have bus transactions on the AHB interface of the processor due to debug accesses. Therefore, an extra signal GATEHCLK is provided to indicate that the processor is sleeping, and there are no on-going bus transactions like debug accesses.

How these signals can be used is device-specific. For example, bus clocks can be gated off, SRAM can enter a lower power state, and some peripherals could be stopped if GATEHCLK is high.

6.3.2 Q-channel low-power interface (Applicable to Cortex-M23, Cortex-M33, Cortex-M35P)

Newer Cortex-M processors (Cortex-M23, Cortex-M33, and Cortex-M35P) support Q-channel, one of the handshaking protocols defined in AMBA 4 Low-power Interface Specification. The specification of this interface protocol can be downloaded from Arm's website:

http://infocenter.arm.com/help/topic/com.arm.doc.ihi0068c/index.html

The new interface protocol enables system designers to create reusable IP for power management. This Low-power Interface Specification describes both Q-channel and P-channel protocols. The use of Q-channels in the Cortex-M processors only started recently with the introduction of Cortex-M23 and Cortex-M33 processors. P-channels are used on recent Cortex-A processors for most complex power control scenarios.

The Q-channel connects between a design unit (e.g., a processor) and a power management unit (device-specific). The interface operates with 4 signals, as shown in Table 6.2. The polarity of these signals must be chosen so that if the interface signals get clamped to 0 in a low-power state, it will not affect the signal levels

Signal	Description
QACTIVE	Indicates the design unit has an outstanding action to perform
QREQn	Active-low signal to request the low-power state
QACCEPTn	Active-low signal to acknowledge that the low-power request is accepted
QDENY	Active high signal to indicate that the low-power request is denied

Table 6.2: Q-channel signals.

A processor can have multiple Q-channels for different power domains, and there can be separated Q-channels for clock gating and power-down operations. In simple designs, the system-level power management hardware can use a Q-channel to control a power domain of a processor.

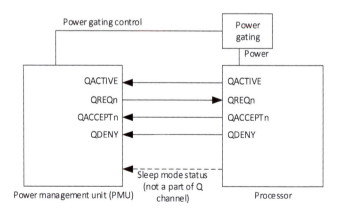

Figure 6.6: A simple example of a Q-channel setup.

The following example shows a power management scenario for a processor's system power domain. At the starting stage of the power-up sequence, the power gating control applies power to the processor. In this scenario, both the QACTIVE and QREQn signals are high before the processor starts (Figure 6.7).

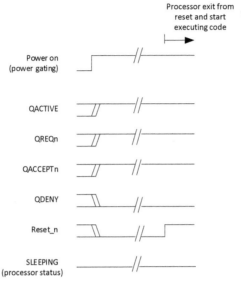

Figure 6.7: Example Q-channel activity for system domain when a processor boots up.

When the processor enters sleep mode, the power management unit detects the sleep operation and then requests to change the processor to low-power state (e.g., SRPG) by asserting QREQn to 0. The processor can then drive QACCEPTn low to indicate that the low-power state request is accepted. After the processor accepts the low-power mode request, it then puts the processor in the targeted low-power state (i.e., SRPG), as shown in Figure 6.8.

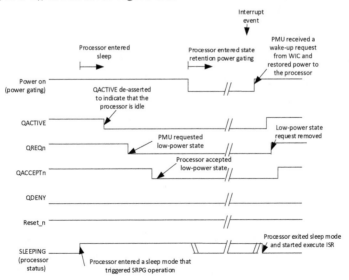

Figure 6.8: Example of Q-channel activity for the system domain when a processor enters a sleep mode that uses state retention power gating.

Assuming that the processor system has a Wakeup Interrupt Controller (WIC) in an always-on power domain or similar hardware features, then a peripheral activity triggering an interrupt request can wake up the system via a separate connection between the WIC and the power management controller. In this scenario, the power management controller can restore the power and clock signal activity to the processor system, and then the Q-channel can complete its handshaking sequence (right-hand side of Figure 6.8).

If an interrupt request arrives just after the processor has entered sleep mode, then it is possible for the processor to reject the low-power state request using the QDENY signal. In such cases, the PMU must not power down the processor in order to allow it to continue its operations, as shown in Figure 6.9.

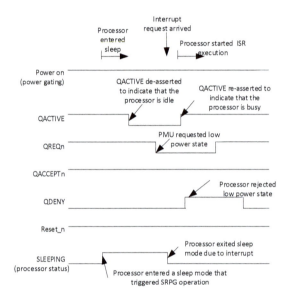

Figure 6.9: Example Q-channel activity for system domain when a processor rejects a low-power state request.

It is possible that some power domains of a processor can start up in a low-power state. For example, the debug power domain of a processor can be in an OFF state when the system starts and turned on only when a debugger is connected. In such cases, the QACTIVE and QREQn signals will have a start-up level of zero instead of one.

In addition to processor systems, the Q-channel can also be used in other system components. Since the handshake protocol is fairly simple and is very generic, it can be deployed for many components of a low-power microcontroller or system-on-chip design.

6.3.3 Sleep hold interface
The sleep hold interface is used to delay the resume of program execution when the processor wakes up from a sleep mode. There would be various reasons for using this interface: one example is that a memory block might need some clock cycles to get itself out of low-power states. Please note, this feature is less likely to be used when the Wake-up Interrupt Controller (WIC) is used because it is possible to hold the processor in sleep mode by gating off all clocks while interrupt detection is handled by the WIC.

The sleep hold interface contains two signals:

Signal name	Description
SLEEPHOLDREQn	Input of processor. When using this feature, set this signal to 1 after entering sleep mode
SLEEPHOLDACKn	Output from processor to indicate sleep hold request is accepted

Table 6.3: Sleep hold request acknowledge interface.

These two signals are active-low and interface with a power management unit (PMU) or the system controller developed by silicon vendors.

The operation of the sleep hold interface is very simple: When the PMU or System Controller detects that the processor core has entered sleep (SLEEPING or SLEEPDEEP signals), it can then assert the SLEEPHOLDREQn signal to the processor. If the processor core responds with the assertion of SLEEPHOLDACKn (pulled low), then the PMU or system controller can then reduce the power by turning off the flash memories, peripherals, PLL, etc. If the processor core does not respond with SLEEPHOLDACKn, then it means the processor core might have received an interrupt or a debug request, so it is going to wake up. In this case, the PMU or system controller should not carry out any further action and de-assert SLEEPHOLDREQn when sleep signals (SLEEPING or SLEEPDEEP) is de-asserted.

If the sleep hold request has been accepted after the system has entered sleep, and an interrupt arrives, the processor core will de-assert the sleep signals. However, the processor core will not resume program execution until SLEEPHOLDREQn from the PMU or system controller is de-asserted (pulled high). When the flash memory voltage supply is resumed, and all the logic is ready, the SLEEPHOLDREQn can be de-asserted, and the execution of the interrupt service routine can be started.

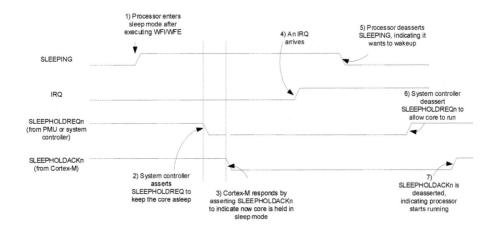

Figure 6.10: Waveform of the sleep hold interface operations.

During the extended sleep, it is possible to stop the HCLK if GATEHCLK is high.

If the sleep hold feature is not needed, the SLEEPHOLDREQn input signal can be tied high.

6.3.4 Wakeup Interrupt Controller (WIC)

If a Cortex-M processor has all of its clock signals gated off or has been put into a state retention power down state, then its NVIC will not be able to detect incoming interrupts or other wake-up events. To solve this problem, the WIC feature was introduced.

The WIC is an optional block that is in a separated always on the power domain that will take the role of interrupt and wake up event detection when the NVIC is stopped or powered down. The exact interface and integration details can be processor-specific. In general, the interface between the WIC and the processor contains:

Signal name	Direction	Description
WICMASKxxx[n:0]	Processor to WIC	Wakeup event mask. Contain mask status for NMI, RXEV, EDBGRQ (for Armv7-M, Armv8-M Mainline) and IRQ signals. The signal width is configurable.
WICLOAD	Processor to WIC	Indicate to WIC that the WICMASK is valid and needs to be captured
WICCLEAR	Processor to WIC	Clear the wake-up event mask inside WIC

Table 6.4: Interface between NVIC and WIC.

The WIC has the following outputs to the system:

Signal name	Direction	Description
WICINT[n:0] / IRQ + other wakeup events	Input	Wakeup events: NMI, RXEV, EDBGRQ (for Armv7-M, Armv8-M Mainline) and IRQ signals. The signal width is configurable.
WAKEUP	Output	Wakeup request to the system controller to indicate that the processor needs to be woken up to serve an interrupt request or other event.
WICPENDxxx[n:0]	Output	Latched version of an interrupt request. Since the incoming interrupt event could be single-cycle, the WIC holds the request status until the processor is back operating and WICCLEAR is asserted. This can be fed to NVIC's interrupt inputs via an OR logic.

Table 6.5: WIC's output.

Finally, there can be an additional interface on the Cortex-M processor to enable/disable the WIC operation, which we will cover later in this section.

The WIC delivered in the Cortex-M product bundle is an example of this small interrupt detection logic, and it is modifiable. In some cases, designers have modified the WIC to enable a latch-based operation so that wake-up events can be detected and captured without any active clocks.
An overview of the WIC operations is as follows:

- When entering sleep mode, the wakeup event mask is transferred from NVIC to WIC using a dedicated hardware interface (WICMASK[] and WICLOAD).

- When a wake-up event is detected, the WIC sends a wake-up request to the system power management control.

■ The power management control then restores the power to the processor and resumes clocking. The processor can pick up the interrupt request (or other wakeup events) and resume operation.

■ The wake-up masking information and pending wake-up event held inside the WIC is cleared by hardware automatically when the processor wakes up from sleep mode (WICCLEAR).

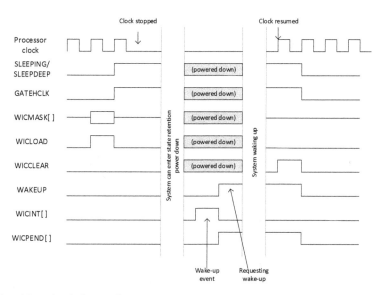

Figure 6.11: Simplified wakeup interrupt controller operations.

In Cortex-M0, Cortex-M0+, Cortex-M3, Cortex-M4, Cortex-M7 and Cortex-M23 processors, the WIC is external to the processor. In Cortex-M33 and Cortex-M35P, the WIC is integrated inside the processor. In different Cortex-M processors, the handling of wakeup event routing is slightly different: In Cortex-M3 and Cortex-M4, the merging of a pending wake-up event with the original source is outside of the WIC. This is merged into the WIC in newer Cortex-M processor designs.

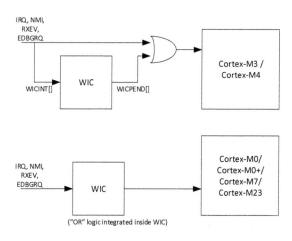

Figure 6.12: Routing of wake-up event signals in different Cortex-M processors.

In Armv7-M or Armv8-M Mainline processor systems, the EDBGRQ signal (external debug request) is included as one of the wake-up events that the WIC monitors. This is because the external debug request can trigger a Debug Monitor exception if it is enabled. In Armv6-M or Armv8-M baseline systems (i.e., Cortex-M23 processor system), the EDBGRQ is not considered to be a wake-up event as the Debug Monitor exception is not available.

The WIC feature can be enabled or disabled with a handshaking signal interface. In the Cortex-M3 and Cortex-M4, this interface involves a pair of handshaking signals between the processor and the WIC, and another pair of handshaking signals between the WIC and the system-level control registers (device-specific).

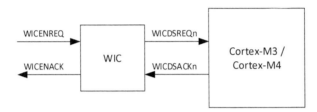

Figure 6.13: The WIC enables handshaking in Cortex-M3 and Cortex-M4.

At the start of the application, the software can write to a register in the system power management unit (outside of the processor, device-specific) to enable the WIC feature. This enables the power management unit that handles state retention power gating. The WIC is then enabled with the following handshaking sequence:

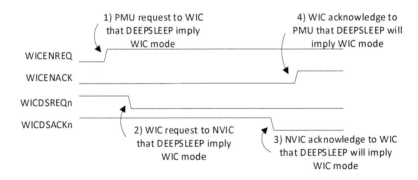

Figure 6.14: The WIC enables handshaking waveform in Cortex-M3 and Cortex-M4.

In later Cortex-M processor designs, the WIC enable/disable interface is simplified so that it only needs the WICENREQ and WICENACK signals. There is no need for additional handshaking between the WIC and the processor.

When using State Retention Power Gating (SRPG), the system designer will need to handle a number of control signals. The control sequences of these signals are process node-specific. In a simple example, you might see the following signals:

Signal	Description
ISOLATEn	Use to isolate the power domain
RETAINn	Use to control, retain and restore state retention logic cells
POWERDOWN	Power down control for power gating

Table 6.6: SRPG support control signals.

System designers need to create a state machine to control the sequence for entering the power-down state and exiting from the power-down state. To support these operations, the power management design also needs to include a status signal to indicate if the power-up has been done (let us assume that this signal is called PWRUPREADY in the following state machine diagrams). When in the power-down state, the WAKEUP signal from the WIC is used to switch the state machine into the wake-up sequence. A simple state transition diagram is shown in Figure 6.15.

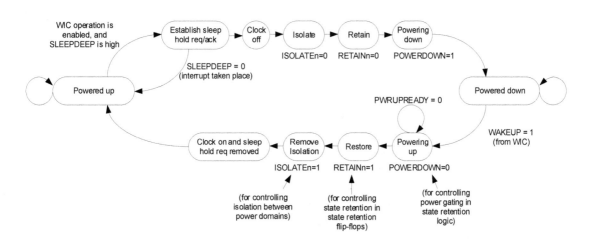

Figure 6.15: Simple state machine for SRPG sequence control.

Silicon vendors might choose different approaches to develop their power control FSM. For example, the FSM can optionally allow the power down sequence to be canceled if the WAKEUP signal is asserted before being powered down to reduce the interrupt latency (Figure 6.16).

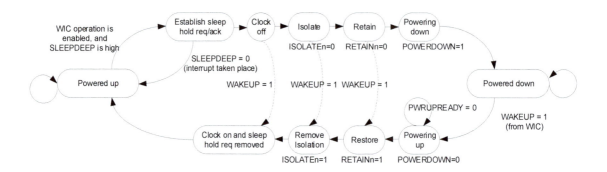

Figure 6.16: State machine for SRPG sequence control that allows the power-down sequence to be canceled.

The design of the FSM is also heavily dependent on other system-level factors (e.g., power control for memories).

6.3.5 SRPG's impact on software
The SRPG feature can greatly reduce the power consumption of sleep modes. However, there are a few areas that application developers must be aware of:

1. The SYSTICK timer will be stopped during power down. As the processor is powered down, the SYSTICK timer inside the processor would be stopped. Embedded applications that use OS will need to use a timer external to the processor core to wake it up for task and event scheduling. Sleep modes that still allow free running processor clocks should not be affected – embedded application programmers should check the sleep mode details from chip manufacturers.

2. The interrupt latency is increased when WIC or SRPG is used. Since it will take a certain duration to power-up the processor, memories, and get the system ready, the interrupt latency can be increased substantially. Please check the datasheet from the silicon vendor for details.

3. Power down is normally disabled when a debugger is attached. This is because debuggers require access to the processor even when the processor core is in sleep modes. In many such cases, the power down FSM is automatically disabled by the WIC interface inside the processor. As a result, testing of deep sleep can show a different set of behaviors and interrupt latency when a debugger is connected.

6.3.6 Software power-saving approach
One of the considerations in software development is to decide whether to:

▪ Run fast and enter sleep mode as much as possible, or,

▪ Run slow to reduce dynamic power.

Unfortunately, there is no golden rule. If the oscillators use large amounts of power, running them slowly might be a good way to reduce power consumption. However, this also has the effect of increasing interrupt latency and overall leakage current.

On the other hand, if the flash memories have a high leakage current, run fast and sleep (while also turning off the flash memory), this could be a good way to reduce overall energy consumption. However, it means that the peak power will be higher.

In addition to that, the peripheral control requirement can also affect the whole picture. Software developers might need to run a number of trials to determine what is the best approach for them.

6.4 Cortex-M processor characteristics that enable low-power designs

6.4.1 High code density

Since the Cortex-M series of processors uses a mixture of 16-bit and 32-bit instructions in its instruction set, it enables high code density, which means an application could fit into a smaller program ROM/flash size.

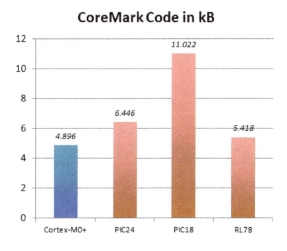

CoreMark Code in kB

Figure 6.17: Thumb instruction set enables high code density for microcontrollers.

High code density can have various advantages. In addition to opportunities to reduce power by using a smaller program ROM/flash, it can also help to:

▧ Reduce cost;

▧ Enable small chip packages.

6.4.2 Short pipeline

Most of the Cortex-M processors (except Cortex-M7) have a fairly short pipeline (2 to 3 stages). In these processor designs, the short pipeline nature enables the processor to have a low branch penalty without having to include branch prediction logic. The shorter pipeline also reduces branch shadows which are instructions after a branch that are fetched by the processor but are discarded if the branch is taken. For example, in the Cortex-M0+ and Cortex-M23 processors, as the pipeline is only 2 stages long, the branch shadow is reduced to just one word. Branch shadows are bad for energy efficiency as they mean that the memory system has used energy to fetch the instructions, but those instructions are not needed.

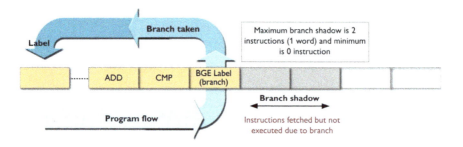

Figure 6.18: Branch shadow in the Cortex-M0+ and Cortex-M23 processors.

6.4.3 Instruction fetch optimizations

While some of the instructions are 16-bit, the Cortex-M processor fetches instructions as 32-bit most of the time (or 64-bit for Cortex-M7 when using 64-bit I-TCM or AXI interface). It means for each instruction fetch, it could obtain up to 2 instructions, and the instruction fetch interface can be idle some of the time to reduce power spent on program memory access.

Figure 6.19: 32-bit instruction fetches enable memory access to be reduced.

The Cortex-M0+ and Cortex-M23 processors also support halfword instruction fetches if a branch target is not word-aligned (bit 1 of address is 1). It means half of the byte lanes for that access can be inactive and could save quite a bit of power in short loops.

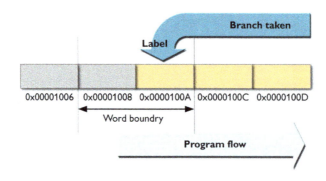

Figure 6.20: Half-word instruction-fetch in non-word-aligned branch target accesses (Cortex-M0+ and Cortex-M23 only).

6.5 System-level design considerations

6.5.1 Low-power designs overview

Low-power design is a very large topic. In addition to utilizing different sleep modes of the processors or extending that to extra sleep modes, all parts of the chip can have an impact on low-power capability and energy efficiency. Typically, clock gating is used in many parts of a microcontroller's design, and if possible, some of the peripherals can also be powered down when they are not being used.

6.5.2 Clock sources

A low-power clock source is one of the key items. Many designs need to have a 32KHz clock that is always on (for real-time clock and power management), and if this clock source is power-hungry, it would have a big impact. Ideally, the 32kHz clock source needs to be ultra-low-power, accurate, and capable of working with wide voltage ranges.

Selection of crystal operation range is also important. While a microcontroller product might be designed to run at 100MHz, having a 100MHz crystal in the design means the product will have a 100MHz clock running all the time and can burn a lot of power. Therefore, it is common to use a relatively slow crystal (4 to 12MHz) and use PLL to generate higher clock frequencies only if they are needed.

6.5.3 Low-power memories

Many memory macros have various sleep/retention modes and a range of 'hooks' to allow system designers to link the memory low-power states to the system's sleep modes. Please note that there are trade-offs between sleep mode power and wake up latency.

For embedded flash, it is also possible to power down the flash completely during sleep as there is no issue of data loss. However, when doing this, be aware of the in-rush current (current spike) when the flash macro is turned on, which potentially can cause a voltage drop in power rails and result in problems affecting other parts of the chip.

Some devices might allow the software to write to flash before brown-out so that crucial data in SRAM can be restored later. This operation might also be needed when the battery of the product is being replaced. If a design needs to support such features, the minimum flash programming voltage and flash power during programming can become a critical issue.

6.5.4 Caches

While adding a cache unit can increase the silicon area and the leakage current, and hence increase the power requirement of a system, sometimes it can help reduce the overall energy efficiency because it reduces the access to the main memories, especially embedded flash, which can be power-hungry. It also has the benefit of enabling higher performance because flash memories are often quite slow (e.g., 30MHz to 50MHz). The AHB flash cache from Arm (in CoreLink SDK-100/101) is available in Cortex-M3 DesignStart Pro, and additional system cache designs are available in other system design kit products (licensable IP).

6.5.5 Low-power analog components
A range of analog components might need to stay on during sleep modes. These include a 32kHz oscillator, real-time clock, brown-out detector, some of the I/O pads (e.g., when an input is used for external interrupt detection), etc.

Many I/O pads have configurable power modes that can reduce power by adjusting drive strengths and skew rates. System designers can make these options programmable by introducing programmable registers to control these configuration signals.

6.5.6 Maximizing clock gating opportunities
In many system designs, it is possible to place clock gating in a range of locations to reduce dynamic power. This includes peripherals and buses. For example, the AHB to APB bridge provided in Arm in the Corstone Foundation IP / Cortex-M System Design Kit provides a clock gating control signal (APBACTIVE) to allow the downstream APB peripheral bus to be clock gated when there is no bus transaction going through.

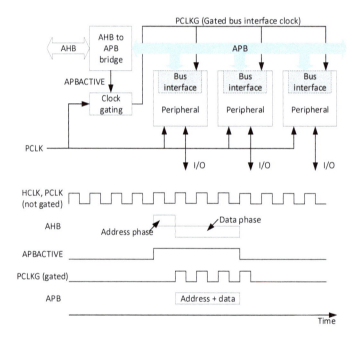

Figure 6.21: AHB to APB bridge in CMSDK has a clock gating control output.

To take advantage of this feature, a peripheral might need to be modified so that it has separate clock signals for the bus interface and peripheral operations.

In some cases, the peripheral buses might be clock gated and software introduced to enable the clock on the peripheral buses before accessing the bus slaves on it.

6.5.7 Sleep mode that completely powers down the processor

It is possible to completely power down the Cortex-M processor and still be able to wake up the system on certain hardware events. However, in such cases:

- The processor states will be lost. Hence, software using this power down arrangement must save critical information to state retention SRAM beforehand.

- The system design needs to have additional hardware logic to handle the hardware wake-up event detection.

If using such an approach, system designers need to add a custom-defined wake-up unit to detect wakeup events, which then:

- Signals to power management hardware to restore power to the processor system;

- Resets the processor system (without resetting the state retention memories and registers);

- Releases resets and the processor can then boot-up and execute software.

In such a system, the design will need a few extra components:

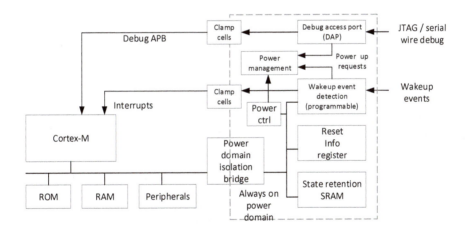

Figure 6.22: Additional hardware needed for sleep mode with full power-down.

- Power ctrl (control) – allows the software to select which sleep mode is used (e.g., whether to enter power down when in deep sleep).

- Reset info register – allows the software to decide if it is a cold boot or wakeup after a power-down 'sleep.'

- State retention SRAM (optional) for holding various program state information.

■ Wakeup event detection – enables the generation of wake-up events from peripherals or I/O. This is likely to be programmable to allow the software to decide if this is enabled or not.

Also, since the wake-up process is going to take time, the design must also hold the wakeup event information so that software can have time to enable NVIC.

Debug access port (DAP) – You might optionally move the SWJ-DP to the always-on power domain to allow the debugger to wake up the system with a debug connection. An alternative solution is to use another hardware mechanism to wake up the system so that debugger can connect to the processor to start the debug sessions.

The downside of this approach is that the processor must boot-up first and will, as a result, take longer time to service the interrupt. It is possible to reduce the boot time by storing most of the key processor's state into retention SRAM before powering down and restoring this after waking up. Using this approach, the C runtime startup could be skipped, and hence, the time needed to setup NVIC could be reduced.

If using this method, the sleep procedure should be handled in privileged thread mode, and if TrustZone is implemented, the sleep procedure should be in Secure privileged thread mode so that all the register states can be accessed easily.

The information that might need to be stored includes:

■ NVIC settings;

■ MPU settings;

■ Potentially SysTick settings;

■ Banked SP (both MSP and PSP might be needed), and if TrustZone is implemented, all four stack pointers and corresponding stack limit registers should be stored;

■ Special registers (PRIMASK, FAULTMASK, BASEPRI, etc.), - and beware that if TrustZone is present, these registers are banked and both versions will need to be saved;

■ FPU settings if FPU is present, and optionally FPU registers if the FPU was used and active;

Note: Depending on the handling of resuming execution, some registers in the register banks might not need to be restored.

Another thing to bear in mind is that if TrustZone is implemented, the security management of retention SRAM is important as Secure information is stored in it when using this power down approach.

CHAPTER 7

Design of
bus infrastructure
components

7.1 Overview

In this chapter, we will go through the basic steps needed to develop a simple AMBA system with a Cortex-M3 processor using the AMBA 5 AHB (AHB5) and APB (AMBA 3) architectures. While the Cortex-M3 processor was designed using the AHB Lite version of AHB protocols in AMBA, here in the featured examples, AHB5 protocol is used because it is the latest protocol and more future proof. However, TrustZone security management with AHB5 is not going to be covered here as the Cortex-M3 processor does not support TrustZone, and it is too complex a topic for beginners. You can use AHB Lite bus masters with AHB5 interconnect, but additional bus wrappers might be needed, for example, to convert exclusive access signals in Cortex-M3/Cortex-M4 to AHB5 equivalents.

For peripheral connections, APB is used in the example, and the APB bus segment is connected via an AHB to APB bridge. As explained in Section 4.5, if you are using Cortex-M3/Cortex-M4/Cortex-M7/Cortex-M33 processors, the PPB (Private Peripheral Bus) interface is primarily for debug components and should not be used for general peripherals.

The example system that we are going to build contains a behavioral model of two memory blocks (Program ROM and RAM) and a number of simple peripherals on the APB including two parallel I/O interface ports, a UART and two simple timers. In addition, a number of basic AMBA infrastructure blocks including an AHB bus bridge to APB and bus slave multiplexers will also be created.

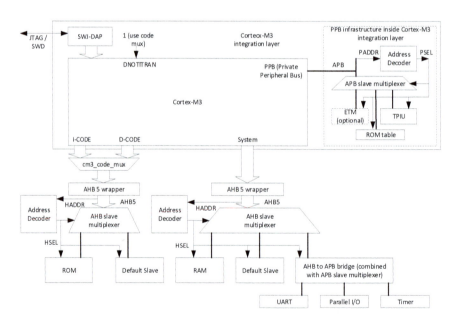

Figure 7.1: A simple Cortex-M3 processor system.

This example system has the following characteristics:

- Two default slaves are needed as there are two AHB bus segments, each of them containing invalid address ranges.

- DNOTITRAN input (applicable for Cortex-M3 and Cortex-M4 processors only) is set to 1 because we are using a code mux module to merge I-CODE bus and D-CODE.

- In this design, the APB slave multiplexer and AHB to APB bridge are combined. It is also absolutely fine to separate the two functions into two modules.

- The PPB bus connections are handled inside the integration layer, and there is no need for them to be handled at a higher level.

- There is no need to do any work on the memory space for NVIC and debug components within the Cortex-M processors. Transfers accessing these components will be routed internally inside the processor and will not be visible from the bus system.

One of the important parts of designing an AMBA system is the determination of the required memory map. In this example, the memory map is based on the one supported in the Cortex-M3 processor, with 64kB for program ROM and data memory, and 64kB of memory space allocated to the APB.

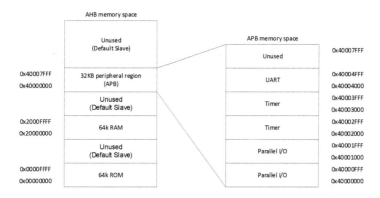

Figure 7.2: Memory map of the simple example Cortex-M system.

Each peripheral block in this example takes 4kB of memory space. Since the transfer size on the APB is limited to word size, we can have up to 1024 hardware registers for each peripheral. However, in normal applications, the required number of registers for each peripheral is likely to be far less than that.

The use of 4kB memory size for peripherals is a common practice, which allows us to create a simple APB slave multiplexer which multiplexes responses using bit fields of PADDR (e.g., bit[15:12] for 16 APB slaves). However, it is fine to use other memory sizes for APB peripherals, although potentially these will require a slightly more complex APB slave multiplexer.

For designs using the Cortex-M3 or Cortex-M4 processors, in cases where the bit-band feature is to be used, then the allocation of an address in the memory map must avoid conflict with the bit-band alias regions.

7.2 Typical AHB slave design rules

Before we start the design process, it is useful to go through some of the rules in AHB operations. In this book, we will only cover the rules for AHB slave operations for AHB LITE, and AHB5 as most FPGA designers will only need to develop AHB slave designs and not AHB masters.

1. An AHB slave must respond with OKAY without a wait state for IDLE or BUSY transfers: When HTRANS is IDLE (0x0) or BUSY (0x01), HSEL is 1 and HREADY (or HREADYIN) is 1, in the next clock cycle HREADYOUT must be 1 and HRESP must be OKAY (0x0).

2. An AHB slave must respond with OKAY without wait state if it is not selected: When HSEL is 0 and HREADY (HREADYIN) is 1, in the next clock cycle HREADYOUT must be 1 and HRESP must be OKAY (0x0).

3. At reset, HREADY output from AHB slaves must be 1 (ready), and HRESP must be OKAY (0x0). This is needed to ensure the AHB system is reset correctly.

4. There should not be any combinatorial path from inputs of the AHB interface to the output of the AHB interface on an AHB slave. The inputs and outputs must be pipelined (separated by register stage) to prevent combinatorial loops.

5. Error signals on HRESP must be two cycles, with HREADY output (HREADYOUT) low in the first cycle and high in the second cycle. An additional wait state(s) before the error response is allowed. Multiple back-to-back transfers can result in multiple back to back error responses, but each of the error responses must still contain the two-cycle waveform.

6. Although the HRESP input in Cortex-M3 and Cortex-M4 is 2-bit wide, the Cortex-M processors and the AHB infrastructure components that we are designing here do not support RETRY and SPLIT responses; therefore, the AHB slaves must not generate these two responses. SPLIT and RETRY responses are not supported in AHB Lite and AHB5.

7. Ideally, the AHB slave should only be able to insert a limited number of wait states to ensure that it will not lock up the whole system. The common recommendation for the maximum number of wait states for a transfer is 16 cycles - but system designers can increase the limit if necessary. Note that this is only a recommendation. In some cases, it is unavoidable to have longer wait states in AHB transfers if the AHB interconnect components or slave has to deal with data transfer across asynchronous clock domains.

8. The minimum memory size of an AHB slave for an ARM system should be 1k bytes. Even if the slave does not need this amount of memory, the remaining memory space should not be used for another AHB slave. Not only does it reduce the complexity of AHB decoder design, but it can also prevent a burst transfer from going across two AHB slaves, which can cause an AHB protocol violation. The starting address of the AHB slave should be aligned to its memory size in order to reduce the complexity of the AHB decoder design.

9. HEXOKAY can only be asserted in the data phase of an exclusive transfer if there is no error response. If a bus slave does not support exclusive transfer, HEXOKAY can be tied low.

With these AHB design rules defined, most AHB slaves can be designed with a simple pipeline logic block, as shown here:

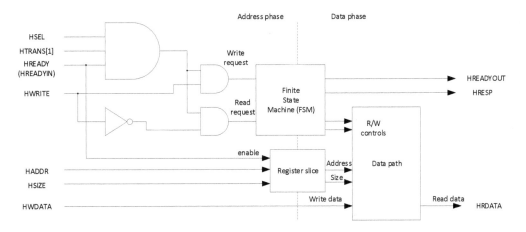

Figure 7.3: Simple AHB slave bus interface design.

In the simplest AHB slaves, the Finite State Machine (FSM) can be implemented as a simple register stage if no wait state is required. If multiple cycles are required, the FSM can be implemented as shown:

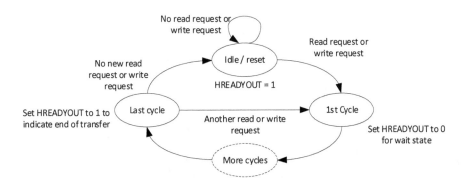

Figure 7.4: Simple Finite State Machine (FSM) for AHB slaves with wait-states.

Additional states will be needed if the device supports error responses on the AHB. The AHB to APB bridge that we will cover in the later chapter of this book is an example of such a design.

7.3 Typical AHB infrastructure components

After familiarizing ourselves with the AHB slave design rules, we can start looking into the development of the AHB system, starting from a few commonly used AHB infrastructure blocks:

7.3.1 AHB Decoders

AHB decoders generate HSEL signals for each AHB slave by decoding the HADDR address signal. The designs of the AHB decoders are system-specific. For the example AMBA system that we are going to develop, the decoders generate the HSEL outputs for the ROM, RAM, APB Bridge, and the default slaves. Two AHB decoders are needed for the example Cortex-M3 system because the AHB bus segment for the I-CODE/D-CODE and the system bus are separated.

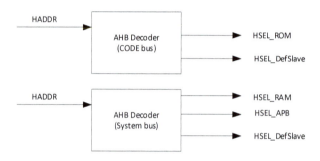

Figure 7.5: AHB decoders for the example Cortex-M3 system.

The default slave is an AHB slave that is selected when the address is invalid (i.e., no valid slave is selected). This subject will be covered in the next section of this chapter. The outputs of the address decoder are combinatorial outputs generated using the address value.

Based on the memory map that we defined earlier, the AHB decoders can be designed as shown here:

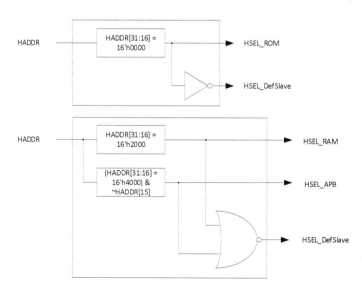

Figure 7.6: Design of the AHB decoders for the example Cortex-M3 system.

In some situations, an AHB decoder might also take an HSEL input to enable the decode operation if the decoder is only for an AHB subsystem, which is part of a larger AHB system. In the case where an optional HSEL input is implemented, the HSEL outputs would be AND together with the HSEL input, so that the output can only be high if the HSEL input is high. This is required in more complex systems where multiple AHB subsystems are developed, and the address decoder of each AHB subsystem requires a HSEL input from a global address decoder.

7.3.2 Default slave

In an AHB system, if the processor tries to access a memory location that is not assigned or not used, the normal practice is to return an error response to generate a fault exception. This mechanism allows the program to detect that something has gone wrong as an unused address range that should not have been accessed. To generate this response, a very simple AHB slave called the Default Slave is used.

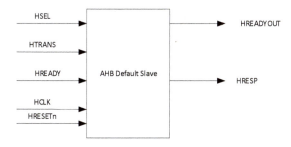

Figure 7.7: AHB Default slave.

The default slave is selected by the AHB address decoder when an invalid address range is output from the processor. If the default slave is selected and the processor (or bus master) issues an active transfer (HTRANS equals NSEQ or SEQ), then the default slave sends out an error response in the data phase of the transfer.

This behavior is different from most 8-bit or 16-bit microcontrollers. In these products, accesses to an invalid address will not normally cause any fault exception. The advantage of using a default slave to respond to invalid accesses is that the processor can remedy this if an error is detected, and thus increase the robustness of the system.

In some designs, the default slave is combined with the AHB slave multiplexer. In this example, we will design it as a separate unit. A simple finite state machine is used to generate the 2-cycle error response as required by the AHB protocol. Since we generate an error response for every transfer with invalid accesses, we do not need to worry about the HWRITE control, HSIZE signals, and data values.

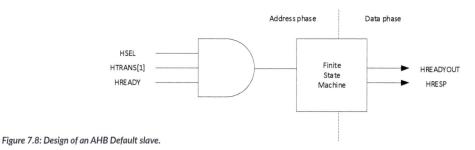

Figure 7.8: Design of an AHB Default slave.

The Verilog RTL of the default slave is as follows:

```
module ahb_defslave (
  input   wire         HCLK,      // Clock
  input   wire         HRESETn,   // Reset
  input   wire         HSEL,      // connect to HSEL_DefSlave from AHB decoder
  input   wire [1:0]   HTRANS,    // Transfer command
  input   wire         HREADY,    // System-wide HREADY
  output  wire         HREADYOUT, // Slave ready output
  output  wire         HRESP      // Slave response output
  );

// Internal signals
wire         TransReq;  // Transfer Request
reg   [1:0] RespState;  // FSM for two cycle error response
wire  [1:0] NextState;  // next state for RespState

// Start of main code
assign TransReq = HSEL & HTRANS[1] & HREADY; // a transfer is issued
 // to default slave because address is invalid

// Generate next state for the FSM
// Encoding : 01 - Idle (bit 0 is HREADYOUT, bit 1 is RESP[0])
//            10 - 1st cycle of error response
//            11 - 2nd cycle of error response
assign NextState = {(TransReq | (~RespState[0])),(~TransReq)};

// Registering FSM state
always @(posedge HCLK or negedge HRESETn)
begin
 if (~HRESETn)
   RespState <= 2'b01; // bit 0 is reset to 1, ensuring HREADYOUT is 1
 else                  // at reset
   RespState <= NextState;
end

// Connect to output
assign HREADYOUT  = RespState[0];
assign HRESP      = RespState[1];

endmodule
```

The default slave does not generate any read data and exclusive responses. When connecting the default slave to an AHB system, the unused HRDATA[31:0] signal and HEXOKAY signal (available in AHB5) can be connected to zero.

7.3.3 AHB Slave multiplexer

The AHB slave multiplexer is needed to connect multiple AHB slaves to an AHB master. In this example, the AHB slave multiplexer connects up to four AHB slaves.

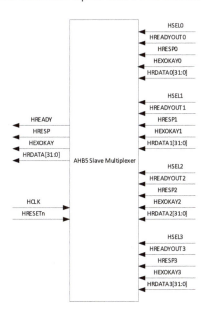

Figure 7.9: Simple AHB5 slave multiplexer with up to four AHB slave connection.

The AHB slave multiplexer takes outputs from each of the AHB slaves, as well as the HSEL outputs from the AHB decoder. Using the multiplexed HREADY signal and the HSEL inputs, the AHB decoder internally generates the pipelined multiplexer control to select the correct data phase output. The design for the four-port AHB Slave multiplexer can be implemented as shown here:

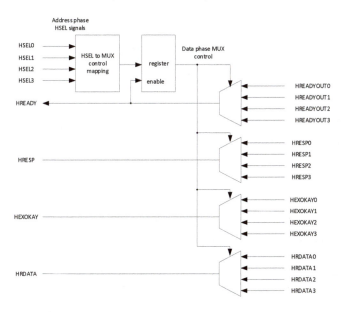

Figure 7.10: Design of a simple AHB5 slave multiplexer with up to four AHB slave connection.

The Verilog RTL code for the slave multiplexer is as follows:

```verilog
module ahb_slavemux (
  input  wire          HCLK,      // Clock
  input  wire          HRESETn,   // Reset
  input  wire          HREADY,       // Bus system level HREADY
  input  wire          HSEL0,        // HSEL for AHB Slave #0
  input  wire          HREADYOUT0, // HREADY for Slave connection #0
  input  wire          HRESP0,       // HRESP  for slave connection #0
  input  wire [31:0]   HRDATA0,      // HRDATA for slave connection #0
  input  wire          HEXOKAY0,     // HEXOKAY for slave connection#0
  input  wire          HSEL1,        // HSEL for AHB Slave #1
  input  wire          HREADYOUT1, // HREADY for Slave connection #1
  input  wire          HRESP1,       // HRESP  for slave connection #1
  input  wire [31:0]   HRDATA1,      // HRDATA for slave connection #1
  input  wire          HEXOKAY1,     // HEXOKAY for slave connection#1
  input  wire          HSEL2,        // HSEL for AHB Slave #2
  input  wire          HREADYOUT2, // HREADY for Slave connection #2
  input  wire          HRESP2,       // HRESP  for slave connection #2
  input  wire [31:0]   HRDATA2,      // HRDATA for slave connection #2
  input  wire          HEXOKAY2,     // HEXOKAY for slave connection#2
  input  wire          HSEL3,        // HSEL for AHB Slave #3
  input  wire          HREADYOUT3, // HREADY for Slave connection #3
  input  wire          HRESP3,       // HRESP  for slave connection #3
  input  wire [31:0]   HRDATA3,      // HRDATA for slave connection #3
  input  wire          HEXOKAY3,     // HEXOKAY for slave connection#3
  output wire          HREADYOUT,  // HREADY output to AHB master and AHB slaves
  output wire          HRESP,      // HRESP to AHB master
  output wire [31:0]   HRDATA,     // Read data to AHB master
  output wire          HEXOKAY     // Exclusive okay
  );

// Internal signals
reg    [3:0] SampledHselReg;

// Registering select
always @(posedge HCLK or negedge HRESETn)
begin
if (~HRESETn)
  SampledHselReg <= {4{1'b0}};
else if (HREADY) // advance pipeline if multiplexed HREADY is 1
  SampledHselReg <= {HSEL3, HSEL2, HSEL1, HSEL0};
end


assign HREADYOUT =
  (SampledHselReg[0] & HREADYOUT0)|
  (SampledHselReg[1] & HREADYOUT1)|
  (SampledHselReg[2] & HREADYOUT2)|
  (SampledHselReg[3] & HREADYOUT3)|
  (SampledHselReg ==4'b0000);

assign HRDATA =
  ({32{SampledHselReg[0]}} & HRDATA0)|
  ({32{SampledHselReg[1]}} & HRDATA1)|
  ({32{SampledHselReg[2]}} & HRDATA2)|
  ({32{SampledHselReg[3]}} & HRDATA3);

assign HRESP =
  (SampledHselReg[0] & HRESP0)|
  (SampledHselReg[1] & HRESP1)|
  (SampledHselReg[2] & HRESP2)|
  (SampledHselReg[3] & HRESP3);
```

```
assign HEXOKAY =
   (SampledHselReg[0] & HEXOKAY0)|
   (SampledHselReg[1] & HEXOKAY1)|
   (SampledHselReg[2] & HEXOKAY2)|
   (SampledHselReg[3] & HEXOKAY3);

endmodule
```

7.3.4 ROM and RAM with AHB interface

A Cortex-M processor system cannot work without memories for program code and data. In this section, we cover the simulation models of simple ROM and RAM memories with AHB5 interfaces for illustration. Please note that, if you are using Cortex-M1 processor, the ROM and RAM are likely to be connected as Tightly Coupled Memories (TCMs) rather than AHB, and the configuration of these memory blocks could be handled by the FPGA design tools.

Two memory models are being developed: a ROM model for program memory and a RAM model for the data memory. Normally, the ROM model is used for program memory, and RAM is used for data memory; however, the RAM model can also be used for program memory if memory initialization is carried out. In this way, we can allow the program to be self-modified or allow an external debugger to change the program code during debugging.

The ROM model that we have illustrated here is a read-only simulation memory model. One of the requirements for this program memory simulation model is that it must allow us to define the program data inside when the simulation starts. Inside the Verilog code of the ROM model, we use the Verilog system function "$readmemh" to initialize the program data array with data from a file called "image. dat". This file contains the hexadecimal values of a compiled binary image for the Cortex-M processor. The RAM model, however, will only initialize the data array to zero values. It is possible to add the "$readmemh" function to initialize the RAM content to other values if it is to be used as program memory.

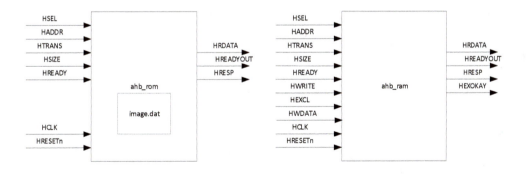

Figure 7.11: Simple memory simulation models with the AHB interface.

In order to simplify the design, the memory models do not insert a wait state and treat burst transfers just like single transfers. Also, these example models only support little-endian.

There are different ways to develop the required AHB memory simulation models. Since the AHB protocol is pipelined, a registering stage is needed inside the memory. For illustration purposes, we will design the ROM model with a registering stage for the data output, while for the RAM, we will use the registering stage for control signal processing.

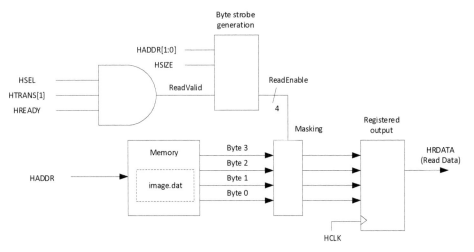

Figure 7.12: Example AHB ROM design for simulation purposes.

For the ROM design, we assumed that all accesses to the ROM are always read transfers. Therefore the HWRITE signal was not used. In the ROM design, we masked the unused read data output for half-word and byte transfers. Note: This is not required in real systems. ARM processors like the Cortex-M3 just ignore the unused data. However, masking the unused data bytes can make the bus activities easier to see during debugging.

The Verilog RTL code of the AHB ROM is as follows:

```
// Simple 64kb ROM with AHB interface
module ahb_rom (
  input  wire        HCLK,     // Clock
  input  wire        HRESETn,  // Reset
  input  wire        HSEL,     // Device select
  input  wire [15:0] HADDR,    // Address
  input  wire [1:0]  HTRANS,   // Transfer control
  input  wire [2:0]  HSIZE,    // Transfer size
  input  wire        HREADY,   // Transfer phase done
  output wire        HREADYOUT, // Device ready
  output wire [31:0] HRDATA,    // Read data output
  output wire        HRESP,      // Device response (always OKAY)
  output wire        HEXOKAY    // Exclusive okay (not used)
  );

  // Internal signals
  reg     [7:0]  RomData[0:65535]; // 64k byte of ROM data
  integer        i;                // Loop counter for ROM initialization
  wire           ReadValid;        // Address phase read valid
  wire    [15:0] WordAddr;         // Word aligned address(addr phase)
  reg     [3:0]  ReadEnable;       // Read enable for each byte(addr phase)
  reg     [7:0]  RDataOut0;        // Read Data Output byte#0(data phase)
```

```verilog
reg     [7:0]  RDataOut1;    // Read Data Output byte#1
reg     [7:0]  RDataOut2;    // Read Data Output byte#2
reg     [7:0]  RDataOut3;    // Read Data Output byte#3

// Start of main code
// Initialize ROM
initial
begin
for (i=0;i<65536;i=i+1)
  begin
  RomData[i] = 8'h00; //Initialize all data to 0
  end
$readmemh("image.dat", RomData); // Then read in program code
end


// Generate read control (address phase)
assign ReadValid = HSEL & HREADY & HTRANS[1];
// Read enable for each byte (address phase)
always @(ReadValid or HADDR or HSIZE)
begin
if (ReadValid)
  begin
  case (HSIZE)
  0 : // Byte
    begin
    case (HADDR[1:0])
      0: ReadEnable = 4'b0001; // Byte 0
      1: ReadEnable = 4'b0010; // Byte 1
      2: ReadEnable = 4'b0100; // Byte 2
      3: ReadEnable = 4'b1000; // Byte 3
default:ReadEnable = 4'b0000; // Address not valid
    endcase
    end
  1 : // Halfword
    begin
    if (HADDR[1])
      ReadEnable = 4'b1100; // Upper halfword
    else
      ReadEnable = 4'b0011; // Lower halfword
    end
  default : // Word
    ReadEnable = 4'b1111; // Whole word
  endcase
  end
else
  ReadEnable = 4'b0000; // Not reading
end


// Read operation
assign WordAddr = {HADDR[15:2], 2'b00}; // Get word aligned address
// Registered read
always @(posedge HCLK or negedge HRESETn)
begin
if (~HRESETn)
  begin
  RDataOut0 <= 8'h00;
  RDataOut1 <= 8'h00;
  RDataOut2 <= 8'h00;
  RDataOut3 <= 8'h00;
  end
else
  begin // Read when read enable is high
  RDataOut0 <= (ReadEnable[0]) ? RomData[WordAddr  ] : 8'h00;
  RDataOut1 <= (ReadEnable[1]) ? RomData[WordAddr+1] : 8'h00;
```

```
    RDataOut2 <= (ReadEnable[2]) ? RomData[WordAddr+2] : 8'h00;
    RDataOut3 <= (ReadEnable[3]) ? RomData[WordAddr+3] : 8'h00;
    end
  end
  // Connect to top level
  assign HREADYOUT = 1'b1; // Always ready (no waitstate)
  assign HRESP     = 1'b0;// Always response with OKAY
  assign HEXOKAY   = 1'b0;// Exclusive accesses not supported in ROM
   // Read data output
  assign HRDATA    = {RDataOut3, RDataOut2, RDataOut1,RDataOut0};

endmodule
```

Unlike the AHB ROM, the pipeline stage of the AHB RAM design takes place at the time of control signal generation. All the actual read and write operations take place during the data phase of the AHB transfer. This ensures that if the data written are read out in the next clock cycle, the updated value will be used for output.

To make it even more interesting, the AHB SRAM example design also adds support for exclusive accesses by having exclusive response generation logic and tag registers (for address and bus master ID) for the exclusive access sequence. Semaphore data are normally placed in SRAM, and if another bus master writes to the same address location during semaphore read-modify-write operations, the access conflict can be detected by the logic added in this model.

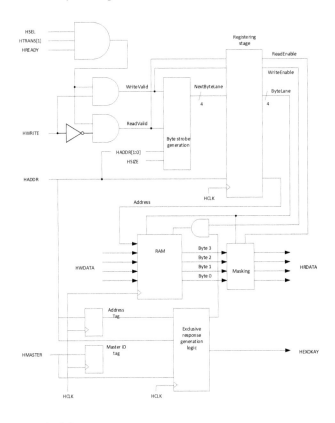

Figure 7.13: Example AHB RAM design for simulation purposes.

The Verilog RTL code of the AHB SRAM (for simulation) is as follows:

```verilog
// Simple 64kb RAM with AHB interface
//
module ahb_ram (
  input  wire        HCLK,     // Clock
  input  wire        HRESETn,  // Reset
  input  wire        HSEL,     // Device select
  input  wire [3:0]  HMASTER,  // Master identification
  input  wire [15:0] HADDR,    // Address
  input  wire [1:0]  HTRANS,   // Transfer control
  input  wire [2:0]  HSIZE,    // Transfer size
  input  wire        HWRITE,   // Write control
  input  wire [31:0] HWDATA,   // Write data
  input  wire        HEXCL,    // Exclusive transfer
  input  wire        HREADY,   // Transfer phase done
  output wire        HREADYOUT, // Device ready
  output wire [31:0] HRDATA,   // Read data output
  output wire        HRESP,    // Device response (always OKAY)
  output wire        HEXOKAY   // Exclusve okay
  );

  // Internal signals
  reg     [7:0]  RamData[0:65535]; // 64k byte of RAM data
  integer        i;             // Loop counter for zero initialization
  wire           ReadValid;     // Address phase read valid
  wire           WriteValid;    // Address phase write valid
  reg            ReadEnable;    // Data phase read enable
  reg            WriteEnable;   // Data phase write enable
  reg     [3:0]  RegByteLane;   // Data phase byte lane
  reg     [3:0]  NextByteLane;  // Next state of RegByteLane

  wire    [7:0]  RDataOut0;     // Read Data Output byte#0
  wire    [7:0]  RDataOut1;     // Read Data Output byte#1
  wire    [7:0]  RDataOut2;     // Read Data Output byte#2
  wire    [7:0]  RDataOut3;     // Read Data Output byte#3
  reg     [15:0] WordAddr;      // Word aligned address

  reg     [15:4] Excl_Tag_Addr; // Exclusive access address
  reg     [ 3:0] Excl_Tag_MID;  // Exclusive access master ID
  reg            Excl_State;    // Exclusive state
  reg            ExclOkay;      // Exclusive Okay status (data phase)
  reg            ExclStoreFail; // Exclusive Failed state (data phase)

  // Start of main code
  // Initialize ROM
  initial
    begin
    for (i=0;i<65536;i=i+1)
      begin
      RamData[i] = 8'h00; //Initialize all data to 0 to avoid X propagation
      end
    //$readmemh("image.dat", RamData); // Then read in program code
    end

  // Generate read control (address phase)
  assign ReadValid  = HSEL & HREADY & HTRANS[1] & ~HWRITE;
  // Generate write control (address phase)
  assign WriteValid = HSEL & HREADY & HTRANS[1] & HWRITE;

  // Read enable for each byte (address phase)
  always @(ReadValid or WriteValid or HADDR or HSIZE)
  begin
```

```verilog
  if (ReadValid | WriteValid)
    begin
    case (HSIZE)
      0 : // Byte
        begin
        case (HADDR[1:0])
          0: NextByteLane = 4'b0001; // Byte 0
          1: NextByteLane = 4'b0010; // Byte 1
          2: NextByteLane = 4'b0100; // Byte 2
          3: NextByteLane = 4'b1000; // Byte 3
      default:NextByteLane = 4'b0000; // Address not valid
        endcase
        end
      1 : // Halfword
        begin
        if (HADDR[1])
          NextByteLane = 4'b1100; // Upper halfword
        else
          NextByteLane = 4'b0011; // Lower halfword
        end
      default : // Word
        NextByteLane = 4'b1111; // Whole word
    endcase
    end
  else
    NextByteLane = 4'b0000; // Not reading
  end

// Registering control signals to data phase
always @(posedge HCLK or negedge HRESETn)
begin
  if (~HRESETn)
    begin
    RegByteLane <= 4'b0000;
    ReadEnable  <= 1'b0;
    WriteEnable <= 1'b0;
    WordAddr    <= {16{1'b0}};
    end
  else if (HREADY)
    begin
    RegByteLane <= NextByteLane;
    ReadEnable  <= ReadValid;
    WriteEnable <= WriteValid;
    WordAddr    <= {HADDR[15:2], 2'b00};
    end
end

// Read operation
assign RDataOut0 = (ReadEnable & RegByteLane[0]) ? RamData[WordAddr  ] : 8'h00;
assign RDataOut1 = (ReadEnable & RegByteLane[1]) ? RamData[WordAddr+1] : 8'h00;
assign RDataOut2 = (ReadEnable & RegByteLane[2]) ? RamData[WordAddr+2] : 8'h00;
assign RDataOut3 = (ReadEnable & RegByteLane[3]) ? RamData[WordAddr+3] : 8'h00;

// Registered write
always @(posedge HCLK)
begin
  if (WriteEnable &  RegByteLane[0] & ~ExclStoreFail)
    begin
    RamData[WordAddr  ] = HWDATA[ 7: 0];
    end
  if (WriteEnable &  RegByteLane[1] & ~ExclStoreFail)
    begin
    RamData[WordAddr+1] = HWDATA[15: 8];
    end
```

```
   if (WriteEnable &  RegByteLane[2] & ~ExclStoreFail)
      begin
      RamData[WordAddr+2] = HWDATA[23:16];
      end
   if (WriteEnable &  RegByteLane[3] & ~ExclStoreFail)
      begin
      RamData[WordAddr+3] = HWDATA[31:24];
      end
 end

 // Exclusive accesses tags - single monitor example
 always @(posedge HCLK or negedge HRESETn)
 begin
 if (~HRESETn)
   begin
   Excl_Tag_Addr <= {12{1'b0}}; // Address
   Excl_Tag_MID  <= {4{1'b0}};  // Master ID
   end
 else if (ReadValid & HEXCL) // Exclusive reads
   begin
   Excl_Tag_Addr <= HADDR[15:4];
   Excl_Tag_MID  <= HMASTER[3:0];
   end
 end

 // Exclusive state
 always @(posedge HCLK or negedge HRESETn)
 begin
 if (~HRESETn)
   Excl_State <= 1'b0;
 else
   if (ReadValid & HEXCL) // Exclusive read
      Excl_State <= 1'b1;
   else if (WriteValid & (HMASTER!=Excl_Tag_MID[3:0]) & (HADDR[15:4]==Excl_Tag_
Addr[15:4]))
      Excl_State <= 1'b0; // Another bus master write to same location
   else if (WriteValid & HEXCL) // Another bus master performed an exclusive write
      Excl_State <= 1'b0;
 end

 // Generate exclusive access response controls
 always @(posedge HCLK or negedge HRESETn)
 begin
 if (~HRESETn)
   begin
   ExclOkay       <= 1'b0;
   ExclStoreFail  <= 1'b0;
   end
 else if (HREADY)
   if (ReadValid & HEXCL)
      begin
      ExclOkay        <= 1'b1;
      ExclStoreFail   <= 1'b0;
      end
   else if  (WriteValid & HEXCL) // Exclusive store
      if ((HMASTER==Excl_Tag_MID[3:0]) & (HADDR[15:4]==Excl_Tag_Addr[15:4]) & Excl_State)
// exclusive Okay
         begin
         ExclOkay        <= 1'b1;
         ExclStoreFail <= 1'b0;
         end
      else // Exclusive failed - either exclusive state is not set, or bus master ID
doesn't match
         begin
```

```
            ExclOkay       <= 1'b0;
            ExclStoreFail <= 1'b1; // Block write
            end
        else
          begin
            ExclOkay       <= 1'b0;  // Not exclusive accesses
            ExclStoreFail <= 1'b0;
            end
    end

    // Connect to top level
    assign HREADYOUT = 1'b1; // Always ready (no waitstate)
    assign HRESP     = 1'b0; // Always response with OKAY
    assign HEXOKAY   = ExclOkay & HREADYOUT;
    // Read data output
    assign HRDATA    = {RDataOut3, RDataOut2, RDataOut1,RDataOut0};

  endmodule
```

For FPGA designs, instead of using the behavioral model for ROM and RAM, the memory will be replaced by either:

▪ Memory blocks within the FPGA device, or

▪ External memory devices.

▪ In cases where the memories are to be implemented inside the FPGA, the design flow can involve:

▪ Using the memory generator in your FPGA development tool to generate the required memory block design file, or

▪ Instantiating the required memory component directly in the FPGA design library.

If the synthesis tool supports the synthesis of memory models, we can create a synthesizable memory model and synthesize the design together with other Verilog files.

In all cases, the implementation details depend on the FPGA product that you are using as well as the development tools. You will need to refer to the documentation or application notes of your FPGA development tool to determine which is the best arrangement for your project.

For example, for users of Synplify, they can choose to synthesize a behavior model of memory, with the possibility of using a standard Verilog function like "$readmemh" to specify the initial content of the memory. The tools will then create the memory from memory blocks in the FPGA. A similar feature is also available from various FPGA tools from different vendors.

For ASIC/SoC designs, the ROM and RAM are normally created using vendor-specific memory compilers and with AHB bus wrappers. An example of an SRAM bus wrapper for AHB Lite can be found in the Cortex-M0 and Cortex-M3 DesignStart bundle called cmsdk_ahb_to_sram.v. This block provides essential write buffering to enable typical SRAM blocks generated from memory compilers to be connected to AHB Lite bus without any wait states. While there is no exclusive monitor functionality in this block, bus level exclusive access monitoring is not normally required in single-processor systems, as described in Section 4.7.

7.3.5 AHB to APB Bridge

The AHB to APB Bridge is needed when connecting peripherals with an APB interface to an Arm processor that has an AHB interface. In this section, we will cover the design of this bus bridge for AHB5 and APBv2 in AMBA 4 (with wait states, error response, and byte strobe support). This bridge can also be used for APB peripherals designed for AMBA 2 and AMBA 3. In such cases, the unused input signals on the bridge such as PREADY input signal can be tied to 1, and the PSLVERR input signal can be tied low.

In AHB, the address value and control information are output from the bus master during the address phase. Since the duration of the address phase is not fixed and the write data is not available until data phase, the bus bridge registers the address and read/write control signal at the end of the address phase and outputs them to the APB during the data phase. In order to generate the required PSEL and PENABLE signals, the bus bridge contains a simple Finite State Machine (FSM) to handle the APB control signals, as well as generating an error response on the AHB when an APB slave error (PSLVERR) is asserted.

The example design also includes an APB slave multiplexer and eight interface ports to APB slaves. The selection of which slave to access is determined by bit-14 to bit-12 of the address value (HADDR[14:12]). It is possible to design the APB Bridge and the APB slave multiplexer as two separated units. However, in this example, they have been designed as a single unit to simplify integration of the AMBA system.

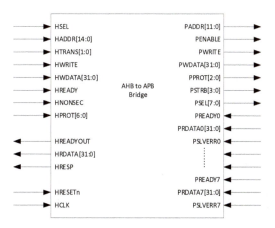

Figure 7.14: AHB5 to APBv2 bus bridge with 8 APB slave interface ports.

The example bus bridge design assumes that HCLK is the same as PCLK. If the AHB system and APB system have different clock frequencies, or if the clock signals are asynchronous, the bus bridge will have to include an extra handshaking mechanism to support the data transfers across different clock domains. This is not supported on the example bridge discussed here.

To keep the design simple, we have also omitted exclusive access support, as semaphore data are normally placed in SRAM rather than in peripherals.

For a simple read operation, the bridge outputs the address and APB control signal at the beginning of the data phase. When the read data is obtained, the read value is sampled in a register and output to the AHB system in the next clock cycle. Since the bridge supports multiple APB slave interfaces, there are multiple PSEL, PRDATA, PSLVERR, and PREADY signals, which have a number as their suffix.

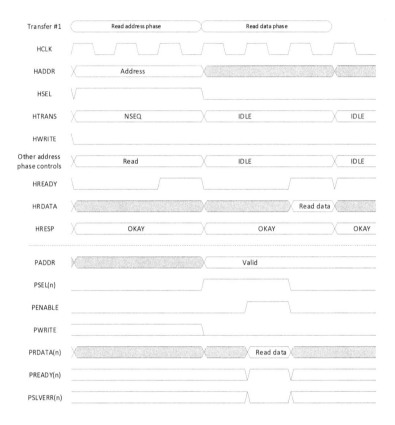

Figure 7.15: AHB5 to APBv2 bus bridge read timing.

It is possible to design the bridge so that as soon as the read data is ready, it is passed on to the AHB system without the sampling cycle. However, this could result in poor timing performance if the output delay of the peripheral system is high, or if the processor core requires a longer setup time for the read data. Registering the read data signal and read response provides better synthesis timing performance for the ASIC/FPGA design. The disadvantage is that it slightly increases the area of the design and adds an extra clock cycle for APB operations.

The write transfer bridging is similar to read transfers. For write data, in most cases, it is not a problem to connect from HWDATA directly to PWDATA because there is no need to add a multiplexer in the write data path (only buffers are needed as the HWDATA signals are connected to a large number of bus slaves). But the PREADY and PSLVERR signals are registered before feeding back to the AHB system.

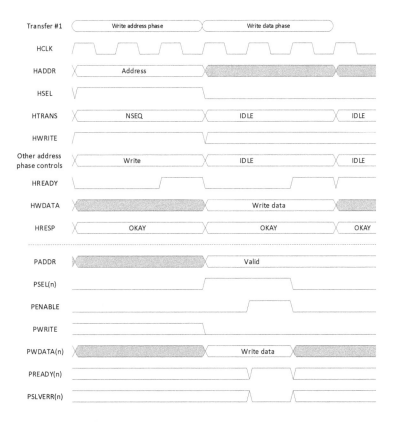

Figure 7.16: AHB5 to APBv2 bus bridge write timing.

In order to generate the read and write control signals, a simple finite state machine (FSM) is used. The FSM is also used to generate the two-cycle error response on the AHB if an error response on the APB is detected.

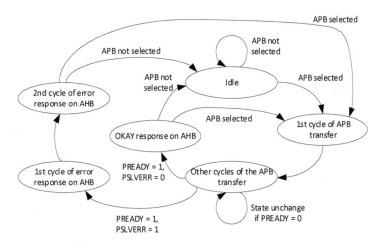

Figure 7.17: AHB5 to APBv2 bus bridge state machine operations.

If a slave error is detected on the APB bus, the APB bridge needs to generate an error response to the AHB master. The error response on the AHB must be two cycles in length. Therefore, two states are assigned in the FSM for this purpose. For example, if an APB receives an error from the peripheral (PSLVERR = 1), the waveform would look like:

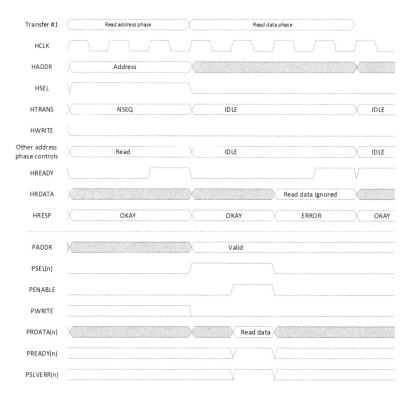

Figure 7.18: AHB5 to APBv2 bus bridge read with error response.

The same applies to the bridging write transfers. If an APB write transfer receives an error response, the bus bridge generates the error response using the same mechanism.

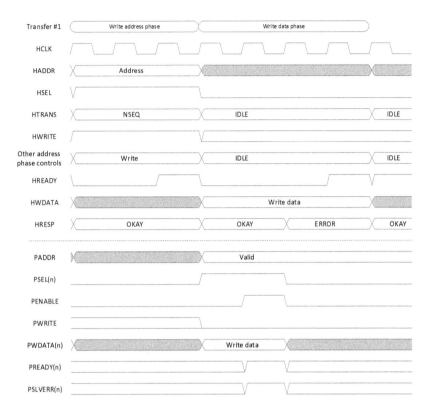

Figure 7.19: AHB5 to APBv2 bus bridge write with error response.

Based on these waveforms, we could design the AHB to APB Bridge, as shown in the following block diagram:

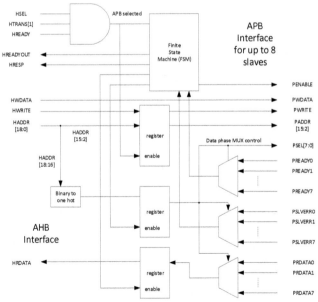

Figure 7.20: Design of the AHB5 to APBv2 bus bridge.

The Verilog RTL of the bus bridge is as follows:

```verilog
// Simple AHB to APB bridge
//
module ahb_to_apb (
  input  wire           HCLK,      // Clock
  input  wire           HRESETn,   // Reset

  input  wire           HSEL,      // Device select
  input  wire  [14:0]   HADDR,     // Address
  input  wire  [1:0]    HTRANS,    // Transfer control
  input  wire  [2:0]    HSIZE,     // Transfer size
  input  wire           HWRITE,    // Write control
  input  wire           HNONSEC,   // Security attribute (TrustZone)
  input  wire  [6:0]    HPROT,     // Protection information
  input  wire           HREADY,    // Transfer phase done
  input  wire  [31:0]   HWDATA,    // Write data

  output wire           HREADYOUT, // Device ready
  output wire  [31:0]   HRDATA,    // Read data output
  output wire           HRESP,     // Device response
                                   // APB Output
  output wire  [11:0]   PADDR,     // APB Address
  output wire           PENABLE,   // APB Enable
  output wire           PWRITE,    // APB Write
  output wire  [2:0]    PPROT,     // APB protection information
  output wire  [3:0]    PSTRB,     // APB byte strobe
  output wire  [31:0]   PWDATA,    // APB write data
  output wire           PSEL0,     // APB Select (8 slaves)
  output wire           PSEL1,
  output wire           PSEL2,
  output wire           PSEL3,
  output wire           PSEL4,
  output wire           PSEL5,
  output wire           PSEL6,
  output wire           PSEL7,
                                   // APB Inputs
  input  wire  [31:0]   PRDATA0,   // Read data for each APB slave
  input  wire  [31:0]   PRDATA1,
  input  wire  [31:0]   PRDATA2,
  input  wire  [31:0]   PRDATA3,
  input  wire  [31:0]   PRDATA4,
  input  wire  [31:0]   PRDATA5,
  input  wire  [31:0]   PRDATA6,
  input  wire  [31:0]   PRDATA7,
  input  wire           PREADY0,   // Ready for each APB slave
  input  wire           PREADY1,
  input  wire           PREADY2,
  input  wire           PREADY3,
  input  wire           PREADY4,
  input  wire           PREADY5,
  input  wire           PREADY6,
  input  wire           PREADY7,
  input  wire           PSLVERR0,  // Error state for each APB slave
  input  wire           PSLVERR1,
  input  wire           PSLVERR2,
  input  wire           PSLVERR3,
  input  wire           PSLVERR4,
  input  wire           PSLVERR5,
  input  wire           PSLVERR6,
  input  wire           PSLVERR7
  );
```

```
// Internal signals
reg  [15:2]  AddrReg;    // Address sample register
reg   [7:0]  SelReg;     // One-hot PSEL output register
reg          WrReg;      // Write control sample register
reg   [2:0]  StateReg;   // State for finite state machine

wire         ApbSelect;  // APB bridge is selected
wire         ApbTranEnd; // Transfer is completed on APB
wire         AhbTranEnd; // Transfer is completed on AHB
reg   [7:0]  NextPSel;   // Next state of One-hot PSEL
reg   [2:0]  NextState;  // Next state for finite state machine
reg  [31:0]  RDataReg;   // Read data sample register
reg   [2:0]  PProtReg;   // Protection information
reg   [3:0]  NxtPSTRB;   // Write byte strobe next state
reg   [3:0]  RegPSTRB;   // Write byte strobe register
wire [31:0]  muxPRDATA;  // Slave multiplexer signal
wire         muxPREADY;
wire         muxPSLVERR;

// Start of main code

// Generate APB bridge select
assign    ApbSelect = HSEL & HTRANS[1] & HREADY;
// Generate APB transfer ended
assign    ApbTranEnd = (StateReg==3'b010) & muxPREADY;
// Generate AHB transfer ended
assign    AhbTranEnd = (StateReg==3'b011) | (StateReg==3'b101);

// Generate next state of PSEL at each AHB transfer
always @(ApbSelect or HADDR)
begin
if (ApbSelect)
  begin
  case (HADDR[14:12]) // Binary to one-hot encoding for device select
  3'b000 : NextPSel = 8'b00000001;
  3'b001 : NextPSel = 8'b00000010;
  3'b010 : NextPSel = 8'b00000100;
  3'b011 : NextPSel = 8'b00001000;
  3'b100 : NextPSel = 8'b00010000;
  3'b101 : NextPSel = 8'b00100000;
  3'b110 : NextPSel = 8'b01000000;
  3'b111 : NextPSel = 8'b10000000;
  default: NextPSel = 8'b00000000;
  endcase
  end
else
  NextPSel = 8'b00000000;
end

// Registering PSEL output
always @(posedge HCLK or negedge HRESETn)
begin
if (~HRESETn)
  SelReg <= 8'h00;
else if (HREADY|ApbTranEnd)
  SelReg <= NextPSel; // Set if bridge is selected
end                   // Clear at end of APB transfer

// Sample control signals
always @(posedge HCLK or negedge HRESETn)
begin
```

```
  if (~HRESETn)
    begin
    AddrReg  <= {10{1'b0}};
    WrReg    <= 1'b0;
    PProtReg <= {3{1'b0}};
    end
  else if (ApbSelect) // Only change at beginning of each APB transfer
    begin
    AddrReg  <= HADDR[11:2]; // Note that lowest two bits are not used
    WrReg    <= HWRITE;
    PProtReg <= {(~HPROT[0]),HNONSEC,(HPROT[1])};
    end
  end

// Byte write strobes
always @(*)
begin
  if (HSEL & HTRANS[1] & HWRITE)
    begin
    case (HSIZE[1:0])
      2'b00: // byte
        begin
        case (HADDR[1:0])
        2'b00: NxtPSTRB = 4'b0001;
        2'b01: NxtPSTRB = 4'b0010;
        2'b10: NxtPSTRB = 4'b0100;
        2'b11: NxtPSTRB = 4'b1000;
        default:NxtPSTRB = 4'bxxxx; // Should not be here.
        endcase
        end
      2'b01: // half word
        NxtPSTRB = (HADDR[1])? 4'b1100:4'b0011;
      default: // word
        NxtPSTRB = 4'b1111;
    endcase
    end
  else
    NxtPSTRB = 4'b0000;
end

always @(posedge HCLK or negedge HRESETn)
begin
if (~HRESETn)
  RegPSTRB<= {4{1'b0}};
else if (HREADY)
  RegPSTRB<= NxtPSTRB;
end

// Generate next state for FSM
always @(StateReg or muxPREADY or muxPSLVERR or ApbSelect)
begin
case (StateReg)
 3'b000 : NextState = {1'b0, ApbSelect}; // Change to state-1 when selected
 3'b001 : NextState = 3'b010;             // Change to state-2
 3'b010 : begin
            if (muxPREADY & muxPSLVERR) // Error received - Generate two cycle
                               // Error response on AHB by
              NextState = 3'b100; // Changing to state-4 and 5
            else if (muxPREADY & ~muxPSLVERR) // Okay received
              NextState = 3'b011; // Generate okay response in state 3
            else // Slave not ready
              NextState = 3'b010; // Unchange
            end
  3'b011 : NextState = {1'b0, ApbSelect}; // Terminate transfer
```

```
                                // Change to state-1 if selected
 3'b100 : NextState = 3'b101;    // Goto 2nd cycle of error response
 3'b101 : NextState = {1'b0, ApbSelect}; // 2nd Cycle of Error response
                                // Change to state-1 if selected
 default : // Not used
          NextState = {1'b0, ApbSelect}; // Change to state-1 when selected
endcase
end

// Registering state machine
always @(posedge HCLK or negedge HRESETn)
begin
if (~HRESETn)
  StateReg <= 3'b000;
else
  StateReg <= NextState;
end

// Slave Multiplexer
assign muxPRDATA = ({32{SelReg[0]}} & PRDATA0) |
                   ({32{SelReg[1]}} & PRDATA1) |
                   ({32{SelReg[2]}} & PRDATA2) |
                   ({32{SelReg[3]}} & PRDATA3) |
                   ({32{SelReg[4]}} & PRDATA4) |
                   ({32{SelReg[5]}} & PRDATA5) |
                   ({32{SelReg[6]}} & PRDATA6) |
                   ({32{SelReg[7]}} & PRDATA7) ;
assign muxPREADY = (SelReg[0] & PREADY0) |
                   (SelReg[1] & PREADY1) |
                   (SelReg[2] & PREADY2) |
                   (SelReg[3] & PREADY3) |
                   (SelReg[4] & PREADY4) |
                   (SelReg[5] & PREADY5) |
                   (SelReg[6] & PREADY6) |
                   (SelReg[7] & PREADY7) ;
assign muxPSLVERR = (SelReg[0] & PSLVERR0) |
                    (SelReg[1] & PSLVERR1) |
                    (SelReg[2] & PSLVERR2) |
                    (SelReg[3] & PSLVERR3) |
                    (SelReg[4] & PSLVERR4) |
                    (SelReg[5] & PSLVERR5) |
                    (SelReg[6] & PSLVERR6) |
                    (SelReg[7] & PSLVERR7) ;

// Sample PRDATA
always @(posedge HCLK or negedge HRESETn)
begin
if (~HRESETn)
  RDataReg <= {32{1'b0}};
else if (ApbTranEnd|AhbTranEnd)
  RDataReg <= muxPRDATA;
end

// Connect outputs to top level
assign PADDR  = {AddrReg[15:2], 2'b00}; // from sample register
assign PWRITE = WrReg;     // from sample register
assign PPROT  = PProtReg; // from sample register
assign PSTRB  = RegPSTRB;
assign PWDATA = HWDATA;   // No need to register (HWDATA is in data phase)
assign PSEL0  = SelReg[0]; // PSEL for each APB slave
assign PSEL1  = SelReg[1];
assign PSEL2  = SelReg[2];
assign PSEL3  = SelReg[3];
assign PSEL4  = SelReg[4];
```

```
    assign PSEL5   = SelReg[5];
    assign PSEL6   = SelReg[6];
    assign PSEL7   = SelReg[7];
    assign PENABLE= (StateReg == 3'b010); // PENABLE to all AHB slaves
    assign HREADYOUT = (StateReg == 3'b000)|(StateReg == 3'b011)|(StateReg==3'b101);
    assign HRDATA = RDataReg;
    assign HRESP   = (StateReg==3'b100)|(StateReg==3'b101);

  endmodule
```

In this design, up to eight APB slaves can be connected to the bridge. The design can be modified easily to support more or fewer APB slaves. This can be done by changing the binary to one-hot logic, the PSEL register, and the multiplexers.

The current design allows each APB to take up 4kB of memory. If the memory range for each APB slave needs to be increased or decreased, the address signal lines connected to the slave multiplexer need to be changed. In most cases, 4kB should be enough for most simple APB slaves.

7.4 Bridging from Cortex-M3/Cortex-M4 AHB Lite to AHB5

A simple bus wrapper component is needed to bridge the AHB interface of Cortex-M3 or Cortex-M4 processors to AHB5 due to:

■ Conversion of memory attribute sideband signals to new AHB5 HPROT signals;

■ Conversion of exclusive access signals.

Please note that there is also a mismatch between the AHB Lite specification and the Cortex-M3 and Cortex-M4's bus interface design. Since the Cortex-M3 was designed before the AHB Lite specification was finalized, the HRESP input signals on the Cortex-M3 processor are 2-bit wide as they are in AHB (AMBA 2), although the RETRY and SPILT responses are not supported. When connecting a Cortex-M3 processor to AHB Lite infrastructure, the bit 1 of the HRESP input in the processor can be tied to 0. Since Cortex-M4 was designed to enable easy migration from Cortex-M3, it kept the same arrangement, and therefore its HRESP inputs are also 2-bit wide.

The Verilog RTL of the bus wrapper is as follows:

```
module cm3ahb_to_ahb5 (
  input  wire          HCLK,    // Clock
  input  wire          HRESETn, // Reset

  input  wire          CM3HREADY,  // HREADY on Cortex-M3/M4
  input  wire          CM3HWRITE,
  input  wire   [3:0]  CM3HPROT,
  input  wire   [1:0]  CM3MEMATTR, // Memory attribute
  input  wire          CM3EXREQ,   // Exclusive request
  output wire          CM3EXRESP,  // Exclusive response
  output wire   [1:0]  CM3HRESP,
```

```
output wire  [6:0]  AHB5HPROT,
output wire         AHB5HEXCL,    // Exclusive request
input  wire         AHB5EXOKAY,   // Exclusive okay
input  wire         AHB5HRESP
);

reg   ExclTransfer; // Indicates data phase of exclusive accesses
//    Cortex-M3                   AHB5
// MEMATTR[1] - shareable     HPROT[6] - shareable
// MEMATTR[0] - allocate      HPROT[5] - allocate
//                            HPROT[4] - lookup
// HPROT[3]   - cacheable     HPROT[3] - modifiable
// HPROT[2]   - bufferable    HPROT[2] - bufferable
// HPROT[1]   - privileged    HPROT[1] - privileged
// HPROT[0]   - data          HPROT[0] - data

assign AHB5HPROT[6]   = CM3MEMATTR[1] & CM3HPROT[3];
assign AHB5HPROT[5]   = CM3HPROT[3] & (~CM3HWRITE | ~CM3MEMATTR[0]);

assign AHB5HPROT[4]   = CM3HPROT[3];
assign AHB5HPROT[3:0] = CM3HPROT[3:0];

assign AHB5HEXCL      = CM3EXREQ;

// Mark data phases of exclusive accesses
always @(posedge HCLK or negedge HRESETn)
begin
if (~HRESETn)
  ExclTransfer <= 1'b0;
else if  (CM3HREADY)
  ExclTransfer <= CM3EXREQ;
end

assign CM3EXRESP = (ExclTransfer & ~AHB5EXOKAY & CM3HREADY);

// Wide matching for HRESP
assign CM3HRESP = {1'b0, AHB5HRESP}; // Only OKAY & ERROR are allowed

endmodule
```

In this bus wrapper, we omitted the HNONSEC (Security Attribute for TrustZone support). If a Cortex-M processor without TrustZone support is used in a TrustZone enabled system, you can use one of two arrangements:

1. The Cortex-M processor is treated as always Non-secure. In this case, the HNONSEC signal(s) of the Cortex-M processor is tied high. The bus system needs to handle permission checking to prevent the processor from accessing Secure memories.

2. The Cortex-M processor is treated as always Secure. In this case, the HNONSEC signal(s) must be generated based on the memory address partitioning (1 for Non-secure addresses and 0 for Secure addresses).

The Corstone system design kits from Arm provide a component called Master Security Controller to handle security management of legacy bus masters in a TrustZone based system.

CHAPTER

Design of
simple peripherals

8

8.1 Common practices for peripheral designs

If you are designing a peripheral for a Cortex-M processor-based system or setting out to develop a wrapper for legacy 8-bit or 16-bit peripheral blocks, a number of standard practices will make the software development easier:

■ Make sure that the peripheral's registers are word-aligned unless you are creating an AHB peripheral with byte-addressable registers. In most cases, peripherals will be connected to the APB bus system. Since there is no transfer size information on this bus and the bus size is always 32-bit wide, it is best to make every register word size and align to word addresses. At the peripheral interface, the address bit [1:0] is unused and can be ignored.

■ When creating peripheral registers, it is important to avoid a status bit that can be cleared by writing a zero to it. For example, if the application needs to perform a read-modify-write operation to change a one-bit bitfield value in a peripheral register, and if another status bit of the same register changed state between the read and the write access, the information of the status bit change would be lost when the write-back takes place. Normally, status bits that indicate events can be implemented as write 1 to clear. In this way, the status bit will not be cleared accidentally.

■ When creating status registers in peripherals, it is best to avoid a status register that changes its value upon read accesses (e.g., clear on read). This is because you might want to read the peripheral memory map through a debugger at the same time as the program is running. Of course, sometimes, this cannot be avoided. In this case, you might want to create a separate address for the debugger accesses to the peripheral status register so that reading of status information by the debugger will not change the behavior of the device.

■ Be aware that the status of the peripheral interface might be in an undefined state during the starting up of an FPGA. Internally to the FPGA, the peripheral can be reset after the FPGA is ready. But the external circuit interface to the peripheral will need to be aware that the FPGA needs a certain period of time to get ready. Most FPGA products have status output to indicate that the starting sequence is completed. This can be used to externally disable the circuit from activation.

■ In most cases, interrupt signals from peripherals are designed as level trigger interrupts. Compared to pulse triggered interrupts, level trigger interrupts can propagate through clock domains with simple synchronizers. Whereas synchronization for pulse trigger interrupt signals is more complex.

■ When developing a complex design, it is often impractical to design all of the required peripherals by yourself. However, there are various offerings available from Intellectual Property providers that can be used to create peripheral solutions that work with Arm processors. Arm also has a range of peripheral products and subsystem products for accelerating time to market.

■ In many cases, a peripheral could operate at a much slower clock speed than the processor. Instead of using bus bridges to convert the bus clock speed to match the peripheral speed, it is often best to have a separated clock for the bus interface of the peripheral and a clock for peripheral functions. The complexity of the peripheral would increase as a result, as there is a need for additional synchronization logic between the clock domains. However, this arrangement avoids high access latency when reading/writing to the peripheral registers, which reduces the energy efficiency of the system and has an impact on interrupt latency.

8.2 Designing Simple APB Peripherals

For the majority of peripheral designs, the AMBA APB protocol is usually chosen because it is very simple. There are, of course, situations where peripherals need to be designed with an AHB interface instead. For example, if a peripheral is required to support any of the following:

■ Transfers of different data sizes (registers are byte/half-word addressable),

■ Exclusive accesses, or

■ Instances in which the peripheral needs to behave differently when other bus-masters have access to it (Note: This requires the HMASTER signal).

In this section, we will cover the design of simple APB peripherals, including a simple parallel I/O interface and a simple timer. First of all, though, we will take a look at APB interface design in general.

APB transfers take two cycles in AMBA 2, or a minimum of two cycles in AMBA 3 and later versions. For read operations, an APB slave must provide valid read data at the last cycle of the transfer, except when it is responding with an error signal (applicable only in AMBA 3 or after). For slower frequency systems, we can generate the read data as soon as possible without any pipeline stage.

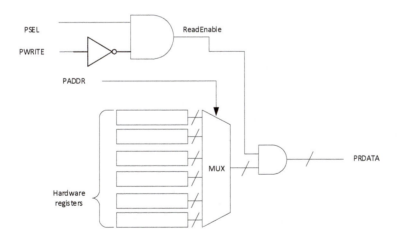

Figure 8.1: Simple APB read data generation.

With the arrangement shown in Figure 8.1, the PRDATA will be valid for all the cycles during the APB transfer. This solution is good enough for some APB systems. However, in systems that require higher operating frequency, this design might not be suitable because of the propagation delay in the read data generation. For example, if an APB slave contains a large number of hardware registers, the read data multiplexer will have a long delay. In addition to that, the APB slave multiplexer at the system-level (in our example the APB slave multiplexer is built-in to the AHB to APB Bridge) also requires some time to multiplex the read data from different APB slaves. As a result, the total propagation delay can be quite significant and can be worse when we include wire connection delays in the calculation. This can reduce the maximum clock frequency of the system, or cause signal routing problems within the FPGA/ASIC designs.

In order to solve this problem, we can insert a register stage in the APB slave read data interface to improve the synthesis timing of the data path. The pipeline stage could be inserted in different positions, depending on your design. One of the possible arrangements is to register the read data multiplexer output.

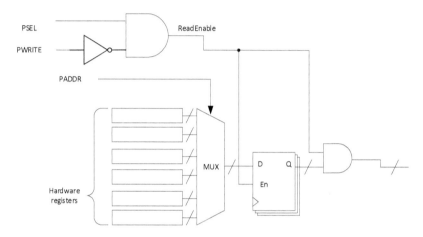

Figure 8.2: Pipelined APB read data generation.

By using this pipeline stage, we can prevent the signal path from hardware registers within the APB slaves to the AHB to APB bridge from getting too long. In addition, an extra registering stage can be placed within the AHB to APB bridge, so in total, a data read takes two clock cycles to get the data value from the peripheral register to the processor. This seems to have increased the read operation latency, but the first registering cycle within the APB slave overlapped with the APB operations (APB transfers take a minimum of two cycles), so the only extra latency cycle is at the registering stage of the AHB to APB Bridge.

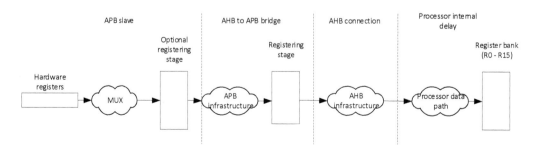

Figure 8.3: The signal path of pipelined APB read data generation.

In the example designs, the register slices for read data only activate if there is a read to the slave. Otherwise, the register is held unchanged to reduce power consumption. The read data output (PRDATA) is masked by a ReadEnable signal to block data output when the APB slave is not being read. Such a blocking mechanism could potentially simplify merging of PRDATA from multiple slaves by using just OR logic if all bus slaves in the APB segment has the same behavior.

The write operation is easier to implement. For example, if each writable hardware register has a corresponding write enable signals, the write enable signal can be generated as:

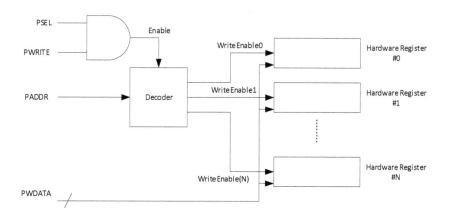

Figure 8.4: APB write implementation.

When designing APB peripherals, we should assign each hardware register to word-aligned addresses and reserve the whole word for the register even if only part of the space is used. This is because the APB interface does not provide transfer size information, so each access is assumed to be the maximum transfer size of the bus (i.e., word size). The common practice is that bit 1 and bit 0 of the PADDR bus are not used, and registers are assigned with word aligned addresses like (0xXXXX0000, 0xXXXX0004, 0xXXXX0008, etc.). Even if the register does not require the whole word, it occupies the whole word address.

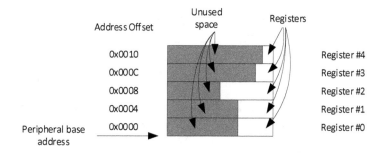

Figure 8.5: Keep peripheral registers word-aligned so that the lowest two bits of an address can be tied off.

For many designers, they might have legacy peripherals that were designed for simple 8-bit or 16-bit microcontrollers and want to reuse them on their Cortex-M processor-based design. In most cases, these peripherals have three read and write control signals: Chip-Select, Read-Enable, and Write-

Enable. If the peripheral has a synchronous (clocked) interface and does not require a tristate data bus, it is normally an easy task to connect this type of peripheral to APB.

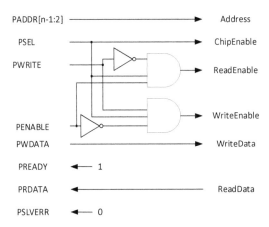

Figure 8.6: Simple APB wrapper for legacy peripherals with a simple synchronous interface.

However, if the peripheral requires a tristate bus interface, or uses an asynchronous interface, the wrapper will have to handle the transfers in multiple clock cycles and create a turn-around cycle if a tristate bus is used (a turn-around cycle is used to prevent current spikes on the data bus when the direction of the data changes, caused by the bus master and bus slave tristate buffers being turned on simultaneously for a very short period of time during the transition). In order to allow multiple cycle operations, the APB system must support the PREADY signal, so the APB for AMBA 3 or later is needed in this situation.

The simplest way to develop a wrapper for such a peripheral is to create a finite state machine and generate the read enable, write enable, and tristate buffer output enable, using the state value. (Note: We assume that the OutputEnable signal is used to enable the tristate buffer for write data, and the ReadEnable is used to enable the tristate buffer for data output on the slaves). If the peripheral accesses take longer, the finite state machine design can be extended easily by adding extra states.

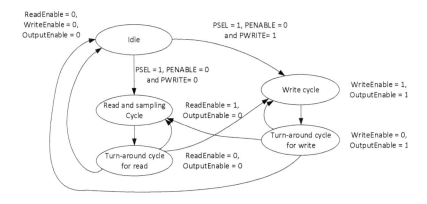

Figure 8.7: State machine to interface APB to asynchronous or tristate buses.

In the example shown in Figure 8.8, a sampling register is used to hold the read data during the turn-around cycle for read. This allows for better synthesis timing performance. Usually, a tristate bus operates slower than a unidirectional bus. Without the sampling register, the delay of the read operation, together with the delay caused by the APB slave multiplexer can become a critical path of the design and limits the maximum clock frequency.

Using the state machine diagram, the wrapper logic to interface an asynchronous peripheral can be developed as follows:

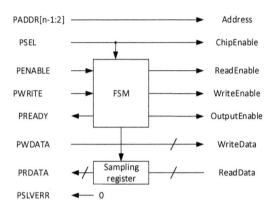

Figure 8.8: APB to simple asynchronous interface wrapper with tristate bus support.

Example Verilog code for this wrapper is listed here.

```verilog
module apb_to_async_wrapper (
    input   wire        PCLK,     // Clock
    input   wire        PRESETn,  // Reset
    // APB interface inputs
    input   wire        PSEL,     // Device select
    input   wire [7:2]  PADDR,    // Address
    input   wire        PENABLE,  // Transfer control
    input   wire        PWRITE,   // Write control
    input   wire [31:0] PWDATA,   // Write data
    // APB interface outputs
    output wire [31:0] PRDATA,    // Read data
    output wire        PREADY,    // Device ready
    output wire        PSLVERR,   // Device error response

    // simple interface's output
    output wire [7:2]  Addr,         // Address
    output wire [31:0] WrData,       // Write Data
    output wire        ReadEnable,   // Read enable
    output wire        WriteEnable,  // Write enable
    output wire        OutputEnable, // Tristate buffer for WrData
    input   wire [31:0] RdData       // Read data
    );

// Cycles for read & write, values are example only. Modify if needed.
localparam  RD_CYCLE=4'h3; // 3 cycles for read
localparam  WR_CYCLE=4'h2; // 2 cycles for write
// Encoding of FSM states
```

```verilog
  localparam  FSM_IDLE=3'b000;    // Idle state
  localparam  FSM_READ_1=3'b100;  // Read operation
  localparam  FSM_READ_2=3'b101;  // Turnaround
  localparam  FSM_WRITE_1=3'b110; // Write operation
  localparam  FSM_WRITE_2=3'b111; // Turnaround

  wire        RdStart;         // Read started
  wire        WrStart;         // Write started
  wire        OpDone;          // Operation done
  reg [3:0]   reg_cycle;       // wait cycle counter
  reg [3:0]   nxt_cycle;       // next state for reg_cycle
  reg [2:0]   reg_fsm_state;   // FSM state register
  reg [2:0]   nxt_fsm_state;   // next state for reg_fsm_state
  reg         reg_ReadEnable;  // Registered ReadEnable output
  reg         reg_WriteEnable; // Registered WriteEnable output
  reg         reg_OutputEnable;// Registered OutputEnable output
  reg [31:0]  reg_rdata;

  assign RdStart = PSEL & ~PENABLE & ~PWRITE;
  assign WrStart = PSEL & ~PENABLE &  PWRITE;

  // Counter to handle multi-cycle operations
  always @(*)
  begin
    if (RdStart)
      nxt_cycle = RD_CYCLE;
    else if (WrStart)
      nxt_cycle = WR_CYCLE;
    else if (|reg_cycle)
      nxt_cycle = reg_cycle - 1'b1;
    else
      nxt_cycle = reg_cycle;
  end

  always @(posedge PCLK or negedge PRESETn)
    begin
    if (~PRESETn)
      reg_cycle <= 4'b0000;
    else
      reg_cycle <= nxt_cycle;
    end

  assign OpDone = (nxt_cycle==4'b0000) & reg_fsm_state[2];

  // FSM
  always @(*)
  begin
    case (reg_fsm_state[2:0])
      FSM_IDLE,FSM_READ_2,FSM_WRITE_2:
        begin
        if (RdStart)
          nxt_fsm_state = FSM_READ_1;
  else if (WrStart)
          nxt_fsm_state = FSM_WRITE_1;
  else
    nxt_fsm_state = FSM_IDLE;
end
      FSM_READ_1:
        nxt_fsm_state = OpDone? FSM_READ_2: FSM_READ_1;
      FSM_WRITE_1:
        nxt_fsm_state = OpDone? FSM_WRITE_2: FSM_WRITE_1;
      default: // should not be here
        nxt_fsm_state = FSM_IDLE;
    endcase
```

```verilog
  end

  always @(posedge PCLK or negedge PRESETn)
    begin
    if (~PRESETn)
      reg_fsm_state <= FSM_IDLE;
    else
      reg_fsm_state <= nxt_fsm_state;
    end

  // Sample read data from bus slave
  always @(posedge PCLK or negedge PRESETn)
    begin
    if (~PRESETn)
      reg_rdata <= {32{1'b0}};
    else if ((reg_fsm_state==FSM_READ_1) & OpDone)
      reg_rdata <= RdData;
    end

  // Registering ReadEnable control
  always @(posedge PCLK or negedge PRESETn)
    begin
    if (~PRESETn)
      reg_ReadEnable <= 1'b0;
    else
      reg_ReadEnable <= (RdStart|reg_ReadEnable) & ~OpDone;
    end

  // Registering WriteEnable control
  always @(posedge PCLK or negedge PRESETn)
    begin
    if (~PRESETn)
      reg_WriteEnable <= 1'b0;
    else
      reg_WriteEnable <= (WrStart|reg_WriteEnable) & ~OpDone;
    end

  // Registering OutputEnable (tristate buffer) control
  always @(posedge PCLK or negedge PRESETn)
    begin
    if (~PRESETn)
      reg_OutputEnable <= 1'b0;
    else
      reg_OutputEnable <= (WrStart|reg_OutputEnable) &
      ~(reg_fsm_state==FSM_WRITE_2);
    end

assign PRDATA       = (PENABLE & ~PWRITE) ? reg_rdata:{32{1'b0}};
assign PSLVERR      = 1'b0;
assign PREADY       =
~((reg_fsm_state==FSM_READ_1)||(reg_fsm_state==FSM_WRITE_1));

// Output to bus slave
assign Addr[7:2]    = PADDR[7:2];
// Note: assumed PADDR is registered in AHB to APB bridge
assign WrData[31:0] = PWDATA[31:0];
// Note: PWDATA should be stable before reaching FSM_WRITE_1

// Connect registered R/W control outputs to top level
assign ReadEnable   = reg_ReadEnable;
assign WriteEnable  = reg_WriteEnable;
assign OutputEnable = reg_OutputEnable;

endmodule
```

8.2.1 General Purpose Input Output (GPIO) interface

In Arm terminology, peripherals that handle a parallel I/O interface are often called General Purpose I/O (GPIO). Some of the commercial I/O interface blocks might be able to support a large number of features, but in here, we are focusing on the APB interface itself, so the design will only provide basic features.

The first stage of the design process is to determine the interface signals required. For basic functionality, we need to have input signals, output signals, and enable control signals for output tristate buffers. We can make the design more flexible by setting the width of the I/O as a Verilog parameter, with a default width of 8-bit. In this way, the block can be reused easily on other designs that need a different I/O width.

Figure 8.9: Simple GPIO peripheral.

The GPIO block will also allow the generation of interrupts to a processor core. In order to make the design more flexible, for each I/O pin, we will provide an interrupt output, as well as a combined interrupt output.

The APB interface will include APB signals for AMBA 3. However, as the design does not require wait state, the PREADY output will be tied to high and PSLVERR signal will be tied to low. This design can be used on APB systems for AMBA 2. In this case, the PREADY and PSLVERR outputs can be ignored.

The next step of the design process is to determine the programmer's model for the GPIO block. The programmer's model is fairly simple, containing only six registers.

Address offset	Name	Type	Reset value	Descriptions
0x000	DataIn	RO	-	Read back value of the IO port
0x004	DataOut	R/W	0x00	Output data value
0x008	OutEnable	R/W	0x00	Output Enable (Tri-state buffer enable)
0x00C	IntEnable	R/W	0x00	Interrupt Enable (for each bit, set to 1 to enable interrupt generation, or clear to 0 to disable the interrupt)
0x010	IntType	R/W	0x00	Interrupt Type (for each bit, set to 1 for edge trigger interrupt, and clear to 0 for level trigger interrupt)
0x014	IntPolarity	R/W	0x00	Interrupt Polarity (for each bit, clear to 0 for rising edge trigger or high-level trigger, and set to 1 for falling edge trigger or low-level trigger)
0x018	INTSTATE	R/Wc	0x00	Bit[7:0] – Interrupt status, write 1 to clear

Table 8.1: Programmer's model for example GPIO block.

With these details in place, we can begin to develop the design for the example GPIO block.

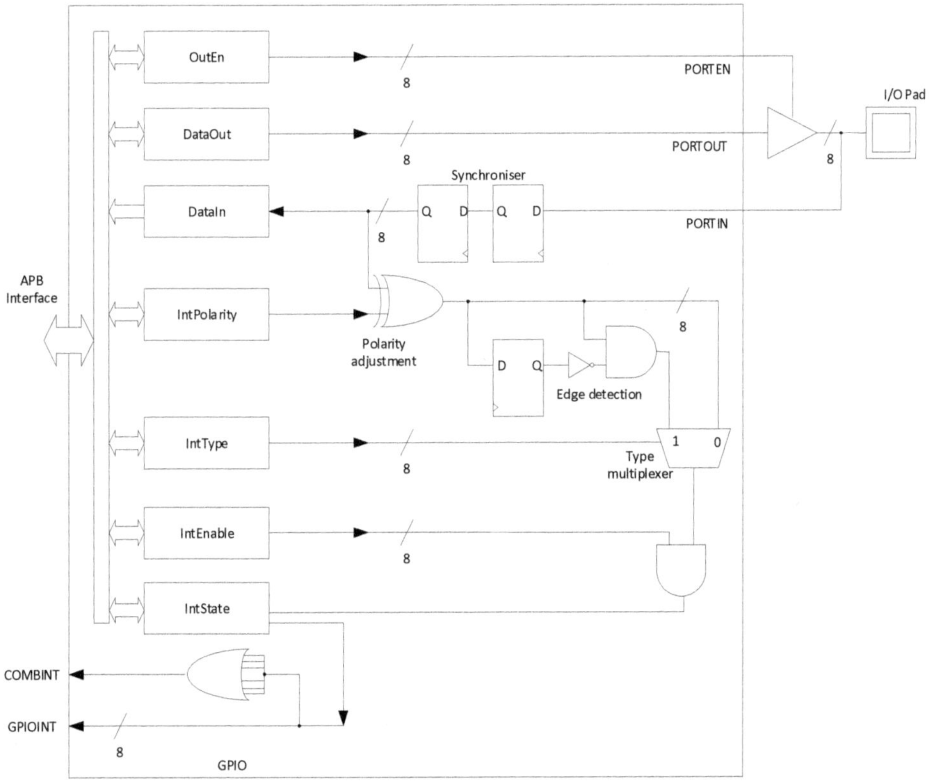

Figure 8.10: Design of a simple GPIO peripheral.

The GPIO design itself does not contain the tristate buffers. These have to be added externally because tristate buffers can be technology-specific, and designers might want to define them manually to match the electrical characteristics needed by the applications. Additionally, in some designs, the I/O pins might need to be shared with other peripherals. In such cases, the tristate buffers would have to be added after the pin multiplexor stage.

The design also contains a dual flip-flop synchronizer. This is used to prevent metastability issues caused by toggling of asynchronous external inputs. The interrupt generation circuit is connected to the synchronizer output. Please note that, with this arrangement, the interrupt generation will not work if the clock is stopped.

For interrupt generation on the Cortex-M processors with this GPIO unit, please note that, aside from enabling the interrupt enable at the GPIO block, it is also necessary to program the interrupt enable register in the NVIC in the Cortex-M processor.

The APB interface design for the example GPIO block is quite simple. First, we use PSEL, PWRITE, and PENABLE to create the enable signals for read and write operations. Then, we combine these signals with the output from address decoding logic to enable write control for each register and to control the read multiplexer for the generation of read data.

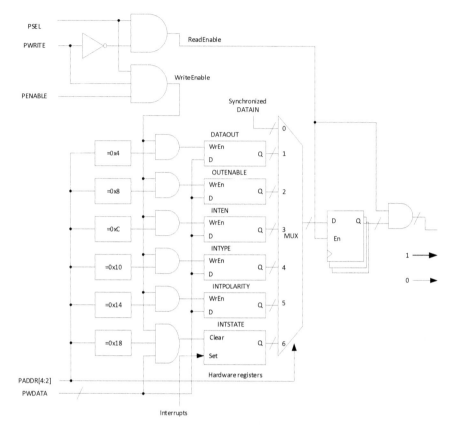

Figure 8.11: APB interface for simple GPIO peripheral.

The Verilog RTL of the example GPIO is as follows:

```
// Simple GPIO
//
//-------------------------------------
// Programmer's model
// 0x00 RO    DataIn
// 0x04 RW    Data Output
// 0x08 RW    Output Enable
// 0x0C RW    Interrupt Enable
// 0x10 RW    Interrupt Type
// 0x14 RW    Interrupt Polarity
// 0x18 RWc   Interrupt State
//-------------------------------------
module apb_gpio #(
  parameter  PortWidth = 8
  ) (
  input  wire         PCLK,    // Clock
  input  wire         PRESETn, // Reset
     // APB interface inputs
  input  wire         PSEL,    // Device select
```

```
  input   wire  [7:2]   PADDR,    // Address
  input   wire          PENABLE,  // Transfer control
  input   wire          PWRITE,   // Write control
  input   wire  [31:0]  PWDATA,   // Write data
   // APB interface outputs
  output  wire  [31:0]  PRDATA,   // Read data
  output  wire          PREADY,   // Device ready
  output  wire          PSLVERR,  // Device error response

  // GPIO Interface inputs and output
  input   wire [PortWidth-1:0] PORTIN,  // GPIO input
  output  wire [PortWidth-1:0] PORTOUT, // GPIO output
  output  wire [PortWidth-1:0] PORTEN,  // GPIO output enable
  // Interrupt outputs
  output  wire [PortWidth-1:0] GPIOINT, // Interrupt output for each pin
  output  wire                 COMBINT  // Combined interrupt
  );

  // Signals for read/write controls
  wire          ReadEnable;
  wire          WriteEnable;
  wire          WriteEnable04; // Write enable for Data Output register
  wire          WriteEnable08; // Write enable for Output Enable register
  wire          WriteEnable0C; // Write enable for Interrupt Enable register
  wire          WriteEnable10; // Write enable for Interrupt Type register
  wire          WriteEnable14; // Write enable for Interrupt Polarity register
  wire          WriteEnable18; // Write enable for Interrupt State register
  reg    [PortWidth-1:0] ReadMux;
  reg    [PortWidth-1:0] ReadMuxReg;

  // Signals for Control registers
  reg    [PortWidth-1:0] RegDOUT;
  reg    [PortWidth-1:0] RegDOUTEN;
  reg    [PortWidth-1:0] RegINTEN;
  reg    [PortWidth-1:0] RegINTTYPE;
  reg    [PortWidth-1:0] RegINTPOL;
  reg    [PortWidth-1:0] RegINTState;

  // I/O signal path
  reg    [PortWidth-1:0] DataInSync1;
  reg    [PortWidth-1:0] DataInSync2;
  wire   [PortWidth-1:0] DataInPolAdjusted;
  reg    [PortWidth-1:0] LastDataInPol;
  wire   [PortWidth-1:0] EdgeDetect;
  wire   [PortWidth-1:0] RawInt;
  wire   [PortWidth-1:0] MaskedInt;

  // Start of main code

  // Read and write control signals
  assign  ReadEnable  = PSEL & (~PWRITE); // assert for whole APB read transfer
  assign  WriteEnable = PSEL & (~PENABLE) & PWRITE; // assert for 1st cycle of write
transfer
  assign  WriteEnable04 = WriteEnable & (PADDR[7:2] == 6'b000001);
  assign  WriteEnable08 = WriteEnable & (PADDR[7:2] == 6'b000010);
  assign  WriteEnable0C = WriteEnable & (PADDR[7:2] == 6'b000011);
  assign  WriteEnable10 = WriteEnable & (PADDR[7:2] == 6'b000100);
  assign  WriteEnable14 = WriteEnable & (PADDR[7:2] == 6'b000101);
  assign  WriteEnable18 = WriteEnable & (PADDR[7:2] == 6'b000110);

  // Write operations
  // Data Output register
  always @(posedge PCLK or negedge PRESETn)
  begin
```

```
    if (~PRESETn)
      RegDOUT <= {PortWidth{1'b0}};
    else if (WriteEnable04)
      RegDOUT <= PWDATA[(PortWidth-1):0];
end

// Output enable register
always @(posedge PCLK or negedge PRESETn)
begin
  if (~PRESETn)
    RegDOUTEN <= {PortWidth{1'b0}};
  else if (WriteEnable08)
    RegDOUTEN <= PWDATA[(PortWidth-1):0];
end

// Interrupt Enable register
always @(posedge PCLK or negedge PRESETn)
begin
  if (~PRESETn)
    RegINTEN <= {PortWidth{1'b0}};
  else if (WriteEnable0C)
    RegINTEN <= PWDATA[(PortWidth-1):0];
end

// Interrupt Type register
always @(posedge PCLK or negedge PRESETn)
begin
  if (~PRESETn)
    RegINTTYPE <= {PortWidth{1'b0}};
  else if (WriteEnable10)
    RegINTTYPE <= PWDATA[(PortWidth-1):0];
end

// Interrupt Polarity register
always @(posedge PCLK or negedge PRESETn)
begin
  if (~PRESETn)
    RegINTPOL <= {PortWidth{1'b0}};
  else if (WriteEnable14)
    RegINTPOL <= PWDATA[(PortWidth-1):0];
end

// Read operation
always @(PADDR or DataInSync2 or RegDOUT or RegDOUTEN or
  RegINTEN or RegINTTYPE or RegINTPOL or RegINTState)
begin
case (PADDR[7:2])
 0: ReadMux =  DataInSync2;
 1: ReadMux =  RegDOUT;
 2: ReadMux =  RegDOUTEN;
 3: ReadMux =  RegINTEN;
 4: ReadMux =  RegINTTYPE;
 5: ReadMux =  RegINTPOL;
 6: ReadMux =  RegINTState;
 default : ReadMux = {PortWidth{1'b0}}; // Read as 0 if address is out of range
endcase
end

// Register read data
always @(posedge PCLK or negedge PRESETn)
begin
  if (~PRESETn)
    ReadMuxReg <= {PortWidth{1'b0}};
  else
```

```
        ReadMuxReg <= ReadMux;
    end

    // Output read data to APB
    assign PRDATA = (ReadEnable) ? {{(32-PortWidth){1'b0}},ReadMuxReg} : {32{1'b0}};
    assign PREADY  = 1'b1; // Always ready
    assign PSLVERR = 1'b0; // Always okay

    // Output to external
    assign PORTEN  = RegDOUTEN;
    assign PORTOUT = RegDOUT;

    // Synchronize input
    always @(posedge PCLK or negedge PRESETn)
    begin
      if (~PRESETn)
        begin
        DataInSync1 <= {PortWidth{1'b0}};
        DataInSync2 <= {PortWidth{1'b0}};
        end
      else
        begin
        DataInSync1 <= PORTIN;
        DataInSync2 <= DataInSync1;
        end
    end

    // Interrupt generation - polarity handling
    assign DataInPolAdjusted = DataInSync2 ^ RegINTPOL;

    // Interrupt generation - record last value of DataInPolAdjusted
    always @(posedge PCLK or negedge PRESETn)
    begin
      if (~PRESETn)
        LastDataInPol <= {PortWidth{1'b0}};
      else
        LastDataInPol <= DataInPolAdjusted;
    end

    // Interrupt generation - positive edge detection
    assign EdgeDetect = ~LastDataInPol & DataInPolAdjusted;

    // Interrupt generation - select interrupt type
    assign RawInt = ( RegINTTYPE & EdgeDetect) |        // Edge trigger, or
                    (~RegINTTYPE & DataInPolAdjusted); // Level trigger

    // Interrupt generation - Enable masking
    assign MaskedInt = RawInt & RegINTEN;

    // Interrupt state
    always @(posedge PCLK or negedge PRESETn)
    begin
      if (~PRESETn)
        RegINTState <= {PortWidth{1'b0}};
      else
        RegINTState <= MaskedInt|(RegINTState & ~(PWDATA[PortWidth-1:0] &
{PortWidth{WriteEnable18}})));
    end

    // Connect interrupt signal to top level
    assign GPIOINT = RegINTState;
    assign COMBINT = (|RegINTState);

endmodule
```

8.2.2 Simple APB Timer

Using a similar approach for the peripheral design, we can also include a simple timer. Unlike the SYSTICK timer, this timer will be based on a 32-bit down counter and has an external input allowing pulse width measurement. The timer can also generate an interrupt when the counter value changes from 1 to 0, and it will automatically reload with a programmable reload value. To make the timer more flexible, we also include an external input signal, which can be used as an external enable control or as an external clock. This allows the timer to be used for a pulse width measurement or frequency meter. The only other interface on this timer block will be the APB interface.

The next step of the design process is to determine the programmer's model for the timer block, which is fairly simple as it contains only four registers.

Address offset	Name	Type	Reset value	Descriptions
0x000	CTRL	R/W	0x00	Control register [3] IntrEN – Interrupt output enable [2] ExtCLKSel – External Clock Select [1] ExtENSel – External Enable Select [0] Enable – Counter Enable
0x004	CurrVal	R/W	0x00	Current Value
0x008	Reload	R/W	0x00	Reload value
0x00C	INTSTATE	R/Wc	0x00	Bit 0 – Interrupt status, write 1 to clear

Table 8.2: Programmer's model for example timer block.

The design of the timer is very simple:

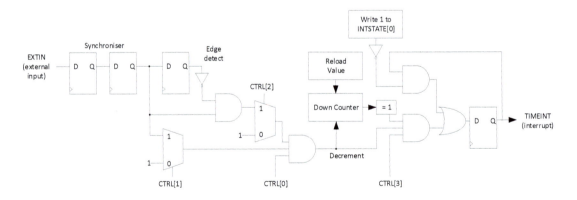

Figure 8.12: Design of a simple timer peripheral.

The APB interface design for the timer is almost the same as the GPIO, hence, it is not covered in detail again here. The Verilog RTL code of the design is as follows:

```
// Simple Timer
//
//-----------------------------------
// Programmer's model
// 0x00 RW    CTRL[3:0]
//            [3] Timer Interrupt Enable
//            [2] Select External input as Clock
//            [1] Select External input as Enable
//            [0] Enable
// 0x04 RW    Current Value[31:0]
// 0x08 RW    Reload Value[31:0]
// 0x0C RWc   Interrupt state
//            [0] IntState, write 1 to clear
//-----------------------------------

module apb_timer (
  input  wire          PCLK,     // Clock
  input  wire          PRESETn,  // Reset
       // APB interface inputs
  input  wire          PSEL,     // Device select
  input  wire [7:2]    PADDR,    // Address
  input  wire          PENABLE,  // Transfer control
  input  wire          PWRITE,   // Write control
  input  wire [31:0]   PWDATA,   // Write data
   // APB interface outputs
  output wire [31:0]   PRDATA,   // Read data
  output wire          PREADY,   // Device ready
  output wire          PSLVERR,  // Device error response

  input  wire          EXTIN,    // External input

  output wire          TIMERINT  // Timer interrupt output
  );

  // Signals for read/write controls
  wire          ReadEnable;
  wire          WriteEnable;
  wire          WriteEnable00; // Write enable for Control register
  wire          WriteEnable04; // Write enable for Current Value register
  wire          WriteEnable08; // Write enable for Reload Value register
  wire          WriteEnable0C; // Write enable for Interrupt state register
  reg    [31:0] ReadMux;
  reg    [31:0] ReadMuxReg;

  // Signals for Control registers
  reg    [3:0]  RegCTRL;
  reg    [31:0] RegCurrVal;
  reg    [31:0] RegReloadVal;
  reg    [31:0] NxtCurrVal;

  // Internal signals
  reg           ExtInSync1;   // Synchronization registers for external input
  reg           ExtInSync2;
  reg           ExtInDelay;   // Delay register for edge detection
  wire          DecCtrl;      // Decrement control
  wire          ClkCtrl;      // Clk select result
  wire          EnCtrl;       // Enable select result
  wire          EdgeDetect;   // Edge detection
  reg           RegTimerInt;  // Timer interrupt output register
  wire          NxtTimerInt;

  assign  WriteEnable08 = WriteEnable & (PADDR[7:2] == 6'b000010);
```

```
// Start of main code
// Read and write control signals
assign  ReadEnable  = PSEL & (~PWRITE); // assert for whole APB read transfer
assign  WriteEnable = PSEL & (~PENABLE) & PWRITE; // assert for 1st cycle of write
transfer
assign  WriteEnable00 = WriteEnable & (PADDR[7:2] == 6'b000000);
assign  WriteEnable04 = WriteEnable & (PADDR[7:2] == 6'b000001);
assign  WriteEnable08 = WriteEnable & (PADDR[7:2] == 6'b000010);
assign  WriteEnable0C = WriteEnable & (PADDR[7:2] == 6'b000011);

// Write operations
// Control register
always @(posedge PCLK or negedge PRESETn)
begin
  if (~PRESETn)
    RegCTRL <= {4{1'b0}};
  else if (WriteEnable00)
    RegCTRL <= PWDATA[3:0];
end

// Current Value register
always @(posedge PCLK or negedge PRESETn)
begin
  if (~PRESETn)
    RegCurrVal <= {32{1'b0}};
  else
    RegCurrVal <= NxtCurrVal;
end

// Reload Value register
always @(posedge PCLK or negedge PRESETn)
begin
  if (~PRESETn)
    RegReloadVal <= {32{1'b0}};
  else if (WriteEnable08)
    RegReloadVal <= PWDATA[31:0];
end

// Read operation
always @(PADDR or RegCTRL or RegCurrVal or RegReloadVal or RegTimerInt)
begin
case (PADDR[7:2])
  0: ReadMux =  {{28{1'b0}}, RegCTRL};
  1: ReadMux =  RegCurrVal;
  2: ReadMux =  RegReloadVal;
  3: ReadMux =  {{31{1'b0}}, RegTimerInt};
  default : ReadMux = {32{1'b0}}; // Read as 0 if address is out of range
endcase
end

// Register read data
always @(posedge PCLK or negedge PRESETn)
begin
  if (~PRESETn)
    ReadMuxReg <= {32{1'b0}};
  else
    ReadMuxReg <= ReadMux;
end

// Output read data to APB
assign PRDATA = (ReadEnable) ? ReadMuxReg : {32{1'b0}};
assign PREADY  = 1'b1; // Always ready
assign PSLVERR = 1'b0; // Always okay
```

```verilog
  // Synchronize input and delay for edge detection
  always @(posedge PCLK or negedge PRESETn)
  begin
    if (~PRESETn)
      begin
      ExtInSync1 <= 1'b0;
      ExtInSync2 <= 1'b0;
      ExtInDelay <= 1'b0;
      end
    else
      begin
      ExtInSync1 <= EXTIN;
      ExtInSync2 <= ExtInSync1;
      ExtInDelay <= ExtInSync2;
      end
  end

  // Edge detection
  assign EdgeDetect = ExtInSync2 & ~ExtInDelay;

  // Clock selection
  assign ClkCtrl    = RegCTRL[2] ? EdgeDetect : 1'b1;

  // Enable selection
  assign EnCtrl     = RegCTRL[1] ? ExtInSync2 : 1'b1;

  // Overall decrement control
  assign DecCtrl    = RegCTRL[0] & EnCtrl & ClkCtrl;

  // Decrement counter
  always @(WriteEnable04 or PWDATA or DecCtrl or RegCurrVal or
  RegReloadVal)
  begin
  if (WriteEnable04)
    NxtCurrVal = PWDATA[31:0];
  else if (DecCtrl)
    begin
    if (RegCurrVal == 32'h0)
      NxtCurrVal = RegReloadVal;
    else
      NxtCurrVal = RegCurrVal - 1;
    end
  else
    NxtCurrVal = RegCurrVal;
  end

  // Interrupt generation
  // Trigger an interrupt when decrement to 0 and interrupt enabled
  assign NxtTimerInt = (DecCtrl & RegCTRL[3] &
                       (RegCurrVal==32'h00000001));

  // Registering interrupt output
  always @(posedge PCLK or negedge PRESETn)
  begin
    if (~PRESETn)
      RegTimerInt <= 1'b0;
    else
      RegTimerInt <= NxtTimerInt|(RegTimerInt & ~(WriteEnable0C & PWDATA[0]));
  end

  // Connect to external
  assign TIMERINT = RegTimerInt;

endmodule
```

8.2.3 Simple UART

A simple UART is also included in the example test bench. Since this chapter focuses on AHB/APB development, we are not going to cover the details of the UART design here. The UART has an APB interface similar to the timer and GPIO. It has the following registers:

Address offset	Name	Type	Reset value	Descriptions
0x000	CTRL	R/W	0x00	Control register (bit[3:0]) [3] Receive interrupt enable [2] Transmit interrupt enable [1] Receive enable [0] Transmit enable
0x004	STAT	R/W	0x00	Status register (bit[3:0]) [3] Receive overrun error, write 1 to clear [2] Transmit overrun error, write 1 to clear [1] Receive buffer full [0] Transmit buffer full
0x008	TXD	R/W	0x00	Write : Transmit data register Read : Transmit buffer full (bit[0])
0x00C	RXD	RO	0x00	Received data register (bit[7:0])
0x010	BAUDDIV	R/W	0x00	Baud rate divider (bit[19:0]) (Minimum value is 32)
0x014	INTSTATE	R/Wc	0x00	Interrupt status [1] – TX interrupt, write 1 to clear [0] – RX interrupt, write 1 to clear

Table 8.3: Programmer's model for example UART.

This simple UART design supports 8-bit data transfers with 1 start bit, 1 stop bit, and without either hardware flow control or parity support. Despite being less than 500 lines of Verilog code, it contains a built-in baud rate generator, and the design supports 16 times oversampling on the serial input for better receive reliability. It also supports interrupt for transmit (when write buffer is emptied) and interrupt for receive (when data is received). For simulation purposes, a UART monitor module is also included in the example testbench to capture the transmitted serial data.

Figure 8.13: Simple UART peripheral.

The Verilog RTL code of the design is as follows:

```
// Simple UART
//
//-------------------------------------
// Programmer's model
// 0x00 RW    CTRL[3:0]   TxIntEn, RxIntEn, TxEn, RxEn
//              [3] RX Interrupt Enable
//              [2] TX Interrupt Enable
//              [1] RX Enable
//              [0] TX Enable
// 0x04 RW    STAT[3:0]
//              [3] RX buffer overrun (write 1 to clear)
//              [2] TX buffer overrun (write 1 to clear)
//              [1] RX buffer full (Read only)
//              [0] TX buffer full (Read only)
// 0x08 W     TXD[7:0]    Output Buffer Data
//       R    TX buffer full - bit[0]
// 0x0C RO    RXD[7:0]    Received Data
// 0x10 RW    BAUDDIV[19:0] Baud divider
//            (minimum value is 32)
//-------------------------------------

module apb_uart (
  input  wire          PCLK,    // Clock
  input  wire          PRESETn, // Reset
  // APB interface inputs
  input  wire          PSEL,    // Device select
  input  wire [7:2] PADDR,      // Address
  input  wire          PENABLE, // Transfer control
  input  wire          PWRITE,  // Write control
  input  wire [31:0] PWDATA,    // Write data
  // APB interface outputs
  output wire [31:0] PRDATA,    // Read data
  output wire          PREADY,  // Device ready
  output wire          PSLVERR, // Device error response

  input  wire          RXD,     // Serial input
  output wire          TXD,     // Transmit data output
  output wire          TXEN,    // Transmit enabled
  output wire          BAUDTICK, // Baud rate (x16) Tick (for testbench)

  output wire          TXINT,   // Transmit Interrupt
  output wire          RXINT    // Receive Interrupt
  );


  // Signals for read/write controls
  wire          ReadEnable;
  wire          ReadEnable10;  // Read baud rate divider
  wire          WriteEnable;
  wire          WriteEnable00; // Write enable for Control register
  wire          WriteEnable04; // Write enable for Status register
  wire          WriteEnable08; // Write enable for TxData buffer
  wire          WriteEnable10; // Write enable for Baud rate divider
  wire          WriteEnable14; // Write enable for Interrupt clear
  reg    [7:0] ReadMux;
  reg    [7:0] ReadMuxReg;
  reg          ReadEnable10Reg; // Read enable for Baud rate divider
                                // (size optimization)
  // Signals for Control registers
  reg    [3:0] RegCTRL;
  reg    [7:0] RegTxBuf;
  reg    [7:0] RegRxBuf;
  reg    [19:0] RegBaudDiv;
```

```verilog
// Internal signals
// Baud rate divider
reg     [15:0] RegBaudCntrI;
wire    [15:0] NxtBaudCntrI;
reg      [3:0] RegBaudCntrF;
wire     [3:0] NxtBaudCntrF;
wire     [3:0] MappedCntrF;
reg            RegBaudTick;
reg            BaudUpdated;
wire           ReloadI;
wire           ReloadF;
wire           BaudDivEn;

// Status
wire     [3:0] UartStatus;
reg            RegRxOverrun;
wire           RxOverrun;
reg            RegTxOverrun;
wire           TxOverrun;
wire           NxtRxOverrun;
wire           NxtTxOverrun;
// Interrupts
reg            RegTXINT;
wire           NxtTXINT;
reg            RegRXINT;
wire           NxtRXINT;

// transmit
reg      [3:0] TxState;    // Transmit FSM state
reg      [3:0] NxtTxState;
wire           TxStateInc; // Bit pulse
reg      [3:0] TxTickCnt;  // Transmit Tick counter
wire     [3:0] NxtTxTickCnt;
reg      [7:0] TxShiftBuf; // Transmit shift register
wire     [7:0] NxtTxShiftBuf;
reg            TxBufFull;  // TX Buffer full
wire           NxtTxBufFull;
reg            RegTxD;     // Tx Data
wire           NxtTxD;
wire           TxBufClear;

// Receive data sync and filter
reg            RxDSync1;   // Double flip-flop synchronizer
reg            RxDSync2;   // Double flip-flop synchronizer
reg      [2:0] RxDLPF;     // Average Low Pass Filter
wire           RxShiftIn;  // Shift Register Input

// Receiver
reg      [3:0] RxState;    // Receiver FSM state
reg      [3:0] NxtRxState;
reg      [3:0] RxTickCnt;  // Receiver Tick counter
wire     [3:0] NxtRxTickCnt;
wire           RxStateInc;// Bit pulse
reg      [6:0] RxShiftBuf;// Receiver shift data register
wire     [6:0] NxtRxShiftBuf;
reg            RxBufFull;
wire           NxtRxBufFull;
wire           RxBufSample;
wire           RxDataRead;
wire     [7:0] NxtRxBuf;

// Start of main code
// Read and write control signals
assign  ReadEnable = PSEL & (~PWRITE); // assert for whole APB read transfer
```

```verilog
  assign  WriteEnable = PSEL & (~PENABLE) & PWRITE; // assert for 1st cycle of write
transfer
  assign  WriteEnable00 = WriteEnable & (PADDR[7:2] == 6'b000000);
  assign  WriteEnable04 = WriteEnable & (PADDR[7:2] == 6'b000001);
  assign  WriteEnable08 = WriteEnable & (PADDR[7:2] == 6'b000010);
  assign  WriteEnable10 = WriteEnable & (PADDR[7:2] == 6'b000100);
  assign  WriteEnable14 = WriteEnable & (PADDR[7:2] == 6'b000101);
  assign  ReadEnable10  = PSEL & (~PWRITE) & (~PENABLE) & (PADDR[7:2] == 6'b000100);

  // Write operations
  // Control register
  always @(posedge PCLK or negedge PRESETn)
  begin
    if (~PRESETn)
      RegCTRL <= {4{1'b0}};
    else if (WriteEnable00)
      RegCTRL <= PWDATA[3:0];
  end

  // Status register
  assign NxtRxOverrun = (RegRxOverrun & ~(WriteEnable04 & PWDATA[3])) | RxOverrun;
  assign NxtTxOverrun = (RegTxOverrun & ~(WriteEnable04 & PWDATA[2])) | TxOverrun;

  always @(posedge PCLK or negedge PRESETn)
  begin
    if (~PRESETn)
      begin
      RegRxOverrun <= 1'b0;
      RegTxOverrun <= 1'b0;
      end
    else
      begin
      RegRxOverrun <= NxtRxOverrun;
      RegTxOverrun <= NxtTxOverrun;
      end
  end

  // Transmit data register
  always @(posedge PCLK or negedge PRESETn)
  begin
    if (~PRESETn)
      RegTxBuf <= {8{1'b0}};
    else if (WriteEnable08)
      RegTxBuf <= PWDATA[7:0];
  end

  // Baud rate divider - integer
  always @(posedge PCLK or negedge PRESETn)
  begin
    if (~PRESETn)
      RegBaudDiv <= {20{1'b0}};
    else if (WriteEnable10)
      RegBaudDiv <= PWDATA[19:0];
  end

  // Read operation
  assign UartStatus = {RegRxOverrun, RegTxOverrun, RxBufFull, TxBufFull};

  always @(PADDR or RegCTRL or UartStatus or RegBaudDiv or
  TxBufFull or RegRxBuf or RegTXINT or RegRXINT)
  begin
  case (PADDR[7:2])
   0: ReadMux =  {{4{1'b0}}, RegCTRL};
   1: ReadMux =  {{4{1'b0}}, UartStatus};
```

```
   2: ReadMux =  {{7{1'b0}}, TxBufFull};
   3: ReadMux =  RegRxBuf;
   4: ReadMux =  RegBaudDiv[7:0];
   5: ReadMux =  {{6{1'b0}}, RegTXINT, RegRXINT};
   default : ReadMux = {8{1'b0}}; // Read as 0 if address is out of range
  endcase
  end

// Register read data
always @(posedge PCLK or negedge PRESETn)
begin
  if (~PRESETn)
    begin
    ReadMuxReg      <= {8{1'b0}};
    ReadEnable10Reg <= 1'b0;
    end
  else
    begin
    ReadMuxReg      <= ReadMux;
    ReadEnable10Reg <= ReadEnable10;
    end
end

// Output read data to APB
assign PRDATA[ 7: 0] = (ReadEnable) ? ReadMuxReg : {8{1'b0}};
assign PRDATA[19: 8] = (ReadEnable10Reg) ? RegBaudDiv[19:8] : {12{1'b0}};
assign PRDATA[31: 20] = {12{1'b0}};
assign PREADY  = 1'b1; // Always ready
assign PSLVERR = 1'b0; // Always okay

// --------------------------------------------
// Baud rate generator
// Baud rate generator enable
assign BaudDivEn    = (RegCTRL[1:0] != 2'b00);
assign MappedCntrF  = {RegBaudCntrF[0],RegBaudCntrF[1],
                       RegBaudCntrF[2],RegBaudCntrF[3]};
// Reload Integer divider
// when UART enabled and (RegBaudCntrF < RegBaudDiv[3:0])
// then count to 1, or
// when UART enabled then count to 0
assign ReloadI      = (BaudDivEn &
       (((MappedCntrF >= RegBaudDiv[3:0]) &
     (RegBaudCntrI[15:1] == {15{1'b0}})) |
(RegBaudCntrI[15:0] == {16{1'b0}}))));
// Next state for Baud rate divider
assign NxtBaudCntrI = (BaudUpdated | ReloadI) ? RegBaudDiv[19:4] :
                      (RegBaudCntrI - {{15{1'b0}},BaudDivEn});
assign ReloadF      = BaudDivEn & (RegBaudCntrF==4'h0) &
                      ReloadI;
assign NxtBaudCntrF = (BaudUpdated) ? RegBaudDiv[3:0] :
                      (ReloadF)     ? 4'b1111 :
                      (RegBaudCntrF - {{3{1'b0}},ReloadI});
always @(posedge PCLK or negedge PRESETn)
begin
  if (~PRESETn)
    begin
    RegBaudCntrI    <= {16{1'b0}};
    RegBaudCntrF    <= {4{1'b0}};
    BaudUpdated     <= 1'b0;
    RegBaudTick     <= 1'b0;
    end
  else
    begin
    RegBaudCntrI    <= NxtBaudCntrI;
```

```
      RegBaudCntrF    <= NxtBaudCntrF;
      // Baud rate updated - to load new value to counters
      BaudUpdated     <= WriteEnable10;
      RegBaudTick     <= ReloadI;
      end
end

// Connect to external
assign BAUDTICK = RegBaudTick;

// --------------------------------------------
// Transmit

// Increment TickCounter
assign NxtTxTickCnt = ((TxState==4'h1) & RegBaudTick) ? 4'h0 :
                        TxTickCnt + {{3{1'b0}},RegBaudTick};

// Increment state (except Idle(0) and Wait for Tick(1))
assign TxStateInc   = (((&TxTickCnt)|(TxState==4'h1)) & RegBaudTick);
// Buffer full status
assign NxtTxBufFull = (WriteEnable08) | (TxBufFull & ~TxBufClear);
// Clear buffer full status when data is load into shift register
assign TxBufClear   = ((TxState==4'h0) & TxBufFull) |
                        ((TxState==4'hB) & TxBufFull & TxStateInc);

// TxState machine
// 0 = Idle, 1 =  Wait for Tick,
// 2 = Start bit, 3 = D0 .... 10 = D7
// 11 = Stop bit
always @(TxState or TxBufFull or TxTickCnt or TxStateInc or RegCTRL)
begin
case (TxState)
  0: begin
    NxtTxState = (TxBufFull & RegCTRL[0]) ? 1 : 0;  // New data is written to buffer
    end
  1: begin  // Wait for next Tick
    NxtTxState = TxState + {3'b0,TxStateInc};
    end
  2,3,4,5,6,7,8,9,10: begin  // Start bit, D0 - D7
    NxtTxState = TxState + {3'b0,TxStateInc};
    end
  11: begin // Stop bit , goto next start bit or Idle
    NxtTxState = (TxStateInc) ? ( TxBufFull ? 4'h2:4'h0) : TxState;
    end
  default: // Illegal state
    NxtTxState = 4'h0;
endcase
end

// Load/shift TX register
assign NxtTxShiftBuf = (((TxState==4'h0) & TxBufFull) |
                        ((TxState==4'hB) & TxBufFull &
      TxStateInc)) ? RegTxBuf :
                        (((TxState>4'h2) & TxStateInc) ?
      {1'b1,TxShiftBuf[7:1]} : TxShiftBuf[7:0]);

// Data output
assign NxtTxD = (TxState==2) ? 1'b0 :
                (TxState>4'h2) ? TxShiftBuf[0] : 1'b1;

// Registering outputs
always @(posedge PCLK or negedge PRESETn)
begin
  if (~PRESETn)
```

```
      begin
      TxBufFull      <= 1'b0;
      TxShiftBuf     <= {8{1'b0}};
      TxState        <= {4{1'b0}};
      TxTickCnt      <= {4{1'b0}};
      RegTxD         <= 1'b1;
      end
    else
      begin
      TxBufFull      <= NxtTxBufFull;
      TxShiftBuf     <= NxtTxShiftBuf;
      TxState        <= NxtTxState;
      TxTickCnt      <= NxtTxTickCnt;
      RegTxD         <= NxtTxD;
      end
  end

  // Generate TX overrun error status
  assign TxOverrun = TxBufFull & ~TxBufClear & WriteEnable08;

  // Connect to external
  assign TXD  = RegTxD;
  assign TXEN = RegCTRL[0];

// --------------------------------------------
// Receive synchronizer and low pass filter

  // Doubling Flip-flop synchronizer
  always @(posedge PCLK or negedge PRESETn)
  begin
    if (~PRESETn)
      begin
      RxDSync1 <= 1'b1;
      RxDSync2 <= 1'b1;
      end
    else
      begin
      RxDSync1 <= RXD;
      RxDSync2 <= RxDSync1;
      end
  end

  // Averaging low pass filter
  always @(posedge PCLK or negedge PRESETn)
  begin
    if (~PRESETn)
      RxDLPF <= 3'b111;
    else if (RegBaudTick)
      RxDLPF <= {RxDLPF[1:0], RxDSync2};
  end

  // Averaging values
  assign RxShiftIn = (RxDLPF[1] & RxDLPF[0]) |
                     (RxDLPF[1] & RxDLPF[2]) |
                     (RxDLPF[0] & RxDLPF[2]);

// --------------------------------------------
// Receive

  // Increment TickCounter
  assign NxtRxTickCnt = ((RxState==4'h0) & ~RxShiftIn) ? 4'h8 :
                        RxTickCnt + {{3{1'b0}},RegBaudTick};
  // Increment state
  assign RxStateInc   = ((&RxTickCnt) & RegBaudTick);
```

```
  // Shift register
  assign NxtRxShiftBuf= (RxStateInc) ? {RxShiftIn, RxShiftBuf[6:1]} : RxShiftBuf;
  // Buffer full status
  assign NxtRxBufFull = RxBufSample | (RxBufFull & ~RxDataRead);

  // Sample shift register when D7 is sampled
  assign RxBufSample  = ((RxState==4'h9) & RxStateInc);

  // Sample receive buffer
  assign NxtRxBuf     = (RxBufSample) ? {RxShiftIn,RxShiftBuf} : RegRxBuf;
  // Reading receive buffer (Set at 1st cycle of APB transfer
  // because read mux is registered before output)
  assign RxDataRead   = (PSEL & ~PENABLE & (PADDR[7:2]==3) & ~PWRITE);
  // Generate RX overrun error status
  assign RxOverrun = RxBufFull & RxBufSample & ~RxDataRead;

  // RxState machine
  // 0 = Idle, 1 =  Start of Start bit detected
  // 2 = Sample Start bit, 3 = D0 .... 10 = D7
  // 11 = Stop bit
  always @(RxState or RxShiftIn or RxTickCnt or RxStateInc or RegCTRL)
  begin
  case (RxState)
    0: begin
       NxtRxState = ((~RxShiftIn) & RegCTRL[1]) ? 1 : 0;  // Wait for Start bit
       end
    1: begin  // Wait for middle of start bit
       NxtRxState = RxState + {3'b0,RxStateInc};
       end
    2,3,4,5,6,7,8,9: begin  // D0 - D7
       NxtRxState = RxState + {3'b0,RxStateInc};
       end
    10: begin // Stop bit , goto back to Idle
       NxtRxState = (RxStateInc) ? 0 : 10;
       end
    default: // Illegal state
       NxtRxState = 4'h0;
  endcase
  end


  // Registering
  always @(posedge PCLK or negedge PRESETn)
  begin
    if (~PRESETn)
      begin
      RxBufFull       <= 1'b0;
      RxShiftBuf      <= {7{1'b0}};
      RxState         <= {4{1'b0}};
      RxTickCnt       <= {4{1'b0}};
      RegRxBuf        <= {8{1'b0}};
      end
    else
      begin
      RxBufFull       <= NxtRxBufFull;
      RxShiftBuf      <= NxtRxShiftBuf;
      RxState         <= NxtRxState;
      RxTickCnt       <= NxtRxTickCnt;
      RegRxBuf        <= NxtRxBuf;
      end
  end

// ----------------------------------------------
// Interrupts
  assign NxtTXINT = RegCTRL[2] & TxBufFull & TxBufClear; // Falling edge of buffer full
```

197

```verilog
      assign NxtRXINT = RegCTRL[3] & RxBufSample; // A new receive data is sampled

      // Registering outputs
      always @(posedge PCLK or negedge PRESETn)
      begin
        if (~PRESETn)
          begin
          RegTXINT <= 1'b0;
          RegRXINT <= 1'b0;
          end
        else
          begin
          RegTXINT <= NxtTXINT|(RegTXINT & ~(WriteEnable14 & PWDATA[1]));
          RegRXINT <= NxtRXINT|(RegRXINT & ~(WriteEnable14 & PWDATA[0]));
          end
      end

      // Connect to external
      assign TXINT = RegTXINT;
      assign RXINT = RegRXINT;

   endmodule
```

8.3 ID registers

Many Arm peripherals and CoreSight debug components contain a range of read-only ID registers at the end of the 4KB memory spaces. These ID values enable debug tools to identify debug components automatically (as described in Section 5.2.7 Debug components discovery), and they allow the software to determine the revision of the design so that it knows what features are available. In some cases, such information is also useful for software to implement a workaround if certain defects in the peripheral design can be overcome by using software measures.

Peripheral IP from Arm normally uses the following peripheral ID format:

Name	Address offset	Type	Descriptions
PID4	0xFD0	RO	Peripheral ID register 4 [7:4] Block count [3:0] jep106_c_code (see Section 5.2.7)
PID5	0xFD4	RO	Peripheral ID register 5, usually tied to 0
PID6	0xFD8	RO	Peripheral ID register 6, usually tied to 0
PID7	0xFDC	RO	Peripheral ID register 7, usually tied to 0
PID0	0xFE0	RO	Peripheral ID register 0 [7:0] Part number [7:0]
PID1	0xFE4	RO	Peripheral ID register 1 [7:4] jep106_id[3:0] (see Section 5.2.7) [3:0] Part number [11:8]
PID2	0xFE8	RO	Peripheral ID register 2 [7:4] Revision [3] jedec_used [2:0] jep106_id[6:4] (see Section 5.2.7)
PID3	0xFEC	RO	Peripheral ID register 3 [7:4] ECO Revision number [3:0] Customer modification number
CID0	0xFF0	RO	Component ID register 0
CID1	0xFF4	RO	Component ID register 1
CID2	0xFF8	RO	Component ID register 2
CID3	0xFFC	RO	Component ID register 3

Table 8.4: Peripheral ID format.

One of the ID registers, PID3, contains an Engineering Change Order (ECO) bit field which can be generated from input signals. The ECO operation enables you to carry out minor design changes in the late stage of a chip design process; for example, at the silicon mask level. By providing an external input to provide ECO input field, it is possible to use tie-off cells on those peripheral inputs to reflect ECO maintenance revisions.

The ID registers are not strictly required for peripheral operation. In ultra-low-power designs, you can remove these ID registers to reduce gate count and power consumption.

When you modify a peripheral from Arm's product range, it is recommended that you alter the JEDEC ID value and the part number in the ID registers to indicate that the peripheral is no longer identical to the original version from Arm. Alternatively, you can remove these ID registers.

8.4 Other peripheral design considerations

8.4.1 Security of system control functions

Typically, a peripheral unit that controls the system (e.g., clock and power control functions) should be privileged access only. If TrustZone security is implemented (for Cortex-M23 and Cortex-M33 processors), these functions could also be Secure access only, and Secure firmware needs to provide APIs for Non-secure software to request system control configuration updates. This prevents untrusted software from stopping critical system functions.

8.4.2 Processor's halting

Potentially some peripherals like watchdog timers might need to suspend their operations when the processor is halted. Otherwise, a reset could be triggered unexpectedly during debugging. Some timers (e.g., SysTick timers inside the Cortex-M processors) also stop counting automatically when the processor is halted to allow single-stepping of application code.

8.4.3 Handling of 64-bit data

In some cases, timers might need to handle 64-bit count values, but the bus interface of a peripheral might be only 32-bit. In such cases, the timer needs to include:

- Include a 64-bit sampling register to allow a 64-bit counter value to be sampled in one go, and then read out using two accesses;

- Include a 64-bit transfer register to allow new 64-bit values to be set up using multiple accesses, and then be transferred into the counter using a separated control register.

Additional information on this topic is available on Arm's website:
https://developer.arm.com/docs/103489550/latest/accessing-64-bit-peripherals-using-cortex-m-processors

CHAPTER 9

Putting the system together

9.1 Creating a simple microcontroller-like system

After designing the bus infrastructure components and peripherals, we can then put together
a processor system and simulate it in a simulator. In this section, we will cover a very simple
microcontroller-like design based on the Cortex-M3 processor (DesignStart) and the components that
we created in the last two chapters.

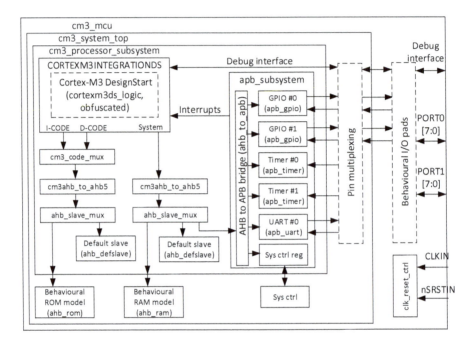

Figure 9.1: Simple microcontroller example.

The design contains multiple levels of design hierarchy – as follows:

▪ The processor subsystem contains the processor and the bus infrastructure components, as well as
the APB subsystem where digital peripherals are located.

▪ The APB subsystem contains the AHB to APB bridge, as well as peripherals (digital parts only).
In this example, we have:

☐ Two GPIO ports (8-bit each);

☐ Two timers;

☐ One UART;

☐ Registers for system control function are also placed here.

- The behavior memory models are one level up in the design hierarchy (cm3_system_top). This level also contains the pin multiplexing.

- The top-level of the microcontroller (cm3_mcu) contains the top-level of the Cortex-M3 system the clock reset control (e.g., clock gating, reset synchronizers) and I/O pads.

This is a simple design just for illustration and educational purposes. In the real world, microcontroller designs are likely to be much more complex; for example:

- Most commercial microcontrollers have a lot more peripherals, including analog peripherals.

- In real microcontrollers, there might be additional bus masters such as DMA controllers.

- In SoC design, RAM, ROM (or embedded flash macros) would be likely to have power management/ control features.

- If embedded flash is used, flash programming support requires additional control registers and a voltage booster (e.g., DC-DC converter).

- Many microcontrollers also have on-chip DC-DC converters to provide lower voltage (~ 1 to 1.2 volts) for digital circuitries. The supply voltage for the chip normally ranges from 1.8 volts to 3.6 volts.

- Additional circuits are needed for chip manufacturing testing. This topic is commonly known as DFT (Design for Testing) and will be covered later.

- Power management in modern microcontrollers can be quite complex. For example, there can be multiple power domains and many clock domains and runtime power mode options. In addition, some of them have separate retention SRAM for holding crucial data while in very low-power sleep modes.

- Various security features might be needed depending on targeted applications.

9.2 Design partitioning

After looking at Figure 9.1, some of you might wonder if there is anything that needs to be considered when defining the design hierarchy? There are indeed several aspects to bear in mind, notably:

- The cm3_processor_subsystem-level contains only synthesizable components. This enables us to synthesize most of the digital parts in one go. If the memory macros require bus wrappers, we can also move the bus wrappers into the processor subsystem in order to synthesize them all in one place.

- A peripheral/APB subsystem is designed as one unit – this allows it to be reused in multiple designs. The system control function is split into two halves: one part of it is in the programmable registers inside the APB subsystem, while the other half is located at a higher level. The reason is that in many SoC designs, the system control function might involve non-synthesizable IP such as voltage control or clock control logic. If a system contains analog peripherals, then it is also possible to use the same arrangement to separate synthesizable and non-synthesizable parts of any analog peripherals in the design hierarchy.

■ Pin multiplexing is also placed outside of the processor subsystem – this enables the same peripheral subsystem to be used with different projects, which can have different chip packages and hence different pin multiplexing arrangements. Another reason for this is that the pin multiplexing might also need to handle pins from analog components at this level.

■ I/O pads are instantiated in the design (in this example, behavioral models of I/O pads are used for simulations). In SoC design, it is often essential to instantiate I/O pads based on electrical characteristics of the pin functions. Usually, various types of input, output, and tristate pads are available for each semiconductor process node with different drive strengths and different speeds. The behavioral models for I/O pads can be used directly in FPGA synthesis, as FPGA development tools can help you to define I/O characteristics using a project's configuration files.

■ Clock gating is handled at a high level in the design hierarchy. This can help simplify the setup of clock tree synthesis. In this case, the clock gating is done in a design unit called clk_reset_ctrl at the top-level.

■ If your SoC design needs to support multiple power domains, it is also important to partition designs based on the power domains. In design units where multiple blocks of different power domains are present; it is best not to have any logic functions inside those hierarchical files to simplify power domain handling in implementation flow.

9.3 What is inside a simulation environment?

A number of Verilog simulators are available on the market. In the majority of Arm Cortex-M processor deliverables, we support the following products: Mentor Modelsim/Questasim, Cadence NC Verilog, and Synopsys VCS. Other simulators could be used, although the deliverables only include the simulation scripts that are mentioned above.

To simulate the simple MCU design, we also need a testbench. A testbench is a simulated environment in which the microcontroller system will be working. In addition to the processor system, which we will call DUT (Device-Under-Test), the simulation environment typically contains a number of other components:

■ Clock and reset signal generator(s).

■ Trickbox(es) that provide input stimulus to the DUT and might also interface with outputs from the DUT. This is optional. In the case of testing a microcontroller-like system, it is possible to use some form of loopback signal connections as a trickbox to test peripheral interfaces.

■ In some cases, simulation models of external memories or external peripherals might also be needed to test some of the interfaces on the DUT. For example, if your system design supports external memories, then you will need to add a model of the external memory in the testbench for testing external memory accesses.

- For a processor testbench, it is also common to add some mechanism to allow message display under the control of software in the processor. For example, when the processor executes a "printf("Hello world\n")" statement, the "Hello world" message can be displayed in the simulator's console.

- Other verification components – one of the techniques for verification is to add a range of verification components like bus protocol checkers in the simulation (some of these components can be inside the DUT). If something goes wrong, for example, illegal bus behavior is observed, the verification component can stop the simulation and report the errors.

In our example testbench, a UART monitor (uart_mon.v) is used to display text messages generated by software (e.g., using printf function). This unit is also used to end the simulation when it receives a special character.

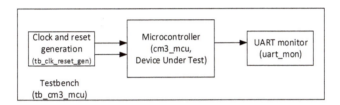

Figure 9.2: Testbench for simple microcontroller example.

To run a system-level simulation, the program memory of the processor system also needs to contain a valid program. Therefore, we need to prepare some minimal software code and a compilation setup to enable us to do a basic simulation.

9.4 Prepare the minimal software support for simulation

9.4.1 Overview of example code based on CMSIS-CORE

For our example simulation, we are going to create our example code based on the CMSIS-CORE software framework. The CMSIS-CORE header files are widely used in the microcontroller industry and can make software development easier. Nevertheless, we do need to create a range of files:

File	Descriptions
cm3_mcu.h	Device-specific header based on CMSIS-CORE. This contains the peripheral register definitions and interrupt assignments.
startup_cm3_mcu.s	Assembly startup file – this contains the reset handler, default handlers, and the vector table
uart_util.c	Simple UART functions to configure the UART and basic UART transmit and receive function. This is used for supporting message display during simulation.
system_cm3_mcu.c	This provides SystemInit(void) usually used for system clock initialization
system_cm3_mcu.h	Header file that declares functions available in system_cm3_mcu.c
hello.c	Simple hello world message display and demo

Table 9.1: Source file created for minimal software support based on CMSIS-CORE.

The assembly startup code (startup_cm3_mcu.s) is toolchain-specific. For this demo, we use Arm assembler from Arm Compiler 5 (this is available as a part of Arm Development Studio as well Keil Microcontroller Development Kit, MDK-ARM).

To support the printf function with redirection to the UART, the Arm software development toolchain Keil MDK-ARM provides the following files:

File	Descriptions
retarget_io.h	Contains low level functions for retargeting I/O functions
RTE_Components.h	Configuration file for retarget_io.h

Table 9.2: Source file created for minimal software support based on CMSIS-CORE.

For applications that do not use I/O functions like printf, puts, gets, etc., these two files are not required.

9.4.2 Device header file, for example, MCU (cm3_mcu.h)

With the CMSIS-CORE software framework, each microcontroller device has its device header file, and the filenames are defined by chip vendors. You can create this file by modifying examples from Arm (e.g., the Cortex-M DesignStart packages contain example files).

One part of the header is Interrupt Number Definition. In our simple MCU example, it has only 6 interrupts, the numbers of which are defined as follows:

```
/*
 * ==========================================================================
 * ---------- Interrupt Number Definition ------------------------------------
 * ==========================================================================
 */

typedef enum IRQn
{
/******  Cortex-M3 Processor Exceptions Numbers  ****************************************
*/
  NonMaskableInt_IRQn      = -14,   /*!<  2 Cortex-M3 Non Maskable Interrupt
*/
  HardFault_IRQn           = -13,   /*!<  3 Cortex-M3 Hard Fault Interrupt
*/
  MemoryManagement_IRQn    = -12,   /*!<  4 Cortex-M3 Memory Management Interrupt
*/
  BusFault_IRQn            = -11,   /*!<  5 Cortex-M3 Bus Fault Interrupt
*/
  UsageFault_IRQn          = -10,   /*!<  6 Cortex-M3 Usage Fault Interrupt
*/
  SVCall_IRQn              = -5,    /*!< 11 Cortex-M3 SV Call Interrupt
*/
  DebugMonitor_IRQn        = -4,    /*!< 12 Cortex-M3 Debug Monitor Interrupt
*/
  PendSV_IRQn              = -2,    /*!< 14 Cortex-M3 Pend SV Interrupt
*/
  SysTick_IRQn             = -1,    /*!< 15 Cortex-M3 System Tick Interrupt
*/
```

```
/****** CM3MCU Specific Interrupt Numbers **********************************************/
  GPIO0_IRQn              = 0,        /*!< Port 0 combined Interrupt
*/
  GPIO1_IRQn              = 1,        /*!< Port 0 combined Interrupt
*/
  TIMER0_IRQn             = 2,        /*!< TIMER 0 Interrupt
*/
  TIMER1_IRQn             = 3,        /*!< TIMER 1 Interrupt
*/
  UARTTX0_IRQn            = 4,        /*!< UART 0 TX Interrupt
*/
  UARTRX0_IRQn            = 5,        /*!< UART 0 RX Interrupt
*/
} IRQn_Type;
```

Another part of this header file that needs some effort to create is the register definitions. In CMSIS-CORE, peripheral registers are defined as C struct and use a pointer declaration to create the peripheral definitions. An example of the C struct for the simple APB timer is as follows:

```
*-------------- Timer (Timer) ------------*/
/** @addtogroup Timer
  memory-mapped structure for Timer
  @{
*/
typedef struct
{
    __IO   uint32_t  CTRL;       /*!< Offset: 0x000 Control Register   (R/ ) */
    __IO   uint32_t  CURRVAL;    /*!< Offset: 0x004 Current Value Register (R/W) */
    __IO   uint32_t  RELOAD;     /*!< Offset: 0x008 Reload Value Register  (R/W) */
    __IO   uint32_t  IRQSTATE;   /*!< Offset: 0x00C Interrupt State Register (R/W) */
} CM3MCU_TIMER_TypeDef;

/*@}*/ /* end of group  Timer */
```

You can also add C macros to declare the bit fields in the registers.

```
#define CM3MCU_TIMER_CTRL_EN_pos          0                                          /*!<
CM3MCU_TIMER_CTRL_EN_Pos: Enable Position */
#define CM3MCU_TIMER_CTRL_EN_Msk          (0x1ul << CM3MCU_TIMER_CTRL_EN_pos)        /*!<
CM3MCU_TIMER ENABLE : Timer Enable Mask */
#define CM3MCU_TIMER_CTRL_ExtENSel_pos 1                                             /*!<
CM3MCU_TIMER_CTRL_ExtENSel_Pos: Ext Enable Sel Position */
#define CM3MCU_TIMER_CTRL_ExtENSel_Msk (0x1ul << CM3MCU_TIMER_CTRL_ExtENSel_pos) /*!<
CM3MCU_TIMER ExtENSel : Timer Ext Enable Sel Mask */
#define CM3MCU_TIMER_CTRL_ExtClkSel_pos 2                                           /*!<
CM3MCU_TIMER_CTRL_ExtClkSel_Pos: Ext Clock select Position */
#define CM3MCU_TIMER_CTRL_ExtClkSel_Msk (0x1ul << CM3MCU_TIMER_CTRL_ExtClkSel_pos)
/*!< CM3MCU_TIMER ExtClkSel : Timer Ext Clock select Mask */
#define CM3MCU_TIMER_CTRL_IRQEN_pos       3                                          /*!<
CM3MCU_TIMER_CTRL_IRQEN_Pos: IRQ Enable Position */
#define CM3MCU_TIMER_CTRL_IRQEN_Msk       (0x1ul << CM3MCU_TIMER_CTRL_IRQEN_pos)     /*!<
CM3MCU_TIMER ENABLE : Timer IRQ Enable Mask */
#define CM3MCU_TIMER_CURRVAL_pos          0                                          /*!<
CM3MCU_TIMER_CURRVAL_pos: Current Value Position */
#define CM3MCU_TIMER_CURRVAL_Msk          (0xFFFFFFFFul << CM3MCU_TIMER_CURRVAL_pos)/*!<
```

```
CM3MCU_TIMER CURRVAL : Current Value Mask */
#define CM3MCU_TIMER_RELOAD_pos             0                                        /*!<
CM3MCU_TIMER_RELOAD_pos: Reload Value Position */
#define CM3MCU_TIMER_RELOAD_Msk            (0xFFFFFFFFul << CM3MCU_TIMER_RELOAD_pos) /*!<
CM3MCU_TIMER RELOAD : Reload Value Mask */
#define CM3MCU_TIMER_IRQSTATE_pos           0                                        /*!<
CM3MCU_TIMER_IRQSTATE_pos: IRQSTATE Position */
#define CM3MCU_TIMER_IRQSTATE_Msk          (0x1ul << CM3MCU_TIMER_IRQSTATE_pos)      /*!<
CM3MCU_TIMER IRQSTATE : IRQ Status Mask */
```

The final part of this file that you need to add is the memory map and peripheral definitions:

```
/*****************************************************************************/
/*                         Peripheral memory map                          */
/*****************************************************************************/
/** @addtogroup CM3MCU_MemoryMap CM3MCU Memory Mapping
   @{
*/


/* Peripheral and SRAM base address */
#define CM3MCU_FLASH_BASE          (0x00000000UL)  /*!< (FLASH     ) Base Address */
#define CM3MCU_SRAM_BASE           (0x20000000UL)  /*!< (SRAM      ) Base Address */
#define CM3MCU_PERIPH_BASE         (0x40000000UL)  /*!< (Peripheral) Base Address */
#define CM3MCU_RAM_BASE            (0x20000000UL)

/* APB peripherals                                                          */
#define CM3MCU_GPIO0_BASE          (CM3MCU_PERIPH_BASE + 0x0000UL)
#define CM3MCU_GPIO1_BASE          (CM3MCU_PERIPH_BASE + 0x1000UL)
#define CM3MCU_TIMER0_BASE         (CM3MCU_PERIPH_BASE + 0x2000UL)
#define CM3MCU_TIMER1_BASE         (CM3MCU_PERIPH_BASE + 0x3000UL)
#define CM3MCU_UART0_BASE          (CM3MCU_PERIPH_BASE + 0x4000UL)

/*@}*/ /* end of group CM3MCU_MemoryMap */


/*****************************************************************************/
/*                         Peripheral declaration                         */
/*****************************************************************************/
/** @addtogroup CM3MCU_PeripheralDecl CM3MCU_CM3 Peripheral Declaration
   @{
*/

#define CM3MCU_GPIO0               ((CM3MCU_GPIO_TypeDef    *) CM3MCU_GPIO0_BASE )
#define CM3MCU_GPIO1               ((CM3MCU_GPIO_TypeDef    *) CM3MCU_GPIO1_BASE )
#define CM3MCU_TIMER0              ((CM3MCU_TIMER_TypeDef   *) CM3MCU_TIMER0_BASE )
#define CM3MCU_TIMER1              ((CM3MCU_TIMER_TypeDef   *) CM3MCU_TIMER1_BASE )
#define CM3MCU_UART0               ((CM3MCU_UART_TypeDef    *) CM3MCU_UART0_BASE )

/*@}*/ /* end of group CM3MCU_PeripheralDecl */
```

9.4.3 Device startup file for example MCU (startup_cm3_mcu.s)

The device startup file can be based on assembly language or C. The requirement and syntax (if using assembly language) is toolchain-specific. Here we use the assembly syntax for Arm assembler. Two parts of modifications are needed when modifying an existing startup code to fit your own devices:

1. Vector table definition;

2. Default handler definition.

The vector table for our example microcontroller is shown below:

```
; Vector Table Mapped to Address 0 at Reset

                AREA     RESET, DATA, READONLY
                EXPORT   __Vectors
                EXPORT   __Vectors_End
                EXPORT   __Vectors_Size

__Vectors       DCD      __initial_sp              ; Top of Stack
                DCD      Reset_Handler             ; Reset Handler
                DCD      NMI_Handler               ; NMI Handler
                DCD      HardFault_Handler         ; Hard Fault Handler
                DCD      MemManage_Handler         ; MPU Fault Handler
                DCD      BusFault_Handler          ; Bus Fault Handler
                DCD      UsageFault_Handler        ; Usage Fault Handler
                DCD      0                         ; Reserved
                DCD      0                         ; Reserved
                DCD      0                         ; Reserved
                DCD      0                         ; Reserved
                DCD      SVC_Handler               ; SVCall Handler
                DCD      DebugMon_Handler          ; Debug Monitor Handler
                DCD      0                         ; Reserved
                DCD      PendSV_Handler            ; PendSV Handler
                DCD      SysTick_Handler           ; SysTick Handler
                DCD      GPIO0_Handler             ; GPIO 0 Handler
                DCD      GPIO1_Handler             ; GPIO 1 Handler
                DCD      TIMER0_Handler            ; TIMER 0 handler
                DCD      TIMER1_Handler            ; TIMER 1 handler
                DCD      UARTTX0_Handler           ; UART 0 TX Handler
                DCD      UARTRX0_Handler           ; UART 0 RX Handler
__Vectors_End
```

Just like the interrupt number assignment in the device-specific header file (cm3_mcu.h), the vector assignment needs to match the IRQ assignments in the Verilog RTL file. The names of the interrupt handlers must also match the name definitions of the default handlers in the startup code, which is the second part of modification as shown below:

```
Default_Handler PROC
                EXPORT  GPIO0_Handler              [WEAK]
                EXPORT  GPIO1_Handler              [WEAK]
                EXPORT  TIMER0_Handler             [WEAK]
                EXPORT  TIMER1_Handler             [WEAK]
                EXPORT  UARTTX0_Handler            [WEAK]
                EXPORT  UARTRX0_Handler            [WEAK]
UARTRX0_Handler
UARTTX0_Handler
GPIO0_Handler
GPIO1_Handler
TIMER0_Handler
TIMER1_Handler
                B       .      ; dead loop
                ENDP
```

9.4.4 UART utilities

After we have the peripheral definitions in the device-specific header (cm3_mcu.h), we can create a C program file to provide simple functions for UART configuration, transmit and receive functions.

```c
#include "cm3_mcu.h"

void uart_config(void);
void uart_putc(char c);
char uart_getc(void);
int stdout_putchar (int ch);

void uart_config(void)
{
  CM3MCU_UART0->BAUDDIV = 32;
  CM3MCU_UART0->CTRL = 1; // Enable TX

  return;
}

void uart_putc(char c)
{
  while (CM3MCU_UART0->STATE & 1); // wait if TX FIFO full
  CM3MCU_UART0->TXD = (uint32_t) c;
  return;
}

char uart_getc(void)
{
  while ((CM3MCU_UART0->STATE & 2)==0); // wait if RX FIFO empty
  return ((char) CM3MCU_UART0->RXD);
}

// Function used by retarget_io.c
int stdout_putchar (int ch)
{
  uart_putc(ch);
  return (ch);
}
```

Combining this utility file and the UART monitor in the testbench, we can output text messages and display them in the simulation console.

9.4.5 System initialization function

The file system_cm3_mcu.c provides a system initialization routine (SystemInit(void)) which is called by the reset handler in the startup code. This function is often used for setting up Phase-Locked Loop (PLL) and clock configurations but might also contain other initialization steps.

In our implementation of system_cm3_mcu.c, the only step carried out by SystemInit is setting up variables which define the system clock speed. These variables can then be used by the application codes - see below:

```c
#include <stdint.h>
#include "cm3_mcu.h"

/*------------------------------------------------------------------
   DEFINES
 *----------------------------------------------------------------*/

/*------------------------------------------------------------------
   Define clocks
 *----------------------------------------------------------------*/

#define XTAL      (50000000UL)               /* Oscillator frequency        */

/*------------------------------------------------------------------
   Clock Variable definitions
 *----------------------------------------------------------------*/
uint32_t SystemCoreClock = XTAL;     /*!< Processor Clock Frequency    */


/*------------------------------------------------------------------
   Clock functions
 *----------------------------------------------------------------*/
void SystemCoreClockUpdate (void)              /* Get Core Clock Frequency    */
{
SystemCoreClock = XTAL;
}

/**
 * Initialize the system
 *
 * @param  none
 * @return none
 *
 * @brief  Setup the microcontroller system.
 *         Initialize the System.
 */
void SystemInit (void)
{
SystemCoreClock = XTAL;

  return;
}
```

The file system_cm3_mcu.h is only used to provide function prototypes of functions available in system_cm3_mcu.c. Application code might call those functions if the application needs to update clock configurations during runtime.

9.4.6 Retargeting

With all these files prepared, you can now create an application that boots up and utilizes the peripherals to do some basic control operations. You can also create a hello world application as follows:

```c
#include "cm3_mcu.h"
#include <stdio.h>

extern void uart_config(void);
extern void uart_putc(char c);

int main(void)
{
  uart_config();
  printf ("Hello world\n");
  uart_putc(4);// end simulation
  while(1);
}
```

When using the printf function, the compilation needs some way of knowing where the message needs to be directed to. The redirection of these messages could be handled by:

- Semi-hosting support in the debugger (note: this is not supported in Keil MDK-ARM);

- Peripheral (e.g., UART);

- Instrumentation Trace Macrocell (ITM) in Armv7-M or Armv8-M Mainline processors via a trace connection (e.g., Serial Wire Output).

The file retarget_io.c supporting multiple redirection methods are listed above. To select UART as standard output (stdout), the file RTE_Components.h defines the following C macros used by retarget_io.h:

```c
#define RTE_Compiler_IO_STDOUT        /* Compiler I/O: STDOUT */
#define RTE_Compiler_IO_STDOUT_User   /* Compiler I/O: STDOUT User */
```

When these C macros are defined, the retarget_io.c selects a user-defined stdout_puchar(int ch) function for standard outputs.

```c
/**
  Put a character to the stdout

  \param[in]   ch  Character to output
  \return          the character written, or -1 on write error.
*/
#if   defined(RTE_Compiler_IO_STDOUT)
#if   defined(RTE_Compiler_IO_STDOUT_User)
extern int stdout_putchar (int ch);
...
```

By defining this stdout_puchar(int ch) function in uart_util.c to output the character to UART, we will be able to collect and display printf messages in simulations.

9.4.7 Other software support package considerations

After creating the basic software support files, a range of system-level simulations can be carried out. However, if you are a SoC designer and you want to make it easier for your customers to adopt your products, there is more work to do:

Device drivers – Typically, chip vendors provide a range of device drivers to access peripheral functions and hence help software developers to create applications quickly. One of the products in the CMSIS is **CMSIS-Driver**, which provides device driver API definitions for a range of communication peripherals. This can help software developers to port their applications to your device.

Device and Board support packages – Typically, chip vendors need to bundle together the relevant software packages to enable users to download all the essential files quickly and easily. To make it even better, the CMSIS team has created a **CMSIS-PACK** framework that is integrated with development toolchains (an Eclipse plug-in for Eclipse-based IDE is also available) to enable software developers to download software packages and dependent packages (if needed). The CMSIS-PACK standard also specifies XML description files that provide essential information about the packages such as the devices supported. Utilities for creating CMSIS-PACK are available from Arm at: https://arm-software.github.io/CMSIS_5/Pack/html/createPackUtil.html. For more information, please visit https://arm-software.github.io/CMSIS_5/Pack/html/index.html

CMSIS-SVD – Another useful part of the CMSIS is the System View Description (SVD), which is an XML-based file to describe a programmer's model of peripherals in the chip. Using this file, debug tools can visualize peripheral register states to allow software developers to analyze the status of the system more easily.

Flash programming – If your chip contains embedded flash memories, you need to prepare flash programming support for your customers. This is provided as part of the CMSIS-PACK, and you can find more information about creating CMSIS-PACK compatible flash programming algorithms at https://arm-software.github.io/CMSIS_5/Pack/html/flashAlgorithm.html

9.5 System-level simulation

9.5.1 Compiling hello world

After the software files are created, you can compile the files either using Keil MDK-ARM or DS-5. For many chip designers using a Linux environment, it is easier to create a "makefile" and handle the compilation in a shell environment. A simple "makefile" for Arm Compiler 5 can be as follows:

```
# Makefile using Arm Compiler 5
INC_DIR1 = cmsis_include
INC_DIR2 = .
USER_DEF =
ARM_CC_OPTS  = --cpu Cortex-M3 -c -O3 -g -Otime -I $(INC_DIR1) -I $(INC_DIR2)
ARM_ASM_OPTS = --cpu Cortex-M3 -g
ARM_LINK_OPTS = "--keep=startup_cm3_mcu.o(RESET)" "--first=startup_cm3_mcu.o(RESET)" \
      --rw_base 0x20000000 --ro_base 0x00000000 --map

all: hello.hex hello.lst
hello.o: hello.c
 armcc $(ARM_CC_OPTS) $< -o   $@

system_cm3_mcu.o: system_cm3_mcu.c
 armcc $(ARM_CC_OPTS) $< -o   $@

uart_util.o: uart_util.c
 armcc $(ARM_CC_OPTS) $< -o   $@

retarget_io.o: retarget_io.c RTE_Components.h
 armcc $(ARM_CC_OPTS) $< -o   $@

startup_cm3_mcu.o: startup_cm3_mcu.s
 armasm $(ARM_ASM_OPTS) $< -o   $@

hello.elf: hello.o system_cm3_mcu.o uart_util.o retarget_io.o startup_cm3_mcu.o
 armlink hello.o system_cm3_mcu.o uart_util.o retarget_io.o startup_cm3_mcu.o $(ARM_LINK_
OPTS) -o $@

hello.hex : hello.elf
 fromelf --vhx --8x1 $< --output $@


hello.lst : hello.elf
 fromelf -c -d -e -s $< --output $@

clean:
 rm *.o
 rm *.elf
 rm *.lst
 rm *.hex
```

To allow the behavior ROM model to load the program image into it, we need to generate a hex file which contains a list of 8-bit hexadecimal values. This is generated with the fromelf utility. If you are using Keil MDK, you can add this in your project options to execute fromelf after compilation is done.

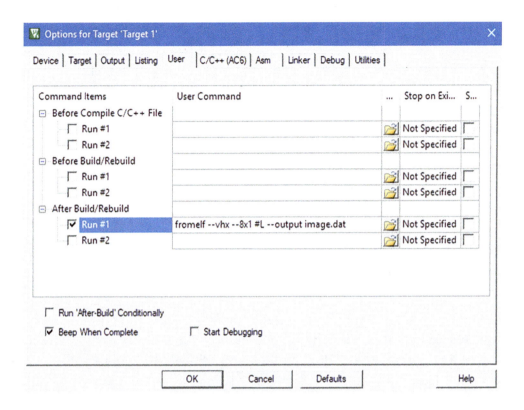

Figure 9.3: Specify additional step to be carried out after compilation in Keil MDK-ARM.

Note: The symbol #L refers to the filename of the generated executable.

9.5.2 Using Modelsim/QuestaSim to compile and simulate the design

There are quite a number of Verilog files in the design. To make the handling of the compile flow easier, a Verilog command file (tbench_cm3.vc) is created:

```
// Verilog Command File for Cortex-M3 simulation
// ============= Verilog library extensions ============
+libext+.v+.vlib

// ============= Module search path =============
-y ../cortex_m3/cortexm3integration_ds_obs/verilog/
-y ../mcu_system
-y .

// ============= Include file search path =============
//+incdir+dirname
+incdir+../cortex_m3/cortexm3integration_ds_obs/verilog/

../cortex_m3/cortexm3integration_ds/verilog/cm3_code_mux.v
tbench_cm3.v
```

This Verilog command file contains the search path, and any additional design files need to be included in the compilation. With this file, we can launch the compilation with the following commands:

```
vlib work   # Create work library - need to do it once only
vlog -incr -lint +v2k -f tbench_cm3.vc -novopt
```

Several options are used in this compilation:

- The option "-incr" means incremental compilation, so if a file hasn't been changed since the last compilation, it can be skipped.

- "-lint" is to enable lint checking, which flags up various possible design errors.

- "-novopt" is used to help maintain all the internal information of the design which can help analysis of its behavior in waveform windows. Without this option, the optimization will remove a lot of internal signal details to speed up the simulation but can be very hard to debug. This option should not be used for regression testing.

After the compilation is carried out successfully, and assuming that the hex file of the software image is prepared and is in the current directory as image.dat, we can start the simulation with:

```
vsim -novopt -gui tbench_cm3
```

The use of "-gui" launches the GUI to allow us to add a waveform window. This is optional. If everything works, you can start the simulation with "run -all." The "Hello world" message should be displayed, and the simulation stop automatically when the program sends a special character (0x4) to the UART monitor.

```
# Reading pref.tcl
# //  Questa Sim
# //  Version 10.6e linux Jun 22, 2018
# //
# //  Copyright 1991-2018 Mentor Graphics Corporation
# //  All Rights Reserved.
# //
# //  QuestaSim and its associated documentation contain trade
# //  secrets and commercial or financial information that are the property of
# //  Mentor Graphics Corporation and are privileged, confidential,
# //  and exempt from disclosure under the Freedom of Information Act,
# //  5 U.S.C. Section 552. Furthermore, this information
# //  is prohibited from disclosure under the Trade Secrets Act,
# //  18 U.S.C. Section 1905.
# //
# vsim -novopt -gui tbench_cm3
# Start time: 22:31:20 on Apr 12,2019
```

```
# ** Warning: (vsim-8891) All optimizations are turned off because the -novopt switch is in
effect. This will cause your simulation to run very slowly. If you are using this switch
to preserve visibility for Debug or PLI features please see the User's Manual section on
Preserving Object Visibility with vopt.
# Loading work.tbench_cm3
# Loading work.tb_clk_reset_gen
# Loading work.cm3_mcu
# Loading work.clk_reset_ctrl
# Loading work.behavioral_clk_gate
# Loading work.cm3_system_top
# Loading work.cm3_processor_subsystem
# Loading work.CORTEXM3INTEGRATIONDS
# Loading work.cortexm3ds_logic
# Loading work.cm3_code_mux
# Loading work.cm3ahb_to_ahb5
# Loading work.ahb_decoder_code
# Loading work.ahb_slavemux
# Loading work.ahb_defslave
# Loading work.ahb_decoder_system
# Loading work.apb_subsystem
# Loading work.ahb_to_apb
# Loading work.apb_gpio
# Loading work.apb_timer
# Loading work.apb_uart
# Loading work.ahb_rom
# Loading work.ahb_ram
# Loading work.sys_ctrl
# Loading work.behavioral_input_pad
# Loading work.behavioral_input_pullup_pad
# Loading work.behavioral_tristate_pullup_pad
# Loading work.behavioral_output_pad
# Loading work.behavioral_tristate_pad
# Loading work.uart_mon
run -all
# ** Warning: (vsim-8233) ../mcu_system/ahb_ram.v(111): Index 1zzzzzzzzzzzzzzzz into array
dimension [0:65535] is out of bounds.
#    Time: 0 ns  Iteration: 0  Instance: /tbench_cm3/u_cm3_mcu/cm3_system_top/u_ahb_ram
# ** Warning: (vsim-8233) ../mcu_system/ahb_ram.v(112): Index 1zzzzzzzzzzzzzzzx into array
dimension [0:65535] is out of bounds.
#    Time: 0 ns  Iteration: 0  Instance: /tbench_cm3/u_cm3_mcu/cm3_system_top/u_ahb_ram
# ** Warning: (vsim-8233) ../mcu_system/ahb_ram.v(113): Index 1zzzzzzzzzzzzzzxz into array
dimension [0:65535] is out of bounds.
#    Time: 0 ns  Iteration: 0  Instance: /tbench_cm3/u_cm3_mcu/cm3_system_top/u_ahb_ram
#             563700 UART: Hello world
#             579700 UART:
#             579700 UART: Simulation End
# ** Note: $finish    : ./uart_mon.v(119)
#    Time: 579700 ns  Iteration: 1  Instance: /tbench_cm3/uart_mon
# 1
# Break in Module uart_mon at ./uart_mon.v line 119
# End time: 22:32:37 on Apr 12,2019, Elapsed time: 0:01:17
# Errors: 0, Warnings: 4
```

9.6 Advanced processor systems and Corstone Foundation IP

The simple system design covered here is adequate for small projects. However, in commercial product development, system designs can be much more complex. For example:

- The bus system might need to support multiple bus masters including a DMA controller, high-speed communication interfaces (e.g., peripherals like USB controller and Ethernet controller can have a bus master interface).

- Additional power management schemes might be needed to enable longer battery life. For example, multiple bus systems can be used, and each of them can be running at different clock speeds to reduce active power.

- Additional security features are often needed, especially when dealing in IoT applications. For example, security control features might be added in peripheral bus bridges to allow peripherals to be allocated to specific tasks, and to make some of the peripherals privileged access only. If a system design is based on Armv8-M processors, the use of the TrustZone security extensions also requires additional system IP to partition memories into Secure and Non-secure spaces.

- Protection of firmware IP (intellectual property) is required for many commercial products. As a result, additional IP (including some form of non-volatile memory) is needed to enable the product's Life Cycle State (LCS) management and debug authentication.

To help reduce time-to-market, Arm has produced and delivered a range of system components and system design products. The Corstone Foundation IP are system design packages containing:

- Subsystems based on Arm Cortex processor, which can be used as a standalone system or as a subsystem in complex SoC designs.

- A wide collection of bus infrastructure components including bus bridges, TrustZone security management components (for Corstone-20x and Corstone-7xx).

- A selection of baseline peripherals.

- Software support.

These IPs are verified, and system designers can integrate these subsystems into their design to accelerate their projects. The Corstone Foundation IP series contains multiple products:

- Corstone-050, 100, 102 – IoT subsystem for Cortex-M3 processor and including deliverables in the previous Cortex-M System Design Kit (CMSDK).

- Corstone-200, 201 – IoT subsystem for Cortex-M33 with TrustZone security, also including CMSDK.

- Corstone-700 – scalable IoT subsystem for small Cortex-A processors and optional Cortex-M subsystems.

For designers that prefer a simpler system design, the previous generation of CMSDK is included in full versions of Corstone Foundation IP, which provides example system designs for Cortex-M0, Cortex-M0+, Cortex-M3, and Cortex-M4 processors.

Corstone-050 is included in the Cortex-M3 DesignStart deliverables.

9.7 Verification

System-level simulation is great for testing the integration of the system (connections between units) and testing of the basic functionality of the design units. In commercial projects, getting a system-level simulation running is only one part of the verification task. There are other verification methodologies needed for SoC designs; notably:

LINT checking
A lint checking tool can be used to analyze the design source code (Verilog / VHDL) to flag up coding errors (e.g., a missing signal in the sensitivity list). The term "lint" originates from the name of a tool for C code checking (https://en.wikipedia.org/wiki/Lint_(software)).

Some Verilog/VHDL simulation tools include LINT checking capability. For example, in the simulation example Section 9.5, we added the "-lint" option in the vlog command to enable lint checking in Modelsim/Questasim.

Formal verification
Since system-level simulation cannot reach corner cases, formal verification is usually needed for component level (smaller design units) verifications. With formal verification, you need to define input constraints for the DUT (Device Under Test) and rules for expected outputs. The formal verification tool then works out all the possible inputs and scenarios to see if the DUT truly follows the rules for the expected output. Take an example in which the DUT is a bus bridge component; a formal verification environment might look like the one shown in Figure 9.4:

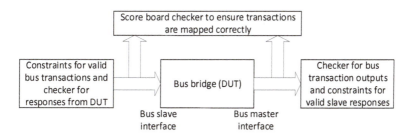

Figure 9.4: Formal verification environment for a bus bridge component.

Due to the long duration for the formal verification runs, usually formal verification is not used at system-level.

Clock Domain Cross (CDC) checks

Many SoC designs contain multiple clock domains that are asynchronous to each other, and appropriate synchronization logic should be in place. CDC checks are used to detect missing synchronization logic (e.g., double flip-flop synchronizers). When using a CDC checker, you might need to add a range of constraints to specified exempted cases (e.g., In some cases, a signal going from one clock domain to another can only change when the destination domain's clock is stopped).

Netlist simulations

After the design is synthesized and has potentially gone through placement and routing flow, it is common to back annotate the netlist and timing to double-check the design using netlist simulations with a subset of tests used in RTL level simulation. Due to additional timing details, typically in the form of SDF (standard delay format) files, netlist simulations are much slower than RTL simulations and therefore re-running all verifications on netlist is typically unfeasible.

While static timing analysis can detect timing violations, netlist simulation is still useful to detect missing or errors in timing constraints. Netlist simulation is also needed to verify scan patterns generated by ATPG (Automatic Test Pattern Generation, see Section 9.9) tools, as scan patterns often contain user-defined setup patterns at the start of the scan test that need to be verified at netlist level.

FPGA prototype

In addition to demonstration purpose, FPGA prototyping is very useful for validating debug connections and related aspects such as pin multiplexing. Since software developers can create applications and execute them on FPGA platforms as in real applications (potentially at a reduced speed), application developers can use FPGA prototypes to develop application-level testing and run the test much quicker than in RTL simulations.

Verifications for designs with multiple power domains

If a design contains multiple power domains, additional verifications are required:

- Power-aware simulations – entering of sleep modes and waking up can be simulated, with some of the power domains powered down during sleep.

- Power intent verification – verification of power intent description (e.g., UPF).

- Low-power formal verification – if a logic operation has moved from one power domain to another due to synthesis optimizations, potentially this can cause incorrect behavior during power down. Low-power equivalent checking can identify such mismatch in behavior.

9.8 ASIC implementation flow

ASIC implementation flow (sometimes also referred to as physical design) can contain many steps:

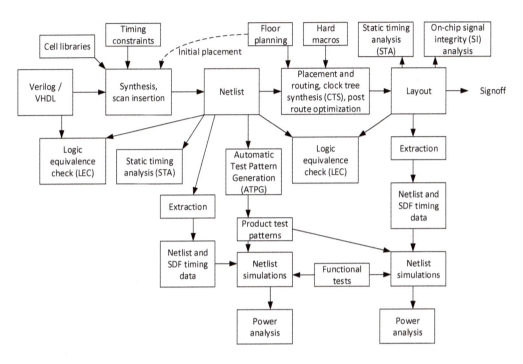

Figure 9.5: Example of implementation flow.

Brief descriptions of some of the key steps in the implementation flow are explained below. Some of the checking (e.g., static timing analysis) might be carried out multiple times during the implementation flow.

Synthesis – Conversion of RTL to netlist. In addition to the RTL, ASIC synthesis tools also need the cell library and various timing constraints for the clock, reset, and interface signals. Synthesis processes might include automatic clock gate generation to help low-power optimization.

Scan insertion – adding of scan chains to the netlist for chip manufacturing testing. See Section 9.9 for more information.

Static timing analysis (STA) – STA tools calculate the timing of the netlist based on timing models of the cell library and check if the design can meet the timing constraint requirements. The analysis involves multiple "corners" to detect potential failures like setup timing violation (circuit running too slow) and hold time violation (a signal changes so fast that a register capturing it can end up with an incorrect value).

Placement and routing – The tool places the logic gates in the chip layout and connects the signals between logic gates. Potentially, the placement can be divided into two stages: initial placement provides a rough location of logic gates to enable better timing optimizations during synthesis, and then a second stage finalizes the locations of the gates.

Clock tree synthesis (CTS) – CTS inserts clock tree buffers to ensure that clock signals reach the different registers at the right time. In a SoC design, two registers receiving the same clock signal might see the clock edge at different times if they are not in the same area on the chip (due to the propagation delay of the clock signal). CTS can balance the clock tree accordingly so that signal paths between the registers still work after placement.

Logic equivalence checking (LEC) – this ensures that the functionality of the design units matches the RTL code. If the LEC check fails, the reason could be an error in the design, missing constraints in the synthesis or LEC setup, or potentially something has gone wrong in the synthesis.

Automatic Test Pattern Generation (ATPG) – ATPG analyzes the netlist and generates scan patterns for chip manufacturing testing. (There can be multiple types of scan patterns for different test purposes).

On-chip signal integrity (SI) analysis – This can help prevent chip failures caused by cross-talk between wires, and static and dynamic voltage drops (known as IR drop) in power rails during circuit activities. Power analysis – this enables designers to confirm that the chip can operate within the power budget.

There can be additional steps required, for example, when dealing with embedded memory macros. Designers need to use memory compilers to generate the memory macros.

9.9 Design for Testing/Testability (DFT)

As transistors get smaller and smaller, a tiny defect in the silicon wafer can easily cause them to fail, and chip manufacturers need to be able to test the chip thoroughly before releasing the product to their customers. While it is possible to carry out some level of testing by running programs on the chip, such a testing methodology is unlikely to get a very high test-coverage and might take a very long time. To enable better testability, modern digital chip design often incorporates additional test circuitries to help manufacturing testing.

Earlier, we mentioned about scan insertion and ATPG in the implementation flow. This is one of the most common approaches used today for testing of digital circuitries. To use scan tests, the flip-flops in the circuit design include additional ports for scan test operations:

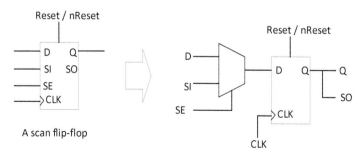

Figure 9.6: Scan D flip-flop.

The extra signals on the scan D flip-flop include:

- SI – scan in;

- SO – scan out;

- SE – scan enable.

After synthesis with scan enable (i.e., scan registers are used), we can then create scan chains using scan insertion in synthesis tools. There can be multiple scan chains in a design (but not too many, as there are restrictions in the chip testers), and the more scan chains you have, the shorter each chain would be and can shorten the time required for running scan tests.

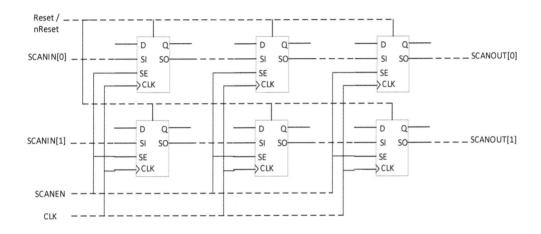

Figure 9.7: Two scan chains inserted (functional logic not shown).

With the scan chain in place, we can then use a tester hardware call Automatic Test Equipment (ATE) to shift in any test patterns to the logic by applying a series of clock pulses with scan enable asserted, and clocked the design with scan enable de-asserted to exercise the functional logic (capture cycle).

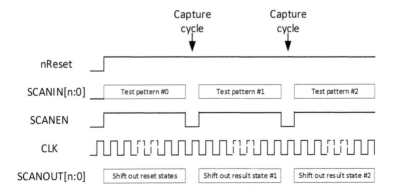

Figure 9.8: Simple scan test operations.

During a scan test, it is often essential to bypass internal clock gating and internal reset generation circuits to allow ATE to have direct control of the clock and reset. Therefore, in Arm IP designs, you might see signals like this:

- CGYPASS – clock gating bypass;

- RSTBYPASS – internal reset generation bypass;

- SCANMODE – Scan mode indication/control to force components to work in certain ways to help test coverage. For example, wrappers of memory macros can route write data to read data so that data paths can be tested easily.

These signals should be high during the whole duration of the scan test, including capture cycles.

In some cases, a setup pattern needs to be added to the beginning of test patterns to enable scan tests. For example, the scan test pins might be multiplexed with other function pins and need a special signal sequence to enable the scan pin accesses. Such a setup pattern is defined by the chip designers.

The ATPG tool can generate different types of test patterns. The typical scan test is targeted at detecting stuck-at faults, which means that it checks the inputs and outputs of logic gates are not stuck with a value of 0 or 1. It is also possible to generate scan test patterns for IDDQ (Idd quiescent) testing, which detects unexpected supply current when a certain logic state is reached, which can be an indication of manufacturing faults.

Scan tests can also be used for at-speed testing of some degree. However, in modern ASICs that run at over 100MHz, many ATE (chip testers) might not be able to support at-speed testing at such a high clock speed and in those cases, traditional functional tests might be more suitable.

Another type of manufacturing test is the memory built-in self-test (BIST). Memory BIST controllers can be inserted by EDA tools and controlled via JTAG or other test interfaces. When memory BIST is enabled, a memory BIST controller automatically creates test patterns to access the memory macros to verify their functions. There can be more than one memory BIST controller in a chip when there is more than one memory block. To help the integration of memory BIST, Arm processors with internal SRAM (e.g., caches) provide memory BIST support. The exact details are processor-specific, so please refer to processor integration manuals for more information.

There are also manufacturing tests that focus on electrical characteristics of input and output pins. Common examples of these tests include:

- Input threshold voltage (VIL, VIH);

- Input leakage current (IIL, IIH);

- Output driving voltage (VOL, VOH) (can also cover output drive current test).

While output pins can be accessed, and their electrical characteristic measured easily, the output signals of input pads are inside the chip and creating a test for checking each of the signals can be tricky. To make it easier, we can add a simple logic to link the input pads' outputs together and test them at the same time.

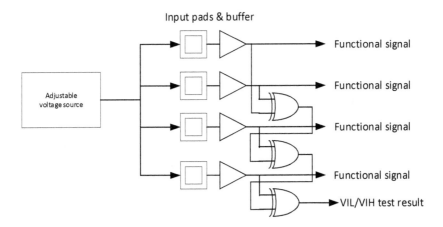

Figure 9.9: Simple XOR tree for VIL/VIH tests.

Assuming that all the input pins have the same electrical characteristics, they should also have the same outputs when the input voltage is in a valid range. Since we know how many input pins are in the XOR tree, we can determine the expected test result easily. By adjusting the input voltage closer to the input threshold voltage level slowly, and if any of the input pins fail to deliver the correct signal, the VIL/VIH test result pin will toggle. Of course, if there are two input pads that fail at the same time at a certain threshold voltage (the chance is low - but it is possible), then the VIL/VIH test result signal will remain unchanged and will not be able to detect the issue.

Depending on other components in the chip design, there can be additional DFT integration requirements. For example, an on-chip Phase-Locked Loop (PLL) module usually has some test pins to enable the PLL to be tested.

CHAPTER

Beyond the
processor system

10.1 Clock system design

10.1.1 Clock system design overview

All processor systems[1] need clock signals to operate. For the majority of microcontroller systems, the clock signals are generated by the following means:

- Internal crystal oscillators with external crystals, or

- Internal oscillators (e.g., R-C oscillators), or

- Internal Phase-Locked-Loop (PLL).

When designing clock systems, several factors are typically considered:

- Accuracy – Many peripherals and external communication interfaces require fairly high accuracy for the clock frequency. For external crystals, the accuracy is often expressed as PPM (Part Per Million), and commercial products usually require 40ppm or better accuracy for the crystal oscillators. Internal R-C oscillators typically are not accurate (some can have up to 20% error).

- Duty cycle – Typically, the clock source should provide a square wave with a 50% duty cycle. For Cortex-M based systems, since all registers in the processor and the bus system trigger at the system clock's rising edge, a small inaccuracy in the duty cycle is unlikely to cause any problems. However, when dealing with an interface with DDR (double data rate) operations, accuracy in clock duty cycle can be very important.

- Low-power – A crystal oscillator running at a high clock speed can consume a lot of power. So if high clock speeds are required, a slower crystal oscillator is often used to generate a reference clock and a PLL to generate a high-frequency clock out of it. When the system does not need the high clock speed, the PLL can be turned off to save power. Another common requirement for low-power systems is to provide an ultra-low-power clock source for Real-Time-Clock (RTC) and a periodic interrupt source for RTOS (Real-Time Operating System). It is therefore relatively common for microcontrollers to have a crystal oscillator for the system clock and a 32kHz crystal oscillator for the RTC clock.

- Clock distribution inside the chip – In Chapter 9, we mentioned the topic of clock tree synthesis during clock design flow. In many system designs, we need to make a clock edge that arrives at different parts of the processor system at the same time. Clock tree balancing during clock tree synthesis is required to achieve this goal. In addition to the clock signal propagation delay, clock tree balancing must also take account of additional delays caused by clock gating cells, and, potentially, additional clock skews and clock jitters (uncertainties). What is more, if all this wasn't enough to make your design flow complicated, the clock tree can use up a considerable amount of power consumption!

  In some cases, application-specific IC designs can have additional clock source requirements. For example, chip designs with USB interfaces might require accurate 12MHz or 48MHz clock sources.

[1] Note: There are processors designed with asynchronous logic, but their bus systems still need clock signals to allow them to interface with the external world and peripherals.

10.1.2 Clock switching

When there are multiple clock sources in the system, one of the design challenges is to handle the switch over from one clock source to another. In a microcontroller application, you might have multiple scenarios in which different clock sources are used – for example:

- When the processor system is running background code, the processor's clock may be driven from the crystal oscillator.

- When the processor system receives a certain processing workload, it needs higher performance and therefore switches from the crystal oscillator's clock to a PLL-generated high-frequency clock.

- When there is nothing to process, the processor enters sleep mode during which only the RTC is running (PLL and other oscillator turned off to minimize power consumption). The processor system might in this state need to use the RTC clock to wake up the memory controllers after an interrupt request is received.

As a result, the clock system design needs to support switching over from one clock source to another, - and this process needs to be glitch-less. If a clock glitch enters the processor system, some of the registers can be affected by metastability issues and enter an undefined state, and the system will not be able to resume normal operations.

One way to provide glitch-free clock switching is to implement a clock switching FSM in each of the clock domains and to enable their clock output only if none of the other clock output FSMs are outputting. Figure 10.1 shows a clock switcher that supports three asynchronous clock sources:

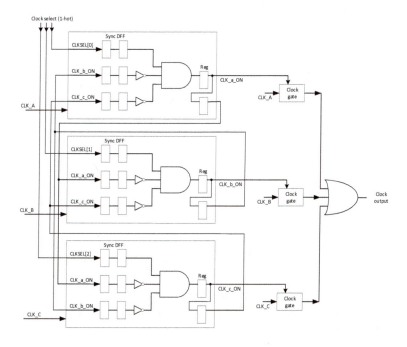

Figure 10.1: Clock switcher that support three clock sources.

The clock gating cells and the OR gate that merge clock sources need to be instantiated and cannot be generated by synthesis. This prevents the synthesis process from reordering logic gates that can result in glitches. The reset values of the flip-flop might need to be customized if you want to allow the system to be started up with the clock running.

10.1.3 Low-power considerations

Crystal oscillators and PLL hardware are often delivered to chip designers as hard macros and simulation models. To enable low-power optimizations at the application level, many of these designs include power control interfaces that allow the oscillator of the PLL to be powered down when they are not being used.

A problem with powering down oscillators and clock sources during sleep is that, in many cases, we still need to have a clock source for various power management hardware, which requires clocks (they might have internal state machines to power up memories). Therefore, chip designers must ensure that either one of the active clock sources is kept active, or that the oscillator's control is designed so that after a wake-up event is triggered, an oscillator could start automatically to support the power-up sequence.

Be careful about the wake-up time required for the oscillator and PLL, including the effect of various operating temperatures and voltages. Typically, a finite state machine (FSM) is needed to ensure that the clock signal to the processor system is gated off until it is fully stabilized. This is why the 32kHz clock is usually left running during sleep mode so that the FSM can rely on this clock to operate.

10.1.4 DFT considerations

An important aspect of clock system design is Design for Testing (DFT). During scan tests, clock signals need to be controllable from the ATE, and that means internal clock switches, clock gates, and internal clock sources such as PLL have to be bypassed. Some of the PLL designs also have scan chains that need to be hooked up and might have additional scan mode control signals.

In addition, some PLL designs provide test modes that can help chip designers to analyze the performance of the PLL in the implemented chips. To use such features, you might need to implement test modes that allow certain PLL signals to be observable at the top-level of the chip.

10.2 Multiple power domains and power gating

In low-power system designs, we often define multiple power domains in a chip and allow some to be powered down when they are not needed. This technique is called power gating.

Unlike clock gating (which simply reduces dynamic leakage), power gating also removes static leakage currents. However, as system states may be lost by removing power, there are some trade-offs to be made – it may take time to save and recover the necessary state information and remove and restore power. A special form of power gating called State Retention Power Gating (SRPG) is available, but SRPG flip-flops are larger than standard flip-flops, have a slightly higher dynamic current, and need an additional power rail to support retention.

To handle power gating and state retention power gating, we need special physical IP for power gating:

▨ Header cells;

▨ Footer cells;

▨ Isolation cells;

▨ State retention flip-flops (registers) (for SRPG only).

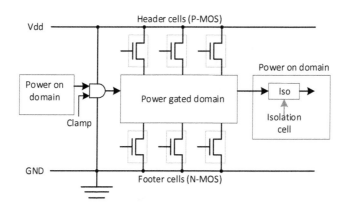

Figure 10.2: Various special cells for power gating.

Footer cells and footer cells - On-chip power gating typically involves inserting large, high- Vt (threshold voltage), low-leakage PMOS (on supply connection side) and/or NMOS (on ground connection) sleep transistors into the chip's power network. This means that the device's power network consists of:

☐ A power network that is permanently turned on (connected to an external supply), and

☐ A number of power islands, to which the power supply may be turned off.

Isolation cells - Isolation cells are special cells that isolate a power-gated block from other parts of the design which remain powered up. These are required to prevent (1) short-circuit currents and (2) the inputs of other blocks from floating (a "clamp" will force such inputs to a logical 0 or 1 when the output of the powered down block has been isolated.)

In some cases, when multiple power domains are used, it is possible to have different voltage levels, and in these situations, level shifters are also needed.

To support power gating design, Arm physical IP products have Power Management Kits (PMK) that contain a range of these special components for multiple power domain designs. Different process nodes need different PMKs libraries. For more information about PMKs, please visit Arm's website: https://www.arm.com/products/silicon-ip-physical/logic-ip

The inclusion of such power gates brings a range of complexity to the physical design:

IR-drop - The voltage supplied to individual functional blocks will be lower than that provided to the chip, due to losses within the on-chip power distribution network. Power gate transistors need to be large in order to reduce the IR drop. In many cases, a number of header cells and footer cells are required to avoid this.

In-rush current – If a voltage island is large and all the header and footer cells are turning on simultaneously, it causes a large 'in-rush current' that can result in problems to the integrity of the device's power grid. In order to prevent this problem, the header and footer cells often have buffered control output to allow-power switching sequences to be chained. This makes the time needed for switching on a power domain longer but can prevent large 'in-rush current' that can cause physical damage to the chip.

Power gating control skew rate - Another potential issue is that power gates themselves can have leakage current, especially if the gating control signal is not well buffered and not reaching optimal voltage. Therefore, the timing of the power gate operation needs to be carefully considered to ensure that the slew rate of the power gate control signal is not too large.

Power-gating also has cost implications in terms of die area and silicon routing. It requires specialist EDA tools and may make timing closure more difficult.

As explained in Chapter 6, there are a number of schemes to preserve the state of a block before it is shut down. While state retention power gating (SRPG) enables the state in the processor system to be retained during sleep, it won't be useful if the states in peripherals and other system components are lost during sleep. So if state retention power gating is used, the components in the system that need to be powered down during sleep mode should also have state-retention power gating (SRPG) implemented to ensure that software can make the most out of SRPG capability.

An alternative method is to store the status of the parts of the applications that need to be preserved to a state retention RAM, before removing power. When power is restored, the software needs to restore the application's state. The state that needs saving might include the processor's registers and peripheral configurations.

Of course, it is also possible to power down and simply restart the system when it is needed.

10.3 Arm processors in a mixed-signal world

10.3.1 Convergence of microcontrollers and mixed-signal designs

Traditionally, many microcontrollers are mostly digital in design with a few analog components, like ADCs (Analog to digital converters) and DACs (Digital to analog converters). In the last 10 years, more and more analog components integrated into microcontrollers:

- PLLs (Phase-Locked Loops) and oscillators;

- ADCs;

- DACs;

- Voltage references;

- Brown-out detector;

- Analog comparators;

- LCD driver;

- Touch sensor / CAP sense;

- Wireless interface, etc.

At the same time, analog components are getting more intelligent. For example, traditional sensor ICs integrate more and more digital logic including, processors and are becoming "smart" sensors. This can bring many advantages by enabling:

- Better calibrations;

- Fault detection and report to devices connected to it;

- Better power management.

Since the Cortex-M processors are small, energy-efficient, and easy to use, they are widely used in microcontrollers and smart analog IC designs. With various sleep mode features and intelligence in software control, a range of mixed-signal designs can reach better levels of energy efficiency and, at the same time, provide more features than before.

When dealing with mixed-signal designs, additional complexities are added to the projects; for example:

- Design flow of analog components can be very different from digital. In some cases, Verilog-AMS can be used, and in others, some analog components are designed with manual chip layout. There is often a need for system-level mixed-signal simulation and verification.

- In some cases, CMOS manufacturing technology is not suitable for certain analog applications (e.g., power electronics, radio frequency circuits). In many cases, BiCMOS is used for mixed-signal designs that combine CMOS, and bipolar transistor technologies on the same silicon die.

- Many analog components need separated power domains (separated from the digital logic). Additional considerations in a chip's power rail design and floor-planning are needed to reduce noise to sensitive analog components. For example, layout implementation techniques such as guard rings and well isolation are common techniques that can be used to prevent switching noise from a digital circuit reaching an analog circuit through silicon substrate coupling.

- Analog components have different manufacturing test requirements.

Many EDA tool vendors have specific offerings to help when dealing with mixed-signal design flows.

10.3.2 Analog to digital conversions

There are many types of ADC available on the market. Depending on the application, there can be different selection criteria for what type of ADC to choose. For example:

- Conversion speed and sampling rate – When dealing with an input signal that has a frequency range of X Hz, the minimum sampling rate needed is 2*X Hz. And in many cases, even 2*X Hz is not enough for quality and reliability reasons. For example, imagine that a 4 kHz sine wave is sampled at 8 kHz: there is a chance that we will sample the input signal at 0 level all the time. Therefore, it is often necessary to have the sample rate more than 4 times that of the input signals. Please note that the input bandwidth of an ADC can be much lower than half of the sampling rate.

- Resolution – This is expressed as the number of bits in the conversion results. For an on-chip ADC, typical resolutions range from 8-bit to 14-bits. The difference between the real value and the measured value is often referred to as the quantization error and is ½ of the LSB of the ADC in ideal cases, as shown in the diagram below:

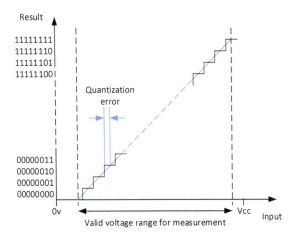

Figure 10.3: ADC resolution and quantization error.

(Please note that many on-chip ADCs have a measurement range less than the supply voltage range.)

■ Signal-to-noise (SNR) ratio – this is often calculated using the number of bits in the results, by assuming the noise level is +/- LSB. SNR is often expressed in decibels, i.e.

$$SNR_{db} = 10log_{10} (P_{signal}/P_{noise})$$

■ Given that the ADC results are in the form of voltage values, we need to convert the formula by squaring the input values (or 2x after log10), thus:

$$SNR_{db} = 20log_{10} (V_{signal}/V_{noise})$$

■ Assuming that the ADC is 8-bit (256 levels), the SNR calculation can be formulated as shown:

$$SNR_{db} = 10log_{10} ((256)^2) = 48db$$

In some cases, you can use oversampling and filtering techniques to reduce noise. But even if the ADC noise level is low, in many cases, noises from other parts of the integrated circuit and on the circuit board, could reduce the signal-to-noise ratio.

■ Suitability for the target process node – One of the challenges for mixed-signal design is that analog circuit design does not scale well to small transistor geometries.

■ Area and power – Silicon area and the type of ADC directly contribute to cost and power. Based on the project requirements, some of the ADC types might not be suitable for these reasons.

■ Operating conditions – If you are designing a chip for industrial (or even automotive) applications, you will need to pay attention to the operating temperature range of ALL the components that you use for the design (not just ADC, DAC, but also oscillators, memories, etc.). Some of the ADCs and DACs might not work at high temperature.

Amongst various types of ADC, successive approximation ADCs are very popular in microcontrollers. Successive approximation contains several parts, as shown in the diagram below:

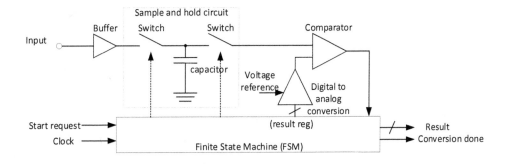

Figure 10.4: Simplified block diagram of a successive approximation ADC.

Using bisection, a successive approximation ADC determines input voltage bit by bit, as illustrated below:

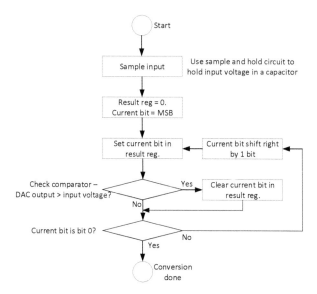

Figure 10.5: Operations of a successive approximation ADC.

With a 14-bit ADC, the finite state machine iterates the operation loop 14 times. While it is not the fastest type of ADC, the conversion speed is acceptable for most applications and delivers relatively high accuracy.

For designs that require very fast conversion speed, a flash ADC can be used. A flash ADC uses an array of voltage comparators to detect the voltage and then converts the results to binary values.

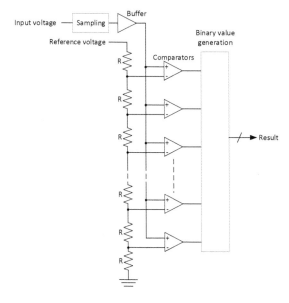

Figure 10.6: Conceptual representation of a flash ADC.

The illustration in Figure 10.6 is a conceptual one. In ASIC design, the resistor network is likely to be replaced by switching capacitor networks as the implementation of resistors in ICs can be challenging in terms of accuracy.

Due to their nature, flash ADCs are usually larger in silicon area, power-hungry, and can offer only limited resolution (e.g., 8-bit). They are commonly used for video signal processing because other ADC methods cannot reach the required speed, and 8-bit is sufficient for video processing needs.

For audio processing, a delta-sigma ADC could be used. Delta-sigma ADCs contains several stages; namely:

▪ A delta sigma modulator;

▪ Digital low pass filter;

▪ Decimation filter.

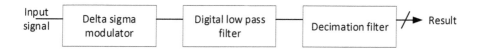

Figure 10.7: Block diagram of a delta sigma ADC.

The delta-sigma modulator runs at several MHz and can generate a bitstream with a feedback loop. The 1-bit DAC in the feedback is simply a switch that switches between +Vref and -Vref based on the result of the 1-bit ADC input. The differential amplifier compares the input signal with the 1-bit ADC, and the integrator works as a lowpass filter of the result.

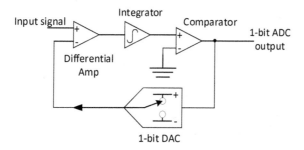

Figure 10.8: Simplified representation of a delta-sigma modulator.

With a delta-sigma ADC, the output is based on the density of ones in the output stream. Due to its nature that high-frequency input will suffer higher quantization errors. For audio processing, this is less of an issue as the human ear is less sensitive to higher frequency sounds, so we can apply a low pass filter to suppress quantization noises.

Since the output is in the form of a bitstream, the application code cannot use this result directly. With a decimation filter, we can convert the bitstream information into multi-bit binary values at a lower sampling rate.

The usable bandwidth of a delta-sigma ADC is a bit lower than the other ADCs mentioned previously. In addition, delta-sigma ADCs are designed to be used with periodic sampling, whereas successive approximation and flash ADC can be turned on and off at any time to skip samples when it is not needed or perform conversions on an ad-hoc basis.

For applications where the sampling rate is very low, for example, in smart sensors when measurement might be needed only for a few times a second, or even a sample every hour, we can use a slower ADC like a dual-slope ADC.

Conceptually, dual slope ADCs can be implemented using an op-amp, a voltage comparator, a binary counter, and a state machine, as illustrated in the diagram below:

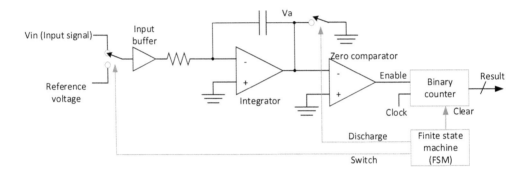

Figure 10.9: Conceptual representation of a dual slope ADC.

When in operation, a dual-slope ADC applies the input voltage to an integrator circuit and integrates the voltage for a fixed duration. A reference voltage of opposite polarity is then applied to the integrator and allowed to ramp until the integrator output returns to zero. The input voltage can then be calculated as a function of the reference voltage, the fixed-length period, and the measured discharge period; which is expressed as follows:

Vin = Vref * (discharge time / fixed_charge_time)

Longer integration times permit higher resolution measurements, and this kind of ADC is particularly suited for very accurate measurement of slowly varying signals.

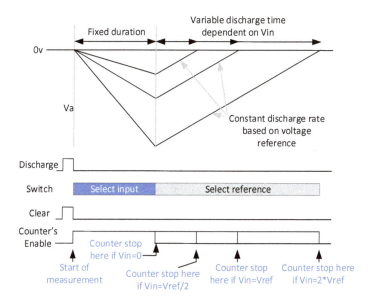

Figure 10.10: Conceptual operation of a dual-slope ADC.

10.3.3 Digital to analog conversions

There are various ways to convert digital values into analog signals. Traditional DACs might use a combination of amplifier and resistor network to obtain analog output, as shown in the diagram below:

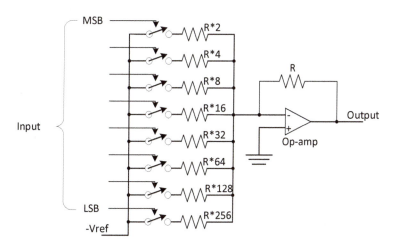

Figure 10.11: Conceptual operation of traditional DAC.

In some cases, when the quality of the output is not critical, we could consider simpler mechanisms for analog output. For example, a simple PWM (Pulse Width Modulation) output could be used to drive a small speaker for audio tone generation.

With a simple analog integrator (either on-chip or off-chip), we can also deploy the delta-sigma technique to produce audio output, as shown here:

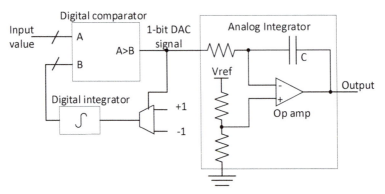

Figure 10.12: Delta-sigma DAC.

10.3.4 Other analog interface approaches

There are several different ways to connect audio/analog interfaces to digital ICs; namely:

I2S interface - For microcontroller-based products, using an external I2S audio codec IC is a common choice. I2S are digital serial interfaces and therefore can be handled as digital peripherals. They can also be implemented on FPGA development boards.

I2C/I3C/SPI interface – External ADC and DAC chips often use serial communication protocols such as I2C/I3C (Inter-IC bus) or SPI (Serial Peripheral Interface). Such an arrangement is suitable for sensor and control applications. I2C and SPI interface peripherals are widely available from various peripheral IP providers. APB interface support is commonly available for these peripheral solutions.

PDM (Pulse Density Modulation) – In recent years, digital microphones with PDM interfaces are becoming more common due to their low cost and simple interfaces. Similar to delta-sigma, a microphone's output is in serial bitstream where the density of '1' indicates a higher analog value. The PDM signals can be converted to analog values using digital filters and be implemented as digital peripheral interfaces.

10.3.5 Connecting ADC and DAC IPs into a Cortex-M system

In instances where you license ADC or DAC IPs, these components usually provide simple digital interfaces. To connect them to a Cortex-M system, the typical integration task includes the following steps:

- Adding an APB bus wrapper for various data and control registers (please note that, potentially, additional level shifters might be needed in the bus wrapper design).

- Adding interrupt handling logic (and registers) to handle completion of conversion or error cases.

- Creation of software driver code and create test codes for system-level simulations.

To help system-level verification, a number of EDA tool vendors offer solutions for mixed-signal verification, including simulators that can handle Verilog and Verilog-AMS co-simulation. For example, Cadence Virtuoso can handle co-simulation of RTL, Verilog-AMS, and wreal:

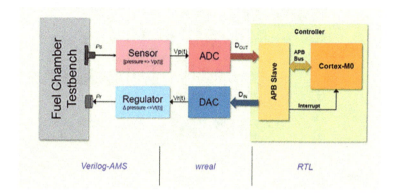

Figure 10.13: A Cadence Virtuoso demo containing a Cortex-M0 based system and mixed-signal IP (diagram in courtesy of Cadence Design Systems).

More information can be found on Cadence's website at the links below:

https://community.cadence.com/cadence_blogs_8/b/ms/posts/arm-based-micro-controllers-using-cadence-s-mixed-signal-solution

https://community.cadence.com/cadence_blogs_8/b/ii/posts/easing-mixed-signal-design-with-the-arm-cortex-m0

10.4 Bringing an SoC to life – Beetle test chip case study

10.4.1 Beetle test chip overview

While Arm does not make silicon chips for sale, test chips are often built to validate new technologies. For the engineers at Arm, because we focus on processors and IP-level development most of the time, we don't often see the whole detailed picture of the system design problems that our customers face. Test chip projects give us first-hand experience of putting a complete SoC design together enabling Arm engineers to create IP that is a better fit with what our customers really need to do the best job for a given design.

Test chip projects can be both exciting and challenging at the same time. One of the test chip projects that I have been involved in is called 'Beetle.' It uses a Cortex-M3 processor and the CoreLink SDK-100 IoT subsystem (rebranded Corstone-100). In addition, it includes a range of peripherals, a true random number generator (TRNG) needed for IoT security, embedded flash, an on-chip PLL, and an integrated Bluetooth interface (Arm Cordio) - see the block diagram below:

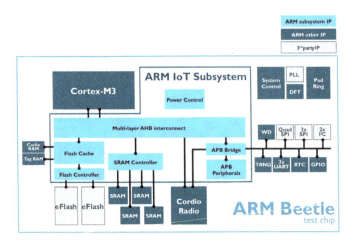

Figure 10.14: Beetle test chip overview.

The chip package that was chosen for the project is a QFN 80 pin package (7mm x 7mm). Several factors were considered in the selection; notably, it needs to be:

▨ A representative package for low-cost IoT endpoints;

▨ Suitable for Bluetooth wireless designs.

While '80 pins' sounds like quite a lot of pins are available in the Beetle chip design, in practice, we are quite tight on pin usage due to the following factors:

▨ Additional pins for multiple voltage supply – since we did not integrate an on-chip DC-DC voltage converter, we need to allocate multiple voltage supply pins for the different voltage levels used by different parts of the chips.

▨ The Cordio IP requires a number of dedicated pins for power, oscillators, and of course antenna and RF interface.

▨ Since we would like to enable all debug features to be used at any time, we did not multiplex debug pins with functional pins.

▨ Several pins are required to control test modes that expose internal signals for testing.

Figure 10.15: Beetle test chip photo.

On the upside, the limited pin situation is not such a problem as it may first seem because:

- The bottom side of the chip provides a large ground connection, so we do not need to have many ground pins; and,

- Oscillators for the Cordio macros are also used by the processor system (shared).

10.4.2 Beetle test chip challenges
The Beetle test chip project proved to be very challenging for our designers in many ways. For example, it is the first Arm test chip with the following features:

- Embedded flash;

- A built-in wireless interface (Cordio Bluetooth 4.2);

- A TSMC 55ULP process node;

- The CoreLink SDK-100 IoT subsystem.

The success of the chip was a really rewarding experience for the project team and everyone involved in the Beetle.

The team was quite small, with only a few designers working on each step of the project. The planning started Q1-2015, and the project officially kicked off in March-2015 with the system design phase. Physical design started in the middle of May-2015, and the Beetle taped out at the beginning of August. We had the chip working and demonstrated it at Arm TechCon 2015. (Here we would like to thank the TSMC team for their help and a fast turnaround achieved for this project).

At the design level, one of the biggest challenges was the issue of handling supply voltage. In this design, various supply voltages were needed for different parts of the Beetle chip; for example:

- The logic cells use 0.9Vnom;

- Due to time pressure and performance requirements, we used 1.2V SRAM;

- Flash memory – 1.2V/2.5V where used for its read/write operations;

- Cordio Bluetooth hard macro – sub-1V.

Making life a little more difficult for us, perhaps, the embedded flash macro had a strict requirement on power-down procedures. Otherwise, it could cause permanent damage to the chip. This led to additional design requirements for the PCB as it had to provide an input signal that would indicate that the supply voltage was dropping. This signal is connected to the on-chip power management control unit, which triggers an internal power control FSM to start the shutdown process. Since the 32kHz oscillator was designed to be always on, the FSM can rely on this to safely shut down the chip before the supply voltage cuts out.

10.4.3 Beetle test chip system design

A key benefit of having a ready-to-use CoreLink SDK IoT subsystem included was envisaged as being improved time to market, and the Beetle test chip project has proven that point without a doubt. The CoreLink SDK-100 IoT subsystem includes the essential system design for the Cortex-M3 processor, and in addition, it comes with the following memory system features in the package:

■ An embedded flash controller for TSMC 55ULP embedded flash;

■ An AHB flash cache for optimizing system performance when running code from flash.

The system design was also created with IoT security requirement in mind. With the TRNG IP, a secure communication protocol stack like mbedTLS can utilize it for entropy generation, which enables better security in session keys generation for encrypted IoT traffic. Another important aspect designed to address IoT security requirements is the Secure firmware update and two banks of embedded flash (128KB each) are included in the package to help support that.

To enable our software support development to start as early as possible, most parts of the beetle test chip were also ported to FPGA to enable our software team to create software support, including software packages and mbedOS support.

While the availability of CoreLink SDK-100 did a great deal to help the design process, there were still several system design tasks to be accomplished at this stage, including the following:

■ Peripheral system integration;

■ Chip-level clock and reset control, including PLL integration;

■ Chip-level power management control;

■ Top-level pin assignment, pin multiplexing;

■ Cordio IP integration;

■ DFT.

Thanks to great support and teamwork from engineering groups within Arm across a number of sites (Cambridge and Sheffield in the UK, Budapest in Hungary, Hsinchu in Taiwan, Austin in the US), system design tasks progressed quickly and were actioned as we had planned from the start.

10.4.4 Implementation of the Beetle test chip

The Beetle test chip was implemented using a standard digital design flow and tools. Although the chip contains wireless support, the Bluetooth IP is a hard macro, and detailed technical documents were available to provide us with guidelines in system-level integration. The presence of the wireless hard macro did add an additional constraint to the chip's floor planning. For example, the hard macro used had to be placed at the corner of the chip, and we needed to keep other, noisy IP like the PLL and charge pump for the embedded flash away from that part of our design.

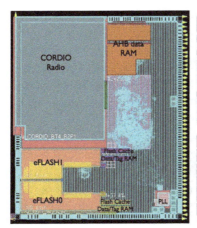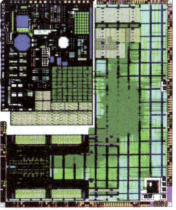

Figure 10.16: Beetle test chip die photo.

10.4.5 Other related tasks

One of the goals of the beetle test chip project was to create a development board as a part of the project for evaluation. So the project didn't stop there after the test chip was designed and made.

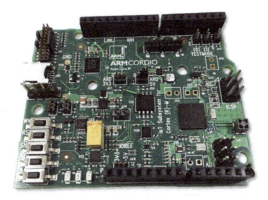

Figure 10.17: Beetle development board.

While we were waiting for the test chip to be delivered, another project team was already busy on the PCB design, and a third team had also started working on the software support. So by the time the chip was back from manufacturing, it could be soldered on the PCB so that software testing could begin. At the same time, a few of our engineers took the test chip samples to our ATE (Automatic Test Equipment) laboratory to test the chip with the DFT supports (e.g., scan testing with ATE) implemented in the chip to see if the design was working properly, while another small engineering team was busy testing the Cordio wireless interface and Bluetooth software support.

When the Beetle test chip was back from the manufacturer, we couldn't get it to work at first, despite the fact that the test chips had all worked during the ATE scan testing. After a few days of head-scratching, we found that the floating pin for scan enable (for scan testing) was the cause of the problem. While the test mode pins were tied to certain logic levels to suppress the scan testing logic, the scan enable pin, - which was shared with a GPIO pin - , was floating and therefore causing a metastability issue. By adding a pull-low resistor on the PCB, the chip booted up! (That was a very nerve-wracking week for all of us in the different teams!)

The Beetle test chip is not the only Cortex-M test chip that Arm has created. Since that time, we have designed and fabricated a series of Cortex-M test chips called Musca, using the Cortex-M33 processor and a more recent CoreLink subsystem. These test chips and development boards have been proving very useful for Trusted Firmware-M development projects. They are also an important way for Arm engineers to learn about the design challenges that other chip designers face so that Arm products can be further enhanced in the process.

CHAPTER

Software development

11

With contribution from Christopher
Seidl, senior marketing manager Keil MDK
and CMSIS, Arm

11.1 Introduction to CMSIS (Cortex Microcontroller Software Interface Standard)

Back in Chapter 9 (Section 9.4 and 9.5), we covered the minimum software support needed to bring up a system-level simulation. In the project created for that, a number of C header files from the CMSIS-CORE project are used. These header files provide a low-level software interface for applications, RTOS and middleware to access various processor level features:

- Register definitions for the processor's hardware blocks.

- A range of access functions for the processor's hardware blocks including NVIC, SysTick timer, Instrumentation Trace Macrocell (ITM).

- A range of functions for accessing special registers inside the processor.

- A range of intrinsic functions for accessing special instructions.

The CMSIS-CORE project also provides a template for a microcontroller's device driver design, including a standardized way to define interrupt assignments, names for system exceptions and a device's system initialization code (e.g., SystemInit() in system_<device>.c).

Like other projects in CMSIS (Cortex Microcontroller Software Interface Standard), CMSIS-CORE is an open-source project driven by Arm. CMSIS is a collection of multiple projects and is widely adopted by the embedded software industry.

The CMSIS project started shortly after the arrival of Cortex-M3 based microcontrollers (Note: Cortex-M3 was the first the Cortex-M processor). The success of Arm Cortex-M based devices created a demand for standardization in the software development area. Engineers don't want to cope with different software development guidelines every time they change from one silicon vendor to the other.

To answer this industry demand, Arm created the Cortex Microcontroller Software Interface Standard (CMSIS). It enables consistent software layers and device support across a wide range of development tools and microcontrollers. CMSIS is a lean software layer with little overhead and provides flexibility to the device manufacturer in defining standard peripherals. The SoC designer can, therefore, support the wide variations of the Cortex-M processor-based devices with this common standard.

The scope of the CMSIS project includes:

- Reduces the learning curve, development costs, and time-to-market for developers. They can write software faster through a variety of easy-to-use, standardized software interfaces.

- Improves the software portability and re-usability by defining consistent software interfaces. With its generic software libraries and interfaces, CMSIS provides a consistent software framework.

- Provides interfaces for debug connectivity, debug peripheral views, software delivery, and device support.

■ Allows the usage of different compilers (such as Arm, GCC, and IAR) via its compiler independent software layer.

CMSIS is defined in close cooperation with silicon and software vendors and provides a common approach to interfacing to peripherals, real-time operating systems, and middleware components. Over the years, the CMSIS project has expanded into multiple areas:

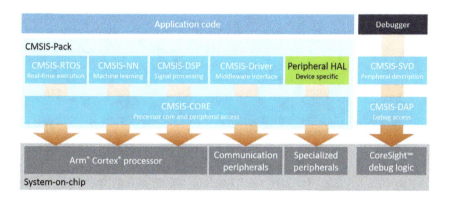

Figure 11.1: Current CMSIS projects.

SoC designers must be aware of the following CMSIS components, to create basic support for their device in various toolchains:

■ CMSIS-CORE is a standardized API for the Cortex-M processor core and peripherals.

■ CMSIS-SVD (System View Description) describes how to display peripherals in IDEs. Create this XML-based file to let tools display the peripherals in debuggers and to create header files with peripheral register and interrupt definitions.

■ CMSIS-Pack is a delivery mechanism for device support and software components. Development tools and web infrastructures use the information included in packs to extract device parameters, software components, and evaluation board configurations.

■ CMSIS-DAP is standardized firmware for a debug probe unit (usually on a separated chip) that connects to the Arm CoreSight Debug Access Port of your SoC design. CMSIS-DAP is well suited for integration on low-cost evaluation boards.

Other components that you should be aware of are:

■ CMSIS-RTOS, a common API for real-time operating systems. It provides a standardized programming interface that is portable to many RTOS and enables software components that can work across multiple RTOS systems.

- CMSIS-Driver, a definition of peripheral driver interfaces for common peripherals such as USB, Ethernet, SPI, and other types. Using this driver interface, middleware becomes reusable across supported devices.

- CMSIS-DSP, a library collection with over 60 signal processing functions.

- CMSIS-NN, a collection of efficient neural network kernels developed to maximize the performance and minimize the memory footprint of neural networks on the Cortex-M processor cores.

- CMSIS-Zone, a tool that helps to describe system resources and to partition these resources into multiple projects and execution areas. This is required for complex microcontrollers that contain multiple cores, memory protection units, or TrustZone for Armv8-M.

An in-depth tutorial is available online that explains how to create device support for a custom device using CMSIS and its pack delivery mechanism. You can find them here: https://arm-software.github.io/CMSIS_5/Pack/html/createPack_DFP.html

11.2 Creating software support for multiple toolchains

11.2.1 What is needed for creating multiple toolchain support?

If you are creating a microcontroller product, your customers are likely to use a range of software development tools, and therefore software support for multiple toolchains is essential. Fortunately, CMSIS-CORE makes this easier, and typically, the required effort for supporting multiple toolchains is limited to:

- Creating startup code for various toolchains – many toolchains use assembly startup code, and the assembly language syntax is toolchain specific.

- Creating compilation setup for various toolchains – this could be in the form of project files for Integrated Development Environments (IDEs) or makefile for Arm Compiler / gcc in Linux environment.

- In creating portable source codes, avoid using compiler/toolchain specific features such as compiler specific intrinsic/attributes. CMSIS-CORE already includes a range of intrinsic functions that is supported across multiple toolchains, and that can be used instead. If a compiler-specific feature is needed, you can add pre-processing macros to make the inclusion of such a feature optional so that the source code can still be compiled by other toolchains.

For chip design project environments, Linux would often be used, and the use of a toolchain in the command-line interface or with makefile is very common. We will look into examples of a simple makefile for Arm Compiler 6 and gcc next.

11.2.2 Compilation with Arm Compiler 6

The project example provided in Chapter 9 demonstrates software compilation with Arm Compiler 5. Currently Arm toolchains – including Keil Microcontroller Development Kit (MDK-ARM) and Arm Development Studio - also support Arm Compiler 6. If you are using Armv8-M processors such as

Cortex-M23 and Cortex-M33, Arm Compiler 6 is needed (Note: Arm Compiler 5 does not support Armv8-M processors).

If using Arm Compiler 6, the compilation command-line needs to be changed:

- Command name changed from armcc to armclang

- Processor option "`--cpu Cortex-M3`" changed to "`--target=arm-arm-none-eabi -mcpu=cortex-m3`"

- Optimization options might need to be updated (e.g., Otime in Arm Compiler 5 is not valid in Arm Compiler 6).

A simple "makefile" for Arm Compiler 6 can be written as follows:

```
# Makefile using Arm Compiler 6
INC_DIR1 = cmsis_include
INC_DIR2 = .
USER_DEF =
ARM_CC_OPTS  = --target=arm-arm-none-eabi -mcpu=cortex-m3 -c -O3 -g -I $(INC_DIR1) -I
$(INC_DIR2)
ARM_ASM_OPTS = --cpu Cortex-M3 -g
ARM_LINK_OPTS = "--keep=startup_cm3_mcu.o(RESET)" "--first=startup_cm3_mcu.o(RESET)" \
    --force_scanlib --rw_base 0x20000000 --ro_base 0x00000000 --map

all: hello.hex hello.lst
hello.o: hello.c
 armclang $(ARM_CC_OPTS) $< -o  $@

system_cm3_mcu.o: system_cm3_mcu.c
 armclang $(ARM_CC_OPTS) $< -o  $@

uart_util.o: uart_util.c
 armclang $(ARM_CC_OPTS) $< -o  $@

retarget_io.o: retarget_io.c RTE_Components.h
 armclang $(ARM_CC_OPTS) $< -o  $@

startup_cm3_mcu.o: startup_cm3_mcu.s
 armasm $(ARM_ASM_OPTS) $< -o  $@

hello.elf: hello.o system_cm3_mcu.o uart_util.o retarget_io.o startup_cm3_mcu.o
 armlink hello.o system_cm3_mcu.o uart_util.o retarget_io.o startup_cm3_mcu.o $(ARM_LINK_
OPTS) -o $@

hello.hex : hello.elf
 fromelf --vhx --8x1 $< --output $@
hello.lst : hello.elf
 fromelf -c -d -e -s $< --output $@

clean:
 rm *.o
 rm *.elf
 rm *.lst
 rm *.hex
```

The assembly startup code, the command-line for assembling and the linker command-lines can remain unchanged when migrating from Arm Compiler 5 to Arm Compiler 6. However, when using new optimization features in Arm Compiler 6, such as LTO (Link Time Optimization), both compilation and linking options need to be updated.

11.2.3 Compilation with gcc

Another popular choice of toolchain is gcc. You can download the gcc toolchain (GNU Arm Embedded Toolchain) for Cortex-M and Cortex-R processor from Arm's developer website:

https://developer.arm.com/tools-and-software/open-source-software/developer-tools/gnu-toolchain/gnu-rm

This toolchain only provides command-line tools but is sufficient for chip designers when compiling projects for simulations. Chip vendors can also create a toolchain package for their customers by providing an IDE built around gcc toolchain.

Unlike when using Arm Compiler 5/6, it is common to merge the compilation and link stages when using gcc or use gcc for both compilation and linking because gcc can invoke the linker (ld) automatically with the correct link options. Linking compiled objects using GNU linker (ld) directly is less common as it is error-prone.

Instead of using the command-line to control memory layout as in previous Arm Compiler 5/6 examples, with gcc, we need to use a linker script to specify memory layout for the linking stage. An example linker script can be written as follows:

```
/* Linker script to configure memory regions.
 * Need modifying for a specific board.
 *    FLASH.ORIGIN: starting address of flash
 *    FLASH.LENGTH: length of flash
 *    RAM.ORIGIN: starting address of RAM bank 0
 *    RAM.LENGTH: length of RAM bank 0
 */
GROUP(libgcc.a libc.a libm.a libnosys.a)

MEMORY
{
  FLASH (rx) : ORIGIN = 0x0,        LENGTH = 0x10000 /* 64KB */
  RAM (rwx)  : ORIGIN = 0x20000000, LENGTH = 0x8000  /* 32KB */
}

INCLUDE "sections.ld"
```

This linker script also pulls in a default linker script sections.ld, which defines the memory layout inside the program image.

Since the assembly language syntax is different between Arm toolchain and GNU assembler, we also need to create a startup code for gcc:

```
startup_cm3_mcu.S
    .syntax unified
    .arch armv7-m

    .section .stack
    .align 3
/*
// <h> Stack Configuration
//    <o> Stack Size (in Bytes) <0x0-0xFFFFFFFF:8>
// </h>
*/

    .section .stack
    .align 3
#ifdef __STACK_SIZE
    .equ    Stack_Size, __STACK_SIZE
#else
    .equ    Stack_Size, 0x200
#endif
    .globl     __StackTop
    .globl     __StackLimit
__StackLimit:
    .space    Stack_Size
    .size __StackLimit, . - __StackLimit
__StackTop:
    .size __StackTop, . - __StackTop


/*
// <h> Heap Configuration
//    <o>  Heap Size (in Bytes) <0x0-0xFFFFFFFF:8>
// </h>
*/

    .section .heap
    .align 3
#ifdef __HEAP_SIZE
    .equ    Heap_Size, __HEAP_SIZE
#else
    .equ    Heap_Size, 0
#endif
    .globl     __HeapBase
    .globl     __HeapLimit
__HeapBase:
    .if     Heap_Size
    .space    Heap_Size
    .endif
    .size __HeapBase, . - __HeapBase
__HeapLimit:
    .size __HeapLimit, . - __HeapLimit


/* Vector Table */

    .section .isr_vector
    .align 2
    .globl __isr_vector
```

```
__isr_vector:
    .long    __StackTop              /* Top of Stack                */
    .long    Reset_Handler           /* Reset Handler               */
    .long    NMI_Handler             /* NMI Handler                 */
    .long    HardFault_Handler       /* Hard Fault Handler          */
    .long    MemManage_Handler       /* MPU Fault Handler           */
    .long    BusFault_Handler        /* Bus Fault Handler           */
    .long    UsageFault_Handler      /* Usage Fault Handler         */
    .long    0                       /* Reserved                    */
    .long    0                       /* Reserved                    */
    .long    0                       /* Reserved                    */
    .long    0                       /* Reserved                    */
    .long    SVC_Handler             /* SVCall Handler              */
    .long    DebugMon_Handler        /* Debug Monitor Handler       */
    .long    0                       /* Reserved                    */
    .long    PendSV_Handler          /* PendSV Handler              */
    .long    SysTick_Handler         /* SysTick Handler             */

    /* External Interrupts */
    .long    GPIO0_Handler           /* 16+ 0: GPIO 0 Handler       */
    .long    GPIO1_Handler           /* 16+ 1: GPIO 1 Handler       */
    .long    TIMER0_Handler          /* 16+ 2: Timer 0 Handler      */
    .long    TIMER1_Handler          /* 16+ 3: Timer 1 Handler      */
    .long    UARTTX0_Handler         /* 16+ 4: UART 0 TX Handler    */
    .long    UARTRX0_Handler         /* 16+ 5: UART 0 RX Handler    */

    .size    __isr_vector, . - __isr_vector

/* Reset Handler */
    .text
    .thumb
    .thumb_func
    .align 2
    .globl   Reset_Handler
    .type    Reset_Handler, %function
Reset_Handler:
/*      Loop to copy data from read only memory to RAM. The ranges
 *      of copy from/to are specified by following symbols evaluated in
 *      linker script.
 *      __etext: End of code section, i.e., begin of data sections to copy from.
 *      __data_start__/__data_end__ : RAM address range that data should be
 *      copied to. Both must be aligned to 4 bytes boundary.  */

    ldr      r1, =__etext
    ldr      r2, =__data_start__
    ldr      r3, =__data_end__

    subs     r3, r2
    ble      .LC1
.LC0:
    subs     r3, #4
    ldr      r0, [r1, r3]
    str      r0, [r2, r3]
    bgt      .LC0
.LC1:

#ifdef __STARTUP_CLEAR_BSS
/*      This part of work usually is done in C library startup code. Otherwise,
 *      define this macro to enable it in this startup.
 *
 *      Loop to zero out BSS section, which uses following symbols
 *      in linker script:
 *      __bss_start__: start of BSS section. Must align to 4
 *      __bss_end__: end of BSS section. Must align to 4
```

```
 */
    ldr r1, =__bss_start__
    ldr r2, =__bss_end__

    movs    r0, 0
.LC2:
    cmp     r1, r2
    itt     lt
    strlt   r0, [r1], #4
    blt     .LC2
#endif /*  __STARTUP_CLEAR_BSS */

#ifndef __NO_SYSTEM_INIT
    /* bl    SystemInit */
    ldr     r0,=SystemInit
    blx     r0
#endif

    bl    _start

    .pool
    .size Reset_Handler, . - Reset_Handler

/*    Macro to define default handlers. Default handler
 *    will be weak symbol and just dead loops. They can be
 *    overwritten by other handlers */
    .macro    def_default_handler    handler_name
    .align 1
    .thumb_func
    .weak     \handler_name
    .type     \handler_name, %function
\handler_name :
    b     .
    .size     \handler_name, . - \handler_name
    .endm

/* System Exception Handlers */

    def_default_handler    NMI_Handler
    def_default_handler    HardFault_Handler
    def_default_handler    MemManage_Handler
    def_default_handler    BusFault_Handler
    def_default_handler    UsageFault_Handler
    def_default_handler    SVC_Handler
    def_default_handler    DebugMon_Handler
    def_default_handler    PendSV_Handler
    def_default_handler    SysTick_Handler

/* IRQ Handlers */

    def_default_handler    GPIO0_Handler
    def_default_handler    GPIO1_Handler
    def_default_handler    TIMER0_Handler
    def_default_handler    TIMER1_Handler
    def_default_handler    UARTRX0_Handler
    def_default_handler    UARTTX0_Handler

    /*
    def_default_handler    Default_Handler
    .weak     DEF_IRQHandler
    .set      DEF_IRQHandler, Default_Handler
    */
    .end
```

Please note that with GNU toolchain, there is a different between filename extension ".S" (upper case) and ".s" (lower case). To enable preprocessing, the filename extension needs to be ".S" (upper case).

The retarget support code is different between gcc and Arm toolchain as well:

retarget.c

```
#include <stdio.h>
#include <sys/stat.h>

extern int stdout_putchar(int ch);

__attribute__ ((used))  int _write (int fd, char *ptr, int len)
{
  size_t i;
  for (i=0; i<len;i++)
  {
    stdout_putchar((int) ptr[i]); // call character output function
  }
  return len;
}
```

To compile the simple hello world project with gcc, the makefile can be made quite simple by merging compilation and linking into one step:

```
# Makefile using gcc (Arm GNU Embedded toolchain)
INC_DIR1 = cmsis_include
INC_DIR2 = .
USER_DEF =
CC_OPTS  = -mthumb -mcpu=cortex-m3 -O3 -g -Otime -I $(INC_DIR1) -I $(INC_DIR2)
LINKER_SCRIPT_PATH = .
LINKER_SCRIPT = mem.ld
LINK_OPTS = -T $(LINKER_SCRIPT)

all: hello.hex hello.lst

hello.elf: hello.c system_cm3_mcu.c uart_util.c retarget.c startup_cm3_mcu.S
 arm-none-eabi-gcc $(CC_OPTS) hello.c system_cm3_mcu.c \
    uart_util.c retarget.c startup_cm3_mcu.S \
    -L $(LINKER_SCRIPT_PATH) $(LINK_OPTS) -o $@

hello.hex : hello.elf
 arm-none-eabi-objcopy -S hello.elf -O verilog  $@

hello.lst : hello.elf
 arm-none-eabi-objdump -S hello.elf > $@

clean:
 rm *.o
 rm *.elf
 rm *.lst
 rm *.hex
```

11.3 Introduction of the Arm Development Studio featuring Arm Keil Microcontroller Development Kit (MDK)

11.3.1 Overview of Keil MDK

Unlike chip designers, microcontroller software developers often use development tools within IDEs (Integrated Development Environments). There are several software development tools available with IDE, and one of these products is Keil MDK (Keil was acquired by Arm in 2005). For chip designers, it is important to test the prototypes (e.g., FPGA prototypes or engineering samples) with these IDEs to ensure that debug and trace connections are correct, and there are no unexpected issues with establishing debug connection to the Cortex-M processor(s).

Keil MDK is an integrated development environment (IDE) that contains compiler, editor, debugger, as well as various utilities such as flash programming tools. Using MDK, software developers can create embedded applications for Arm Cortex-M processor-based devices, program the application images into the flash memories and verify their correct operations using the integrated debugger. The full version of the Keil MDK also includes a set of middleware and two choices of IDEs.

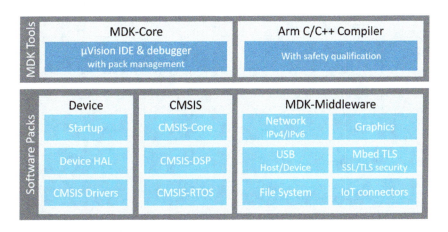

Figure 11.2: Full packages in Keil MDK professional.

For microcontroller software developers, the user interface they are most familiar with is the μVision IDE. From there, you can create/modify projects, edit source codes, compile codes, program the devices, and debug the applications. The rest of this section is focused on μVision IDE, which most microcontroller software developers use.

CMSIS support is closely integrated within the μVision IDE. For example, when creating a project, the project wizard can utilize CMSIS-PACK to download the appropriate software packages required. Software packs contain device support, CMSIS libraries, middleware, board support, code templates, and example projects. These can be added any time to the toolchain. The IDE manages the provided software components that are available for the application as building blocks.

Note: While you need to start with the IDE to set up a project, you can use the command-line afterward to automatically build, flash, and debug your application.

11.3.2 Keil MDK Installation

Keil MDK is available for Windows platform only. There are multiple versions of Keil MDK at different price points. The free MDK-Lite edition supports devices with a code size of up to 32 kB and can be used for professional development of commercial products. Download MDK from www.keil.com/download. To install the product on your PC, follow the installation guide: www.keil.com/mdk5/install

After installing the Keil MDK, the CMSIS-PACK installer will start, and you need to download software packs for the microcontroller devices you want to use. If you are a chip designer and creating your own Cortex-M based device, then you only need to install the base CMSIS-CORE packages.

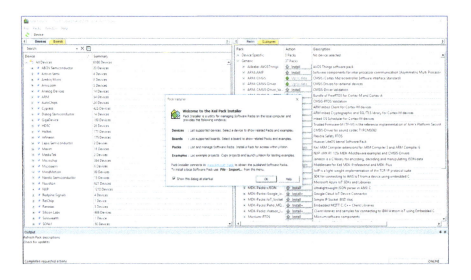

Figure 11.3: CMSIS-Pack installer startup screen.

Additional software utilities might be needed:

- Debug probe driver - Depending on the debug probe that you are going to use, you might need to install the correct device driver for it. The Keil MDK installation by default includes a number of these drivers in <installation_dir>\ARM\<Segger/SiLabs/STLink/TI_XDS/ULINK>. Please double-check the documentation that comes with your debug probe hardware to see the driver installation requirements.

- UART Terminal (or virtual COM port terminal) – If you want to redirect printf text message into a UART connection and display that on your PC, you need a UART terminal program such as TeraTerm or Putty. Since most modern PCs do not have RS232 ports anymore, you will need to get a USB-UART adaptor, and that also has its hardware device driver to install. (Note: printf message display using Cortex-M's instrumentation Trace Macrocell (ITM) does not require such drivers as Keil MDK can display the prinrf message in the debug IDE. But remember: the ITM feature is not available in Armv6-M and Armv8-M Baseline processors).

Please note that there are two types of USB-UART adaptors:

■ Adaptors that provide DB9 connectors and use RS232(C) signal protocol

■ Adaptors that provide jumper wire connections and use logic level signaling (usually 3.3v but can also be TTL compatible).

Silicon designs normally use 3.3v signaling for top-level I/O, and if RS232 signaling is needed, a separate signal converter chip is required. Make sure that you have the right kind of USB-UART adaptor when connecting your boards, as a direct connection between digital logic and RS232 can result in permanent damage to the circuits.

11.3.3 Create an application

In this section, we will create a project based on a FPGA platform with a Cortex-M3 processor. Unlike software development using microcontrollers, FPGA platforms do not have internal flash memories, and the program is downloaded into the program RAM directly. Also, we do not have the chip-vendor prepared software packs as in many microcontroller devices. However, many of the project flow concepts are similar.

We go through the following steps to create an application:

1. Create a project and select the device along with the relevant CMSIS components.

2. Create and add the source code files to the project.

3. Edit the source files and add the required code.

4. Compile and link the application for downloading it to the on-chip Flash memory.

5. Debug the application and verify the correct operation.

For this project, we will create the following application files:

1. The main.c file contains the main() function that initializes essential hardware, the peripherals, and starts the LED blinky execution.

2. The LED.c file contains functions to initialize and control the GPIO port. The LED_Initialize() function initializes the GPIO port pin. The functions LED_On() and LED_Off() control the port pin that interfaces to the LED.

3. The LED.h header file contains the function prototypes for the functions in LED.c and is included in the file main.c.

11.3.4 Using the project wizard to create a project

To create a blank Cortex-M3 project, we can use the project wizard, accessible from the pull-down menu: Project → New μVision Project.

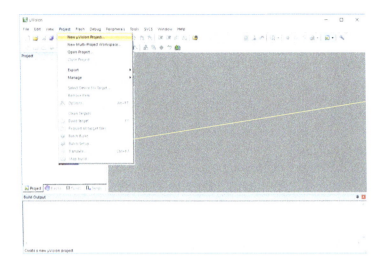

Figure 11.4: A new project.

It will then ask you where the project should be placed. For this example, we selected an empty folder called "C:\work\CM3_Blinky_1".

The project wizard then asks which device this project will be based on. For this project, which is starting from scratch, the generic Cortex-M3 processor (ARMCM3) is selected.

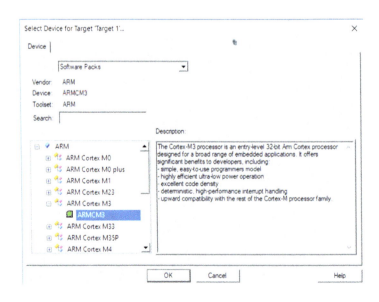

Figure 11.5: Target select to ARMCM3.

The project wizard then opens the Run-Time Environment window, which allows us to include a range of software components in the project. For the basic project that we are creating, we need the CMSIS-CORE support and a device startup file. However, since we are creating our own startup code with our specific vector table, only the CMSIS-CORE software component is selected, and we will add the startup code to the project manually.

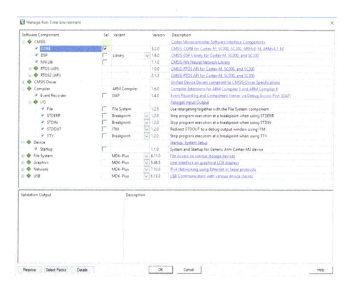

Figure 11.6: Select Run-time environment options.

If we want to include printf support in our example code, we should also include Compiler → I/O → STDOUT [e.g., ITM/User]. The first project we demonstrate here does not require printf, so this is not selected.

Now we have an empty project, as shown in Figure 11.7.

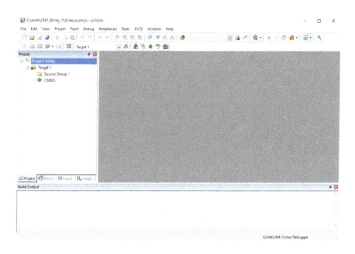

Figure 11.7: A blank project.

You can add/modify the project's source groups and add the source file to the project:

▨ Rename a source group – single click on the name of the source group.

▨ Add a new source group – right-click on the Target name (Target 1) and select "Add Group ...".

▨ Add a source file to a source group - by double-click on the Source Groups.

For this example, I have modified the project to have two source groups, as shown in Figure 11.8, and added some files to it:

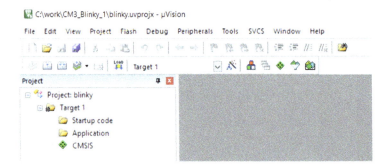

Figure 11.8: Project modified to have two source groups.

11.3.5 Create and add source files

There are several ways to create and add source files to the project:

▨ Create the source file in µVision IDE using File→New, write the code and "Save as" the file type you need, and then add to the project.

▨ Right click on a source group, select "Add New item to Group '<group name>'"

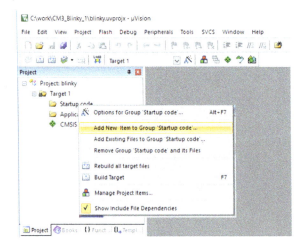

Figure 11.9: Add a new item to a source group.

When using the second method, the following window will appear and allow you to define the file type and the filename.

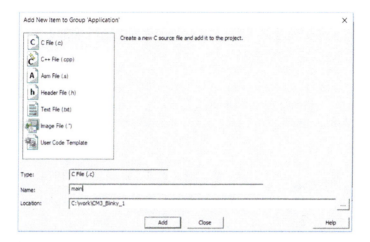

Figure 11.10: Define file type and filename when adding a new item to a source group.

We can reuse some of the previously created projects such as startup code and system initialization code, create the new source files (main.c, LED.c, and LED.h), and add these to the project.

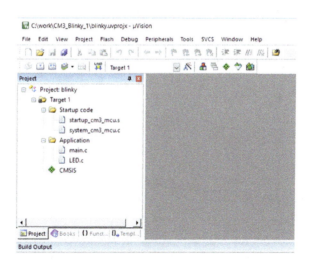

Figure 11.11: Project with source files added.

11.3.6 Edit the source files

We use the built-in editor in μVision to edit the source files; however, you can also use the editor of your choice. The files are created and available in the project's home directory. The μVision editor includes features like code completion, dynamic syntax checking, code navigation, or function finding. The editor margin can contain signs for bookmarks, breakpoints, error indicators, program counter, code execution, or performance indicators.

We start with the last file LED.c and its associated header file LED.h. Based on the system-level header file (cm3_mcu.h) created in previous chapters, the source code for LED utilities can be written using the peripheral definitions defined in the cm3_mcu.h. The example code for LED.h is written as follows:

LED.h

```
#include "stdint.h"  // Required for the return type of LED initialize
int32_t LED_Initialize (void); // function prototype for LED_Initialize
void     LED_On          (void); // function prototype for LED_On
void     LED_Off         (void); // function prototype for LED_Off
```

Here, we define the three functions that will be available to users. The actual content of the functions is available in LED.c. Open this file and add the following code (Assuming the LED pin is GPIO 0 - pin 0):

LED.c

```
#include "LED.h"
#include "cm3_mcu.h"

void     LED_On          (void)
{
  CM3MCU_GPIO0->DATAOUT |= (0x01UL); // Set data output to 1
  return;
}
void     LED_Off         (void)
{
  CM3MCU_GPIO0->DATAOUT &= ~(0x01UL); // Set data output to 0
  return;
}

int32_t LED_Initialize (void)
{
  CM3MCU_GPIO0->DATAOUT &= ~(0x01UL); // Set data output to 0
  CM3MCU_GPIO0->OUTEN   |= 0x1UL; // Enable bit 0 as output
  return (0);
}
```

The file main.c contains an endless loop that use the LED functions to toggle the LED. The toggling delay is implemented using SysTick, which increments an integer variable SysTickCntr at 1KHz.

main.c

```
#include "cm3_mcu.h"
#include "LED.h"

volatile  uint32_t SysTickCntr=0;
void      TickDelay(int32_t);

int main(void)
{
  LED_Initialize();
  SysTick_Config((SystemCoreClock/1000)-1); // 1KHz Ticks
  while(1){
    LED_On();
    TickDelay(500);
    LED_Off();
    TickDelay(500);
  }; // end while
}

void TickDelay(int32_t tnum)
{
  uint32_t LastTick=0, NewTick=0, DivideCntr=0;
  LastTick = SysTickCntr;
  NewTick = LastTick;
  DivideCntr = tnum;
  while (DivideCntr>0) {
    NewTick = SysTickCntr;
    if (NewTick!=LastTick) { // SysTickCntr changed
      LastTick = NewTick;
      DivideCntr--;
    }
  }
  return;
}

void SysTick_Handler(void)
{ // Trigger at 1KHz
  SysTickCntr++;
  return;
}
```

11.3.7 Defining project options

Before we can compile and test our application, we need to define your project options. You can access to project options by right-clicking on the target name on the project hierarchy window, or click on the project option button:

Figure 11.12: Access to project options.

Since this project is for our own system design, we need to tell the tool what the memory map looks like. Therefore, in the target tab of the project option, we define the memory size for our system, as shown in the example value in Figure 11.13:

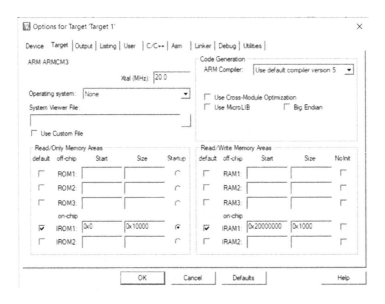

Figure 11.13: Memory addresses and sizes in the project options.

We also need to tell the linker to use this memory layout for linking operations. This option ("Use Memory Layout from Target Dialog") is available in the linker option tap. (This option is not set by default).

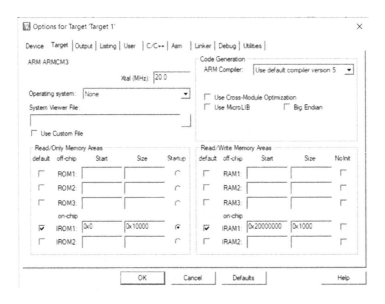

Figure 11.14: Linker options, including the option to force the linker to use memory layout in the target dialog.

We can optionally define the compiler options in the C/C++ compiler options, as shown in Figure 11.15:

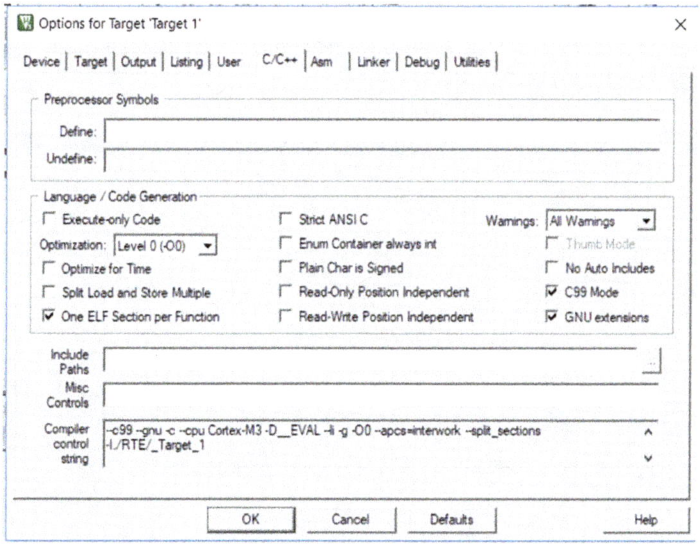

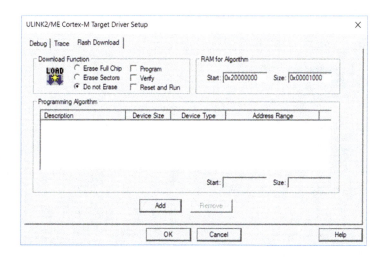

Figure 11.15: Compiler options, including optimization options, preprocessing flags, include paths and C/C++ coding rules.

If you are using an FPGA prototype, then there is no flash programming algorithm, and the download option needs to be set up accordingly, as shown in Figure 11.16. To gain access to this dialog, either:

■ Click on debug option tab, then click on the "Settings" button on the right of the selected debug probe choice, or

■ Click on the Utilities tab, then click on the "Settings" button.

Figure 11.16: Specify no flash download for FPGA projects.

11.3.8 Compile the project

Once everything is in place, we can now compile and test our project. Go to Project – Build Target and use F7 to build the application. This step compiles and links all related source files. The Build Output window shows information about the build process. An error-free build displays program size information, zero errors, and zero warnings:

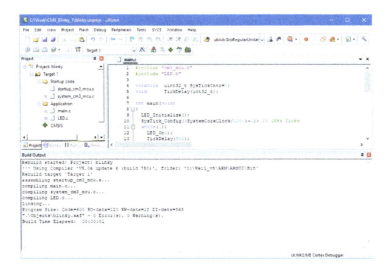

Figure 11.17: Specify no flash download for FPGA projects.

11.3.9 Download and debug the application

The debug session can be started by hotkey "Ctrl-F5", via a pull-down menu (Debug→Start/Stop debug session) or by clicking on the "(d)" button in the toolbar just below the pull-down menu. By default, the code stops at the beginning of main() when the debug session starts (this behavior is controllable from debug options):

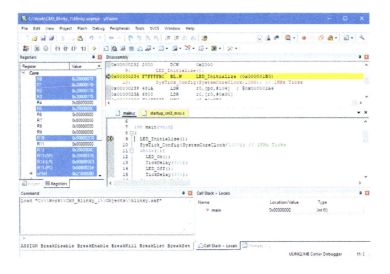

Figure 11.18: Debug session start screen.

Please note that in the debug session, the buttons in the toolbar are different from the coding screen. You can see a description of the button by moving the mouse cursor on top of it.

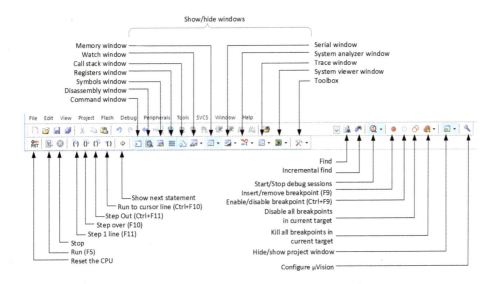

Figure 11.19: Toolbar during debug session.

The µVision debugger connects to various debug/trace adapters and supports traditional features like simple and complex breakpoints, watch windows, and execution control. Using trace, additional features like event/exception viewers, system analyzer, execution profiler, and code coverage are supported. Component viewer and event recorder help you to gain insight into the operation of third-party software, such as Keil RTX.

In the **Registers** window, you see the content of the registers of the Cortex-M processor. The **Disassembly** window shows the program execution in assembly code intermixed with the source code (when available). When this is the active window, all debug stepping commands will then work at the assembly level. The **Call Stack + Locals** window shows the function nesting and variables of the current program location. You can use the **Command** window to enter debug commands.

The application has run to main and is ready to be run. If we do that now, we will see the LED toggles at 2Hz (i.e., blinks at 1Hz). If you want to look at the toggling operations in detail, you can add a breakpoint to the loop, such as line 12 of main.c (LED_on()). This can be done by simply left-clicking the grey area next to this line, and you will see a red dot that shows the breakpoint set. Go to **Debug – Run** or press **F5** to run to this breakpoint. Use the **Step** function (**F11**) to step into the code. The next line will be highlighted by two arrows. Step again, into the LED_On function. The scope changes, and the LED.c file comes into the foreground. Step twice to see how the LED is lit and to go back to main.c.

As you don't want to step many times in the TickDelay function, use **Step Over (F10)** to step over this function and stop at LED_Off. If we step into it and step out again, we will see that the LED is off.

11.3.10 Using ITM for text message output (printf)

In Chapter 9, Section 9.4.6, we demonstrated how to redirect printf output messages to a UART interface. You can do the same on FPGA platforms or your microcontroller designs and capture the output messages with a USB-UART adaptor.

Instead of using a UART (since your chip might have only one usable UART, which you could, need that for your application), you can use ITM (Instrumentation Trace Macrocell) to handle the printf text message. The trace message output can pass through a trace connection (e.g., either SWO pin or trace data pins) and be collected by the debug host, and then be displayed in real-time.

To use this feature:

- The processor needs to be an Armv7-M or Armv8-M Mainline processor. (Cortex-M0/M0+/M1/M23 processors do not support ITM).

- A trace connection needs to be available (e.g., when using Serial-Wire debug, the TDO pin can be switched into SWO for low-cost trace connection).

- The debug probe and the debug environment must support ITM trace (e.g., Using Keil MDK and ULINK2 debug probe allows us to collect trace message via the TDO pin).

To do that, several small changes are needed in the project we demonstrated before. The first step is to include the STDOUT support in the Run-Time Environment. You can open the Run-Time environment dialog by clicking on the button on the toolbar, as shown in Figure 11.20:

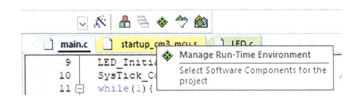

Figure 11.20: Open Manage Run-Time Environment dialog.

Inside the manage Run-time environment dialog, enable the STDOUT redirection to ITM, as shown in Figure 11.21:

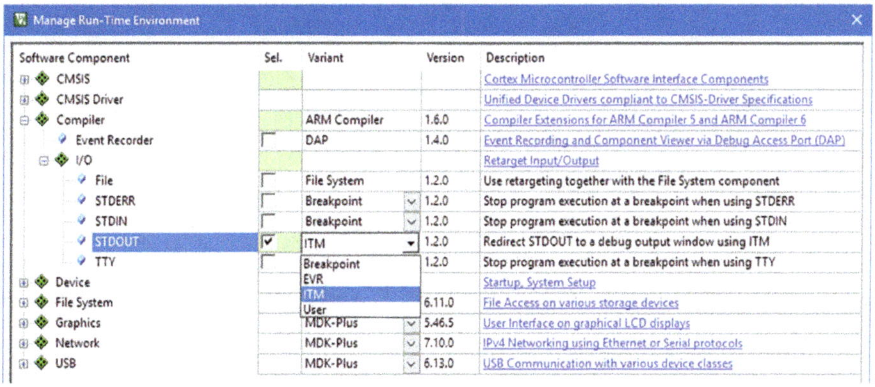

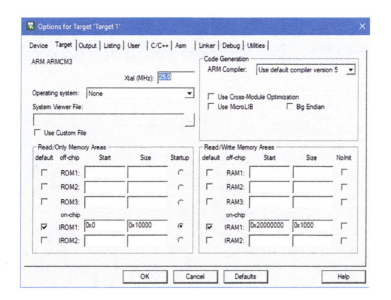

Figure 11.21: Adding STDOUT support in Run-Time Environment configuration.

If using a SWO trace connection, you will need to make sure the clock frequency setup is correct.

Figure 11.22: Target clock frequency setup in the project.

If using the SWO that is multiplexed with the TDO pin, we must select Serial-Wire Debug mode in the debug connection setting:

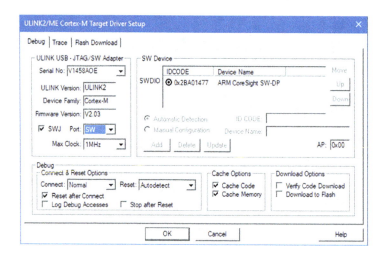

Figure 11.23: If using SWO signal for trace, select Serial-Wire debug mode so that TDO pin can be used for SWO.

Now click on the 'Trace' tab of the debug probe settings and enable trace. Please also double-check that the clock frequency setting is correct.

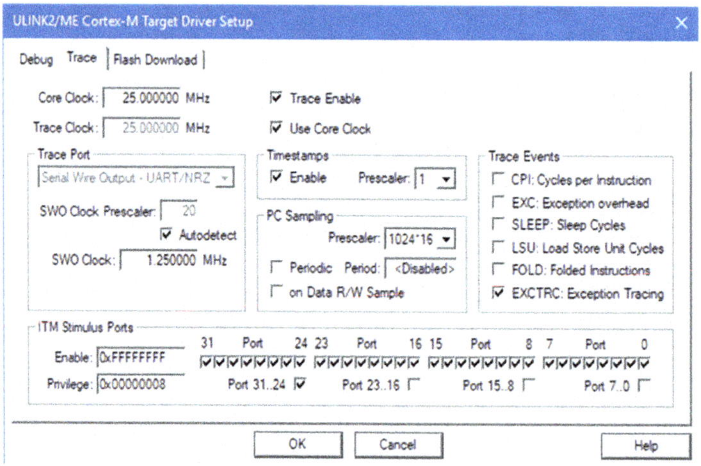

Figure 11.24: Enable trace option.

Notes:

◼ Starting from MDK version 5.28, there are separated clock settings for Core and Trace clocks.

◼ If you find you are losing some of the trace messages, you can disable timestamp package generation to reduce the bandwidth of the trace output. That might help avoid some of the trace data being lost.

The program main.c is then modified to generate printf messages:

main.c (for ITM printf demo)

```c
#include "cm3_mcu.h"
#include "LED.h"
#include <stdio.h>

volatile  uint32_t SysTickCntr=0;
void      TickDelay(int32_t);

int main(void)
{
  uint32_t counter=0;
  LED_Initialize();
  printf ("Hello world\n");
  SysTick_Config((SystemCoreClock/1000)-1); // 1KHz Ticks
  while(1){
    LED_On();
    TickDelay(500);
    LED_Off();
    TickDelay(500);
    counter++;
    printf("%d\n", counter);
  }; // end while
}

void TickDelay(int32_t tnum)
{
  uint32_t LastTick=0, NewTick=0, DivideCntr=0;
  LastTick = SysTickCntr;
  NewTick = LastTick;
  DivideCntr = tnum;
  while (DivideCntr>0) {
    NewTick = SysTickCntr;
    if (NewTick!=LastTick) { // SysTickCntr changed
      LastTick = NewTick;
      DivideCntr--;
    }
  }
  return;
}

void SysTick_Handler(void)
{ // Trigger at 1KHz
  SysTickCntr++;
  return;
}
```

We can now compile the project and start the debug session as before. In the debug session, before we start the program execution, we need to open the printf display console: this is accessible from the pull-down menu View→Serial Windows→Debug (printf) viewer:

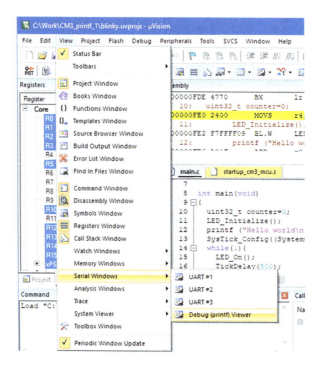

Figure 11.25: Access to debug (printf) viewer in a debug session.

You should then be able to see the debug (printf) viewer in the bottom right-hand corner of the IDE screen. When the program starts, you can then see the printf message being displayed in this window:

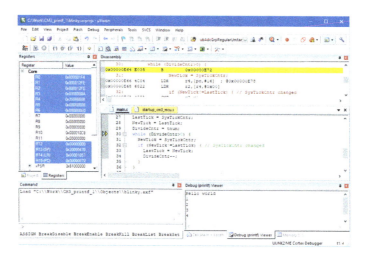

Figure 11.26: Debug (printf) viewer showing the printf message received via a trace connection.

11.3.11 Software development in collaborative environments

Today, development teams are distributed across various locations, often worldwide. To be able to work on the same project, collaborative tools are used to grant access to every team member, no matter where they are located. Currently, the most widely used tool is Git, which was established as the version control system for the Linux kernel.

Development tools, like Keil MDK, have interfaces to Git so that developers can efficiently submit their code to the repository and update the code base with contributions from other team members.

Git is so popular today that there are a lot of excellent tutorials out there to help you get started, and since an in-depth introduction to Git is beyond the scope of this introductory chapter, we recommend that you select one suitable for your needs and study the subject. It is worth bearing in mind though before you are tempted to find other ways to collaborate that using Git is a good idea even for very small development teams as each member has the complete repository available, in case the original one fails for any reason and has to be recreated.

11.4 Using an RTOS

Before showing an example with RTOS, we will explore the two software concepts that can be used for creating an embedded application.

11.4.1 RTOS software concepts

In an **infinite loop design**, the program runs in an endless loop. Program functions (threads) are called from within the loop, while interrupt service routines (ISRs) perform time-critical jobs including some data processing.

Simple embedded applications can safely be run in an endless loop. Time-critical functions, typically triggered by hardware interrupts, are executed in an ISR that also performs the required data processing. The main loop contains only basic operations that are not time-critical and run in the background.

In an **RTOS-based design**, multiple threads run in the multitasking environment provided by the real-time operating system (RTOS). The RTOS provides inter-thread communication and time management functions. A pre-emptive RTOS reduces the complexity of interrupt functions because high-priority threads can perform time-critical data processing.

RTOS kernels are based on the idea of parallel execution threads (tasks). Just like in the real world, an application usually must fulfill multiple different tasks. An RTOS-based application recreates this model in software and makes sure that:

- Thread priority and run-time scheduling are handled by the RTOS kernel, using a proven code base.

- Inter-thread communication is handled using the API provided by the RTOS.

- Larger teams can safely work on various aspects of the software. A pre-emptive multi-tasking concept simplifies the progressive enhancement of an application as new functionality can be added without risking the response time of more critical threads.

- Polling for interrupts is not required. Infinite loop software concepts often poll for occurred interrupts. In contrast, RTOS kernels themselves are interrupt driven and can largely eliminate polling. This allows the CPU to sleep or process threads more often.

- Hard real-time requirements can be met because the RTOS kernel is usually transparent to the interrupt system. Communication facilities can be used for IRQ-to-task communication and allow top-half/bottom-half handling of your interrupts.

11.4.2 Using Keil RTX

The Keil RTX implements the CMSIS-RTOS API v2 as a native RTOS interface for the Cortex-M processor-based devices. CMSIS-RTOS is one of the projects within CMSIS. It provides a common RTOS software interface to application and middleware. The RTX is an Arm implementation of a small RTOS kernel based on this open RTOS API standard.

While RTX RTOS is not part of CMSIS, it is an open-source project of its own, and it builds into Keil MDK library support. Note: Software developers can include RTX in their software project for free!

Once the execution reaches main(), we use the recommended order to initialize the hardware and start the kernel. We should implement in main() at least the following in the given order:

1. Initialization and configuration of hardware, including peripheral, memory, pin, clock, and interrupt system.

2. Update of the system clock frequency using the CMSIS-CORE function **SystemCoreClock**.

3. Initialize the CMSIS-RTOS kernel using **osKernelInitialize**.

4. Optionally, we can create a new thread using **osThreadNew**, for example, app_main. In the following example, this is used as the main thread. Alternatively, threads can also be directly created in main(). We will use this approach later in our little example project.

Start the RTOS scheduler using **osKernelStart**.

To add RTX into the project, we can enable the RTX library in the Manage Run-Time environment dialog:

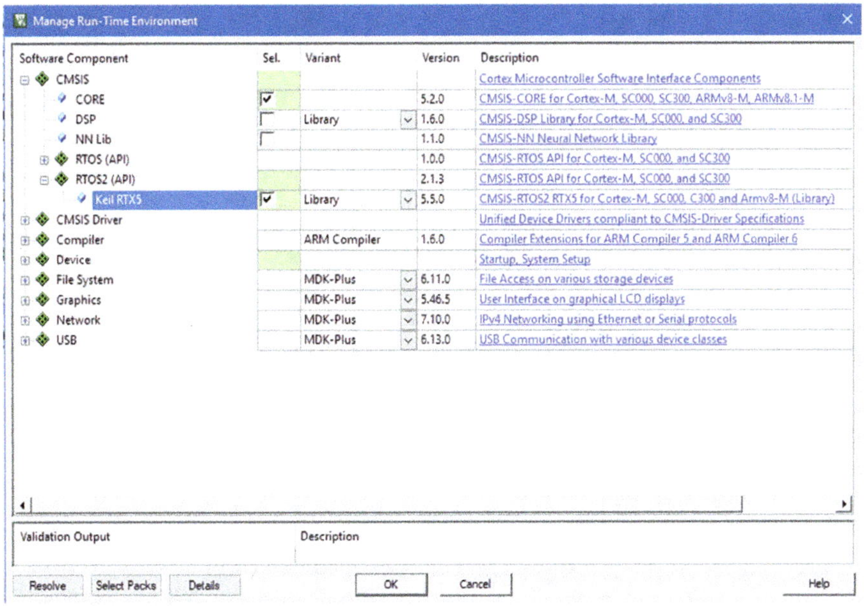

Figure 11.27: Adding RTX in run-time environment option.

When using Keil RTX5, the project wizard specified that default device startup code and system initialization must be used. Therefore, we enabled the option, and the project wizard added the default Cortex-M3 startup code and system initialization code into the project. Since we cannot have two versions of startup code in the project, the original startup code is removed, and the custom-defined vector table is then transferred into the new default startup code. We also do the same for the system initialization code.

Next, we modify the main.c to utilize the RTX kernel. In this example, we have only one thread for toggling the LED:

main.c

```
#include "cm3_mcu.h"
#include "LED.h"
#include "cmsis_os2.h"

void thread_led (void *arg);

int main(void)
{
  LED_Initialize();
  osKernelInitialize(); // Initialize CMSIS-RTOS
  osThreadNew(thread_led, NULL, NULL); // create thead for thread_led
  osKernelStart();                     // Start thread execution
  for (;;) {}
```

```
  }

  void thread_led (void *argument) {
    while(1){
      LED_On();
      osDelay(500);
      LED_Off();
      osDelay(500);
    }; // end while
  }
```

Now we can compile the code and test it, and it should toggle the LED in the same way as the first example.

For more information on using RTX and CMSIS-RTOSv2 API, please visit:
https://www.keil.com/pack/doc/CMSIS/RTOS2/html/index.html

11.4.3 Optimizing memory usage
11.4.3.1 The need for RAM usage analysis
While our little program now behaves as expected, a software developer might face the problem that the overall memory usage is too high. In RTOS based system, each thread needs to have its own stack, and the RTOS itself also requires memory allocation for various objects (e.g., semaphores, mailboxes). Although toolchains often have the capability to report stack usage of a function tree, there are limitations:

- If the code calls a library function and the library does not provide stack usage, C usage reports will not be able to analysis the stack usage needed for the library calls.

- If the code contains function calls to function pointers which are dynamically assigned, the toolchain cannot determine a static call tree for stack usage analysis.

Even if the toolchain can report the RAM usage, it might not be clear how the RAM is used per thread. The last build output should have shown a RW memory usage of roughly 3 kB. This is already quite a lot for some devices that have a small amount of RAM. How can we reduce this? Let's use some more enhanced debug features to check our code.

11.4.3.2 Configure RTX for stack watermarking
Although the RTX kernel is added to the project in library form, it is still configurable, and a number of settings can be controlled in RTX_Config.c and RTX_Config.h (you can see them in the project hierarchy window).

The file RTX_Config.h contains a number of markups in its code comments to enable easy configuration via a Configuration Wizard. Underneath the code window, you can see a Configuration Wizard tab. Click on it, and you can then browse and edit each option in the file easily. In Figure 11.28, we enable the Stack Usage Watermark feature – make sure you save this file before you recompile the project!

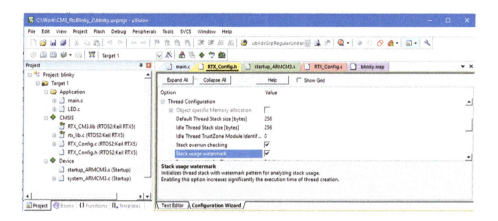

Figure 11.28: Enabling stack usage watermark for stack size measurement in RTX.

After the project is compiled, start the debug session as usual, and the program should stop at the beginning of main().

11.4.3.3 RTX RTOS viewer in Watch windows

After enabling the stack usage watermark feature in RTX, we can then report the stack usage of each thread using the RTX RTOS viewer during a debug session.

The RTX RTOS viewer can be enabled in a debug session via pull-down menu View→Watch windows→RTX RTOS. This shows some of the configuration information about the RTX kernel, including memory configuration parameters (e.g., default stack size for threads) and states of stack overflow detection features.

When the RTX RTOS viewer is open at the start of the application (before the OS start), this window does not show any thread information. But once the program has run for a bit and then halted, the RTX RTOS viewer will show the information about the threads as well as the OS kernel. Let the program run for a while and then stop. In the **RTX RTOS** window, expand **Threads**, and then the thread that is marked as thread_led. Observe the **Stack** usage:

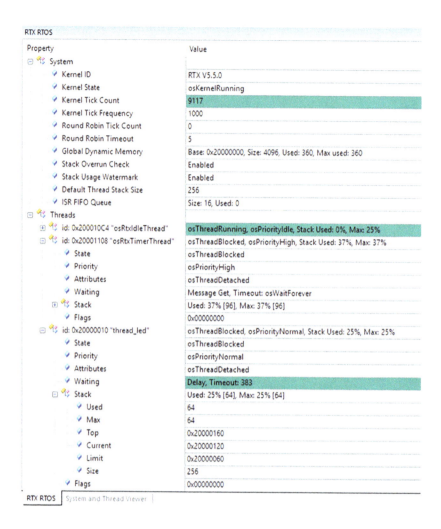

Figure 11.29: Stack usage of each thread is shown in the RTX RTOS viewer.

Both stack values, the (currently) used one, and the maximum used one are shown in bytes. Observe that the actual stack usage is very low. Also, the timer and the idle thread require very little stack. The Global Dynamic Memory shows that only 360 bytes are consumed.

Previously, we have specified in the RTX_Config.h file that all objects can consume up to 4096 bytes.

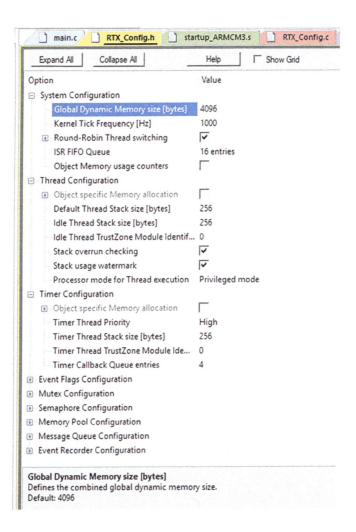

Figure 11.30: Memory usage configuration on RTX_Config.h.

With the new information, we can now reduce the memory sizes of the RTX by editing various options in RTX_Config.h. For example, we can:

▪ Change the global dynamic memory size to only 512 bytes.

▪ Reduce the stack size for Timer thread and Idle thread.

Save the file and recompile. You should see a reduction of RAM usage in your project. Do not forget to disable the stack usage watermark feature afterward – as this can increase OS operation overhead.

11.5 Other toolchains

The example above used Arm's toolchain and IDE for microcontroller software development, MDK. There are multiple toolchains and IDEs available on the market for developing software for Arm Cortex-M based processors. In Section 11.2.3, we briefly mentioned the GNU Arm Compiler, a popular open-source toolchain available for download at: https://developer.arm.com/open-source/gnu-toolchain/gnu-rm/downloads. Keil MDK can be used with this toolchain. For more information, please refer to Keil documentation.

A commercial alternative to MDK is the IAR Embedded Workbench for Arm (EWARM), available at: www.iar.com/arm

If you are looking for an open-source implementation of an Eclipse-based IDE, you might want to take a look at GNU MCU Eclipse (https://gnu-mcu-eclipse.github.io/). This enables you to develop your software using Linux or even Mac OS machines.

Glossary of terms

ACE	(AXI Coherency Extensions) - ACE provides additional channels and signaling to an AXI interface to support system-level cache coherency.
ADI	(Arm Debug Interface) - The ADI connects a debugger to a device. The ADI is used to access memory-mapped components in a system, such as processors and CoreSight components. The ADI protocol defines the physical wire protocols permitted, and the logical programmers model.
Advanced eXtensible Interface	See AXI
Advanced High-performance Bus	See AHB, AHB5
Advanced Microcontroller Bus Architecture	See AMBA
Advanced Peripheral Bus	See APB
Advanced Trace Bus	See ATB
AHB Access Port	See AHB-AP
AHB, AHB5	(Advanced High-performance Bus) - An AMBA bus protocol that supports pipelined operation, with the address and data phases occurring during different clock periods. This means the address phase of a transfer can occur during the data phase of the previous transfer. AHB provides a subset of the functionality of the AMBA AXI protocol. AHB5 is a specific release of AHB specification defined in AMBA 5. See also Advanced Microcontroller Bus Architecture (AMBA) and AHB-Lite.
AHB-AP	(AHB Access Port) - An optional component of the DAP that provides an AHB interface to a SoC. CoreSight supports access to a system bus infrastructure using the AHB-AP in the Debug Access Port (DAP). The AHB-AP provides an AHB master port for direct access to system memory. Other bus protocols can use AHB bridges to map transactions. For example, you can use AHB to AXI bridges to provide AHB access to an AXI bus matrix. See also Debug Access Port (DAP).
AHB-Lite	A subset of the AMBA 2 AHB protocol specification. It provides all of the basic functions required by the majority of AMBA AHB slave and master designs, particularly when used with a multi-layer AMBA interconnect.

AMBA	(Advanced Microcontroller Bus Architecture) - The AMBA family of protocol specifications is the Arm open standard for on-chip buses. AMBA provides solutions for the interconnection and management of the functional blocks that make up a System-on-Chip (SoC). Applications include the development of embedded systems with one or more processors or signal processors and multiple peripherals.
APB	(Advanced Peripheral Bus) - An AMBA bus protocol for ancillary or general-purpose peripherals such as timers, UARTs, and I/O ports. Using APB to connect to the main system bus through a system-to-peripheral bus bridge can help reduce system power consumption.
API	(Application Programming Interface)
Arm Compiler for DS-5	Arm Compiler for DS-5 is a suite of tools, together with supporting documentation and examples, that you can use to write and build applications for the Arm family of processors. Arm Compiler for DS-5 supersedes RealView Compilation Tools. DS-5 has now been superseded. See Arm Development Studio entry for information; See also armasm, armcc, fromelf.
Arm Debug Interface	See ADI
Arm instruction	An instruction executed by a core that is in AArch32 Execution state and A32 Instruction set state. A32 is a fixed-width instruction set that uses 32-bit instruction encodings. Previously, this instruction set was called the Arm instruction set. Arm instructions are not used in the Cortex-M processors.
armasm	The Arm assembler. This converts Arm assembly language into machine code.
armcc	The Arm compiler for C and C++ code in Arm Compiler 5. See Development Studio 5 (DS-5) and Keil MDK.
armclang	The Arm compiler for C and C++ code in Arm Compiler 6. See Development Studio 5 (DS-5) and Keil MDK.
ATB	(Advanced Trace Bus) - An AMBA bus protocol for trace data. A trace device can use an ATB to share CoreSight capture resources. Use AMBA ATB on first use, and ATB thereafter.
ATPG	(Automatic Test Pattern Generation) - A method to create a test vector for chip production testing based on scan chain hardware.
Automatic Test Pattern Generation	See ATPG

AXI	(Advanced eXtensible Interface) - An AMBA bus protocol that sets up the rules for how different modules on a chip communicate with each other, requiring a handshake-like procedure before all transmissions. Having a protocol such as this allows a true "system" rather than a "collection" of modules to be established as the protocol connects and provides an effective medium for transfer of data between the existing components on the chip. See also AXI Coherency Extensions (ACE).
AXI Coherency Extensions	See ACE
big-endian	In the context of the Arm architecture, big-endian is defined as the memory organization in which the least significant byte of a word is at a higher address than the most significant byte, for example: A byte or half-word at a word-aligned address is the most significant byte or half-word in the word at that address. *A byte at a halfword-aligned address is the most significant byte in the halfword at that address.
BPU	(Breakpoint Unit) - A hardware unit inside the Cortex-M processor to provide hardware comparators for breakpoint functionality. In early Cortex-M processors like Cortex-M3 and Cortex-M4, their BPU is also known as Flash Patch and Breakpoint unit (FPB).
breakpoint	A debug event triggered by the execution of a particular instruction. It is specified by one or both of the address of the instruction and the state of the processor when the instruction is executed. See Watchpoint.
Breakpoint Unit	See BPU
Bus master multiplexer (master MUX)	A bus interconnect component that allows several bus masters to connect to a single bus slave. Typically, it has its own arbitration logic to decide which bus master can drive the downstream bus. The output signals are then multiplexed into a single bus by forwarding the address and control signals from the highest priority master to downstream AHB slaves.
Bus matrix	An on-chip bus interconnect component that allows multiple bus masters to communicate with multiple bus slaves simultaneously.
Bus slave multiplexer (slave MUX)	A bus interconnect component that allows a bus master to connect to multiple bus slaves by multiplexing their return read data and response signal into a single bus for feedback to the bus master.
cacheable	A memory attribute that defines whether the data is allowed to be cached to enable faster accesses.

clock gating	A design technique for reducing power consumption in an integrated circuit. Gating a clock signal for a macrocell or functional block with a control signal and using the modified clock that results to control the operating state of the macrocell or block.
CMSIS	(Cortex Microcontroller Software Interface Standard) - A collection of software components that enables consistent device support and simple software interfaces to the processor and its peripherals. It is designed to simplify reuse, reduce the learning curve for microcontroller developers, and reduce the time to market for new devices. CMSIS has several components, including CMSIS-CORE which contains APIs for the processor core and peripherals.
core	Core is used to describe a single processing unit. In the processor context, we can further define core as something that has exclusive use of its own Program Counter (PC).
CoreSight ECT	A modular system that supports the interaction and synchronization of multiple triggering events with an SoC. It comprises Cross Trigger Interface (CTI), and Cross Trigger Matrix (CTM).
Cortex Microcontroller Software Interface Standard	See CMSIS
CoreSight ETB	A Logic block that extends the information capture functionality of a trace macrocell.
CoreSight ETM	A hardware macrocell that, when connected to a processor, outputs trace information on a trace port. The ETM provides processor driven trace through a trace port compliant to the ATB protocol. An ETM always supports instruction trace and might support data trace.
Cross Trigger Interface	See CTI
Cross Trigger Matrix	See CTM
CPSR	(Current Program Status Register) – A register that holds the APSR (Application Program Status Register) flags, the current processor mode, interrupt disable flags, current processor state, endianness state (on ARMv4T and later), execution state bits for the IT block (on ARMv6T2 and later).
CTI	(Cross Trigger Interface) - Part of an Embedded Cross Trigger (ECT) device. In an ECT, the CTI provides the interface between a processor or ETM and the CTM. The CTI enables the debug logic, ETM, and PMU, to interact with each other and with other CoreSight components. This is called cross triggering. For example, you can configure the CTI to generate an interrupt when the ETM trigger event occurs.

CTM	(Cross Trigger Matrix) - A block that controls the distribution of trigger requests.
DAP	(Debug Access Port) - A hardware block that acts as a master on a system bus and provides access to the bus from an external debugger. It contains a Debug Port interface for handling JTAG or Serial Wire Debug protocols and Access Port interface, which is the bus master.
Data Watchpoint and Trace	See DWT
Debug Access Port	See DAP
Default Slave	A bus slave in an AHB system that is used to return a bus error response to the bus master when a transfer to an illegal address is detected. If the bus master is a processor, a fault exception is then triggered, and it can deal with the error accordingly.
Design for Testing/ Testability	See DFT
Arm Development Studio	A one suite tool that provides a comprehensive embedded C/C++ dedicated software development solution. Arm Development Studio includes (1) Arm debugger and Keil µVision debugger; (2) Embedded C/C++ Arm Compiler 6; (3) Streamline performance analyzer for system-wide optimization on Linux, Android or bare-metal; (4) Royalty-free CMSIS-compliant middleware blocks for MCUs; (5) Armv7 and Armv8 Fixed Virtual Platforms for software development without a hardware target; and (6) Graphics debugger compatible with OpenGL ES, Vulkan and OpenCL.
DFT	(Design for Testing/Testability) - Various methodologies to enable a manufactured chip to be tested for manufacturing defects.
DS-5 Debugger	An Arm software development tool that enables you to make use of a debug agent to examine and control the execution of software running on a debug target. Note: DS-5 has been superseded by the Arm Development Studio.
DWT	(Data Watchpoint and Trace) - A component in the Cortex-M processors for data watchpoint, and also for processors that support trace (Armv7-M processors, and Armv8-M processors with Main Extension). DWT can be used for supporting data trace, event trace, and profiling trace.
Eclipse	An open-source IDE (Integrated Development Environment) that can be configured to work with various development tools. Note: DS-5 has been superseded by the Arm Development Studio.

Eclipse for DS-5	Eclipse for DS-5 is based around the Eclipse IDE and provides additional features to support the Arm development tools provided in DS-5. See Development Studio 5 (DS-5). Note: DS-5 has been superseded by Arm Development Studio (see entry).
Embedded Trace Buffer	See ETB
Embedded Trace Macrocell	See ETM
endianness	The scheme that determines the order of the successive bytes of data in a larger data structure when that structure is stored in memory.
ETB	(Embedded Trace Buffer) - A logic block that extends the information capture functionality of a trace macrocell.
ETM	(Embedded Trace Macrocell) - A hardware macrocell that, when connected to a processor, outputs trace information on a trace port. The ETM provides processor driven trace through a trace port compliant to the ATB protocol. An ETM always supports instruction trace and might support data trace.
exception	A mechanism to handle a fault, error event, or external notification. For example, exceptions handle external interrupts and undefined instructions.
exception vector	When an exception occurs, the processor must execute the handler code that corresponds to the exception. The location in memory where the handler is stored is called the exception vector. In Arm architectures, exception vectors are stored in a table, called the exception vector table.
Field Programmable Gate Array	See FPGA
Flash Patch and Breakpoint	See FPB
FPB	(Flash Patch and Breakpoint) - A hardware unit in the Cortex-M processor that provides hardware comparators for breakpoint functionality (see breakpoint). In Cortex-M3 and Cortex-M4 processors, these comparators can also be used for code patching. See also BPU.
FPGA	(Field Programmable Gate Array) - An integrated circuit that is configured by a designer (hence, field-programmable) using a hardware description language (HDL), which is similar to that used for an Application-Specific Integrated Circuit (ASIC). FPGAs contain programmable logic blocks, which can be configured to perform complex combinational logic functions and reconfigured as required.

FPU	(Floating Point Unit) - A hardware unit inside a processor for handling floating-point data.
fromelf	The Arm image conversion utility. This accepts ELF format input files and converts them to a variety of output formats. fromelf can also generate text information about the input image, such as code and data size.
Generic Interrupt Controller	See GIC
GIC	(Generic Interrupt Controller) - An exclusive block of IP that performs critical tasks of interrupt management, prioritization, and routing. GICs are primarily used for boosting processor efficiency and supporting interrupt virtualization. GICs are implemented based on Arm GIC architecture, which has evolved from GICv1 to the latest version GICv3/v4. Arm has a number of multi-cluster CPU interrupt controllers that provide a range of interrupt management solutions for all types of Arm Cortex-A and Cortex-R processor systems. For Cortex-M systems, NVIC is used instead and is integrated inside the processor rather than as a separated component.
host	A computer that provides data and other services to another computer. In the context of an Arm debugger, a host is a computer providing debugging services to a target being debugged.
IDAU	(Implementation Defined Attribution Unit) - A customer-defined component in Armv8-M processors system with TrustZone, in the form of a hardware lookup table that works closely with a Security Attribution Unit (SAU) to determine the partitioning of Secure and Non-secure address ranges in the address space.
IDE	(Integrated Development Environment) - An application running on a debug host (e.g., a PC) to provide code editor, easy access to software project management, the various project flows (e.g., compilation), and debug control.
IEEE 754	A standard for floating-point data format and operations
Implementation Defined Attribution Unit	See IDAU
Instrumentation Trace Microcell	See ITM
Integrated Development Environment	See IDE
interrupt	A signal emitted by hardware or software to the processor, indicating that an event needs immediate attention.

IRQ	(interrupt requests) – Interrupts are hardware lines over which devices can send interrupt signals to the microprocessor.
ITM	(Instrumentation Trace Microcell) - A component in Armv7-M processors, and Armv8-M processors with Main Extension, for software to generate trace data. This can be used for redirecting debug message (e.g., printf) and for OS awareness in debug.
Joint Test Action Group	See JTAG
JTAG	(Joint Test Action Group) - An IEEE group focused on silicon chip testing methods. Many debug and programming tools use a Joint Test Action Group (JTAG) interface port to communicate with processors. See IEEE Std 1149.1-1990 IEEE Standard Test Access Port and Boundary-Scan Architecture specification (available from the IEEE Standards Association).
LEC	(Logic Equivalent Checking) - A formal verification method to ensure that the output netlist of a design from synthesis matches the original RTL design.
little-endian	In the context of the Arm architecture, little-endian is defined as the memory organization in which the most significant byte of a word is at a higher address than the least significant byte. See also big-endian.
Load/Store architecture	A processor architecture where data-processing operations only operate on register contents, not directly on memory contents. The Arm architecture is a Load/Store architecture.
Logic Equivalent Checking	See LEC
MBIST	(Memory Built-In Self-Test) MBIST is the industry-standard method of testing embedded memories. It writes and reads all locations of the RAM to ensure that the cells are operating correctly. This process gives additional test coverage of the address and data paths that MBIST uses.
MCU	(Microcontroller Unit) - A type of general purposed SoC designed for various types of control applications.
MDK / Keil MDK	(Microcontroller Development Kit) - A development toolchain for microcontroller software development.
Memory Built-In Self-Test	See MBIST
Memory Management Unit	See MMU
Memory Protection Unit	See MPU

Micro Trace Buffer	See MTB
Microcontroller Development Kit	See MDK / Keil MDK
Microcontroller Unit	See MCU
MMU	(Memory Management Unit) - An MMU provides detailed control of the memory system in Arm Cortex-A processors. Most of the control uses translation tables that are held in memory. An MMU is the major component of an Arm Virtual Memory System Architecture (VMSA). Not available in Cortex-M processors, which provide MPU instead.
MPU	(Memory Protection Unit) - A hardware unit that controls a limited number of protection regions in memory. An MPU is the major component of an Arm Protected Memory System Architecture (PMSA).
MTB	(Micro Trace Buffer) - The MTB provides a simple execution trace capability to M-series processors. It has a low-cost option for instruction trace requirements for software development. Unlike the Embedded Trace Macrocell (ETM) or the Program Trace Macrocell (PTM) trace solutions, the MTB does not require a dedicated trace connection and trace data can be collected using a JTAG or Serial Wire Debug connection. However, the amount of trace history provided by the MTB is limited by the size of SRAM allocated for trace operations.
Nested Vectored Interrupt Controller	See NVIC
NMI	(Non-Maskable Interrupt) - A special type of interrupt request in Cortex-M processors. Can be used for critical interrupt events from a watchdog timer, brown-out detector, etc.
Non-Maskable Interrupt	See NMI
nTRST	Abbreviation of TAP Reset. nTRST is the electronic signal that causes the target system TAP controller to be reset. This signal is known as nICERST in some documentation. See also nSRST and Joint Test Action Group (JTAG).
NVIC	(Nested Vectored Interrupt Controller) - A component inside a Cortex-M processor that deals with interrupts and exceptions handling.
Operating System	See OS
OS	(Operating System) - Software that provides multitasking capability and in some cases also provides access APIs for various system functions. See also RTOS.

Phase-Locked Loop	See PPL
PLL	(Phase-Locked Loop) - A component that generates a clock signal with a frequency ratio based on a reference clock. In microcontrollers, PLLs are often programmable, so software developers can define the operating frequency of the system at different stages of program execution.
Program Trace Macrocell	See PTM
PTM	(Program Trace Macrocell) - A real-time trace module that provides instruction tracing of a processor.
Real-time Operating System	See RTOS
register	A processor register usually consists of a small amount of fast storage, which in some designs can be allocated to specific hardware functions, and may be read-only or write-only. Arm processors provide general-purpose and special-purpose registers. Some additional registers are available in privileged execution modes.
RTOS	(Real-time Operating System) - A type of OS that can respond to events (e.g., events caused by peripheral hardware) in a well-defined time period.
SAU	(Security Attribution Unit) - A component in Armv8-M processors with TrustZone. This unit works together with the Implementation Defined Attribution Unit (IDAU, configured by SoC designers) to define the partitioning of Secure and Non-secure address ranges.
SDF back-annotation	Using the timing delay values extracted from post-layout data (stored in a SDF file) to update the netlist ('back-annotate' it) during a netlist simulation.
Security Attribution Unit	See SAU
Serial Wire Debug	See SWD
Serial Wire Debug Port (SW-DP):	See SW-DP
SIMD	(Single Instruction, Multiple Data) - In the Arm instruction sets, supported SIMD instructions can perform parallel operations on the bytes or halfwords of the Arm core registers or vector operations (i.e., they perform parallel operations on vectors held in multiword registers). Note: Different versions of the Arm architecture support and recommend different instructions for vector operations. See the appropriate Arm Architecture Reference Manual for more information.

Single Instruction, Multiple Data	See SIMD
SoC	(System-on-Chip) - A SoC combines computer components onto a complete electronic substrate system (the chip) that may contain analog, digital, mixed-signal, or radio frequency functions. SoC can be seen in contrast to motherboard-based PC architecture, which separates the components based on function and uses a central interfacing circuit board to connect them. SoCs integrate all these components into a single integrated circuit that includes both the hardware and the software. SoC designs are characterized by low-power consumption, high levels of performance, small footprint, and reliability when compared to equivalent multi-chip systems.
SRPG	(State Retention Power Gating) - A method to reduce leakage power of a chip design when the system is idle/inactive.
STA	(Static Timing Analysis) – A type of analysis used to verify that the output design from synthesis or placement & routing can meet the timing requirements.
SP	(Stack Pointer) On Arm cores, SP refers to the stack pointer for the hardware-managed stack.: In AArch32 state, the SP is register R13 in the general-purpose register file. In AArch64 state, there is a dedicated SP for each implemented Exception level.
Standard Delay Format	See SDF
State Retention Power Gating	See SRPG
Static Timing Analysis	See STA
SWD	(Serial Wire Debug) - A debug implementation that uses a serial connection between the SoC and a debugger. This connection normally requires a bidirectional data signal and a separate clock signal, rather than the four to six signals required for a JTAG connection.
SW-DP	(Serial Wire Debug Port) - The interface for Serial Wire Debug
SWI	(SoftWare Interrupt) - The SWI instruction causes a SWI exception. This means that the processor mode changes to Supervisor, the CPSR is saved to the Supervisor mode SPSR and execution branches to the SWI vector
System-on-Chip	See SOC

SysTick timer	(System Tick timer) - A hardware unit in Cortex-M processor that provides periodic interrupts for OS operations. The SysTick timer is controlled by software, and CMSIS-Core support for Cortex-M processor-based devices provide APIs that generate interrupt requests on a regular basis. Example use of the SysTick timer and its interrupt include allowing an OS to carry out context switching to support multiple tasking. For applications where OS is not required, SysTick can be used for timekeeping, time measurement, or as an interrupt source for tasks that need to be executed regularly.
TAP	(Test Access Port). See also TAP Controller
TAP Controller	Logic on a device that enables access to some or all of that device for debug or test purposes. The circuit functionality is defined in IEEE1149.1. See also Joint Test Action Group (JTAG).
Target	In the context of an Arm debugger, the part of your development platform to which you connect the debugger, and on which debugging operations can be performed. A target can be: (1) A runnable target, such as a core that implements the Arm architecture. When connected to a runnable target, you can perform execution-related debugging operations on that target, such as stepping and tracing. (2) A non-runnable CoreSight component. CoreSight components provide a system-wide solution to real-time debug and trace.
TCK	(Test Clock) - The electronic clock signal that times data on the TAP data lines TMS, TDI, and TDO. See also Test Data Input (TDI) and Test Data Output (TDO).
TCM	(Tightly-Coupled Memory) - An area of low latency memory that provides predictable instruction execution or data load timing, for cases where deterministic performance is required. TCMs are suited to holding critical routines such as for interrupt handling scratchpad data types whose locality is not suited to caching critical data structures, such as interrupt stacks.
Test Clock	See TCK
Tightly-Coupled Memory	See TCM
TPIU	(Trace Port Interface Unit) - A hardware block to convert trace data from an ETM or other trace sources into parallel trace protocol for trace probe to collect the data via top-level pins.
Trace Port Interface Unit	See TPIU

TrustZone technology	The hardware and software that enable the integration of enhanced security features throughout a SoC. It is widely used in Cortex-A processors and has been introduced to the latest Cortex-M processors such as Cortex-M23, Cortex-M33, and Cortex-M35P.
Wake-up Interrupt Controller	See WIC
WIC	(Wakeup Interrupt Controller) - An optional component closely coupled or built into a Cortex-M processor to generate wakeup requests from interrupt request signal. This is used when the processor is powered down with (e.g., with State Retention Power Gating (SRPG)), or when all clocks to the processor logic are stopped. The wake-up request from WIC can be used to restore power and clock signals.

References

The designs in this book are based on the following AMBA specifications:

Specifications	Url
AMBA 5 AHB Protocol Specification (ARM IHI0033B)	https://developer.arm.com/docs/ihi0033/latest/arm-amba-5-ahb-protocol-specification
AMBA APB Protocol Specification (ARM IHI0024C)	https://developer.arm.com/docs/ihi0024/latest/amba-apb-protocol-specification

Other AMBA specifications (including older versions of AHB and APB specifications) were also mentioned:

Specifications	Url
AMBA 2 Specification (ARM IHI0011A, 1999)	https://developer.arm.com/docs/ihi0011/latest/amba-specification-rev-20
AMBA 3 AHB-Lite Protocol Specification v1.0 (ARM IHI0033A)	https://developer.arm.com/docs/ihi0033/a/amba-3-ahb-lite-protocol-specification-v10
AMBA 3 APB Protocol Specification (ARM IHI0024B)	https://developer.arm.com/docs/ihi0024/b
AMBA 4 ATB Protocol Specification (ARM IHI0032B)	https://developer.arm.com/docs/ihi0032/b
AMBA 3 ATB Protocol Specification (ARM IHI0032A)	https://developer.arm.com/docs/ihi0032/a
AMBA Low-power Interface Specification (ARM IHI0068C)	https://developer.arm.com/docs/ihi0068/latest/amba-low-power-interface-specification

The Cortex-M3 example system design is based on:

Cortex-M	Access
Cortex-M3 DesignStart Eval r0p0-02rel0 (functionally same as Cortex-M3 r2p1 with restrictions on configurability and features)	https://developer.arm.com/ip-products/designstart

The Keil Microcontroller Development Kit (MDK-ARM) introduction materials in Chapter 11 are based on version MDK-ARM 5.27. For evaluation and education, you can use Keil MDK Lite for free (code size limited to 32KB). You can find the latest version here: http://www2.keil.com/mdk5

Several other toolchains are covered in this book:

Arm Compiler 6 can be downloaded from:	https://developer.arm.com/tools-and-software/embedded/arm-compiler/downloads/version-6
Arm Compiler 5 can be downloaded from:	https://developer.arm.com/docs/ihi0024/latest/amba-apb-protocol-specification
GNU Arm Embedded Toolchain (gcc)	https://developer.arm.com/tools-and-software/open-source-software/developer-tools/gnu-toolchain/gnu-rm

Index

Arm Education Media
Online Courses

Our online courses have been developed to help students learn about state-of-the-art technologies from the Arm partner ecosystem. Each online course contains 10-14 modules, and each module comprises lecture slides with notes, interactive quizzes, hands-on labs and lab solutions. The courses will give your students an understanding of Arm architecture and the principles of software and hardware system design on Arm-based platforms, skills essential for today's computer engineering workplace.

Available now:

 Efficient Embedded Systems Design and Programming

 Rapid Embedded Systems Design and Programming

 Digital Signal Processing

 Internet of Things

 Graphics and Mobile Gaming

 System-on-Chip Design

 Real-Time Operating Systems Design and Programming

 Advanced System-on-Chip Design

 Embedded Linux

 Mechatronics and Robotics

Contact: edumedia@arm.com

Introduction to System-on-Chip Design
Online Courses

The Internet of Things promises devices endowed with processing, memory, and communication capabilities. These processing nodes will be, in effect, simple Systems-on-Chips (SoCs). They will need to be inexpensive, and able to operate under stringent performance, power and area constraints.

The Introduction to System-on-Chip Design Online Course focuses on building SoCs around Arm Cortex-M0 processors, which are perfectly suited for IoT needs. Using FPGAs as prototyping platforms, this course explores a typical SoC development process: from creating high-level functional specifications to design, implementation, and testing on real FPGA hardware using standard hardware description and software programming languages.

Learning outcomes:

Knowledge and understanding of
- Arm Cortex-M processor architectures and Arm Cortex-M based SoCs
- Design of Arm Cortex-M based SoCs in a standard hardware description language
- Low-level software design for Arm Cortex-M based SoCs and high-level application development

Intellectual
- Ability to use and choose between different techniques for digital system design and capture
- Ability to evaluate implementation results (e.g., speed, area, power) and correlate them with the corresponding high-level design and capture

Practical
- Ability to use commercial tools to develop Arm Cortex-M based SoCs

Course Syllabus:

Prerequisites: Basics of hardware description language (Verilog or VHDL), Basic C, and assembly programming.

Modules
1. Introduction to Arm-based System-on-Chip Design
2. The Arm Cortex-M0 Processor Architecture: Part 1
3. The Arm Cortex-M0 Processor Architecture: Part 2
4. AMBA 3 AHB-Lite Bus Architecture
5. AHB SRAM Memory Controller
6. AHB VGA Peripheral
7. AHB UART Peripheral
8. Timer, GPIO, and 7-Segment Peripherals
9. Interrupt Mechanisms
10. Programming an SoC Using C Language
11. Arm CMSIS and Software Drivers
12. Application Programming Interface and Final Application

Discover more at www.armedumedia.com

Arm Education Media
Books

The Arm Education books program aims to take learners from foundational knowledge and skills covered by its textbooks to expert-level mastery of Arm-based technologies through its reference books. Textbooks are suitable for classroom adoption in Electrical Engineering, Computer Engineering, and related areas. Reference books are suitable for graduate students, researchers, aspiring and practicing engineers.

Available now:

Embedded Systems Fundamentals with Arm Cortex-M based Microcontrollers: A Practical Approach
By Dr. Alexander G. Dean
ISBN 978-1-911531-03-6

Digital Signal Processing using Arm Cortex-M based Microcontrollers: Theory and Practice
By Cem Ünsalan, M. Erkin Yücel, H. Deniz Gürhan
ISBN 978-1-911531-16-6

Coming soon:

Operating Systems Foundations with Linux on the Raspberry Pi
By Wim Vanderbauwhede, and Jeremy Singer
ISBN 978-1-911531-20-3

Contact: edumedia@arm.com

www.ingramcontent.com/pod-product-compliance
Lightning Source LLC
LaVergne TN
LVHW062305060326
832902LV00013B/2060